Bearsted and Thurnham
At Play

Other local books

Bearsted and Thurnham Remembered (edited Kathryn Kersey)

Robert Fludd of Bearsted
(edited by Kathryn Kersey on behalf of Bearsted & District Local History Society)

Also by Kathryn Kersey

A School at Bearsted

'Dutifulness and Endurance' Bearsted and Thurnham 1914-1918, 1939-1945

The Lost Manor of Ware

Bearsted and Thurnham
At Play

Kathryn Kersey and Ian Lambert

with contributions
from

Alan Ferrell, Angela Legood
Rosemary Pearce, Michael Perring and Roger Vidler

First published in 2008 by Kathryn Kersey

Kathryn Kersey
5 Greensand Road, Bearsted, Maidstone, Kent ME15 8NY

All rights reserved © Kathryn Kersey, Alan Ferrell, Ian Lambert, Angela Legood, Richard Odell, Rosemary Pearce, Michael Perring and Roger Vidler 2008

The rights of Kathryn Kersey, Alan Ferrell, Ian Lambert, Angela Legood, Richard Odell, Rosemary Pearce, Michael Perring and Roger Vidler to be authors, and Kathryn Kersey to be editor of this work, have been asserted by them in accordance with section 77 of the Copyright, Designs and Patent Act 1988.

This book is sold subject to the condition that is shall not, by way of trade or otherwise, be lent, resold, hired out or otherwise circulated without the publisher's prior consent in any form of binding or cover other than that in which it is published and without a similar condition being imposed upon the subsequent purchaser.

British Library Cataloguing in Publication Data

ISBN 9780954583149

Front and back covers:
An impression of Bearsted and Thurnham Carnival and Fayre in 2007: the biggest opportunity in the year for residents of all ages from Bearsted and Thurnham to be At Play, in watercolour by local artist, Richard Odell.

Text digitally set in 11, 12, 14 and 16pt Garamond, 8 and 10pt Times New Roman
Printed and bound in Great Britain by Parchment (Oxford) Limited

Acknowledgements

There is a massive debt of gratitude due to those involved in the production of this book.

First of all, our thanks to: Stuart Bligh, Julie Gregson and the staff at the Centre for Kentish Studies in Maidstone in fulfilling countless requests for information, and their generous permission to use it, Simon Lace and Fiona Woolley at Maidstone Museum and Bentlif Art Gallery for permission to include a sketch by Edward Pretty of The Royal Oak public house circa 1860, the staff at Maidstone Reference Library, and the Bearsted and Madginford branches of Kent Library Service.

Particular thanks to: Danielle Masters for permission to use photographs from the 2004 Curtis Cup; Cambridge University Press for permission to reproduce a portrait of the cricketer, Alfred Mynn; Sally Goldfield and Glenys Williams of the MCC and Lords Cricket Ground for locating the portrait of Lewis Cage, 1768, and most generous permission to reproduce a photograph of it. Further thanks are due to the MCC for permission to use the print believed to have been executed by William Alexander, of Maidstone around 1800, during a game of cricket.

Huge thanks also to Fran and Geoff Doel and all of the Tonbridge Mummers for an evening of peerless folk entertainment which included a performance of the Bearsted Play, together with most generous permission to use information about it.

We have been able to include many photographs and reports through the courtesy and generosity of Barry Hollis, Steve Crispe, David Antony Hunt, Peter Still, John Wardley, John Westhorp, and the team at Kent Messenger newspaper group, Adscene newspaper, also Denis Fowle and the team at Downs Mail.

Deep thanks and high appreciation to Richard Odell for creating his beautiful impression of Bearsted and Thurnham Carnival and Fayre in 2007 in watercolour, and most generous permission to use his work on the covers of this book.

We would like to acknowledge the kind assistance, together with most generous permission to quote and use as a source of information/illustrations, the following people and organisations:

Frank and Gill Alston, Bearsted Badminton Club, Bearsted Brownies and Guides, Bearsted Cricket Club, Bearsted Football Club, Bearsted Golf Club, Bearsted Green Women's Institute, Bearsted Rifle Club, Bearsted Scout Group, Bearsted and District Local History Society, Bearsted and Thurnham Bowling Club, Bearsted and Thurnham Carnival and Fayre Committee, Bearsted and Thurnham Lawn Tennis Club, Bearsted and Thurnham Women's Institute, Bearsted Scout Group, Bearsted Woodland Trust, Alex Bensley, David Bracey, John Blamire Brown, Sister Mary Margaret OHP (née Margaret Blamire Brown), Don and Philip Bramall, Doris Britcher, Anthony Chadwick, Douglas Chenery, Terry Clarke, Anne and James Clinch, Trevor Coleman, Jean Corps, Alan Croucher, Evelyn and the late Bernard Croucher, Robin Cunningham, Brenda Donn, David and Theresa Elliott, David J Elliott, Martin Elms, Alan and the late Joy Ferrell, Barbara Foster, Sheila and the late Tony Foster, George Frampton, John and Simon France, Evelyn Fridd, the late Dennis Gibbons, the Gibson family, Debbie, Richard, and the late Thomas Gilbert, Norah Giles (née Pettipiere), Irene Hales, John Hardy, Gerry Harris, the late Ellen Hodson (née Byam), Holy Cross church, Maureen Homewood (née Rumble), Clive Horton, Jenni Hudson, Chris and Sue Hunt, George Hunt, Roy Ingleton, Norman King, Ian and Mary Lambert, the late Lucy Lang, John Lawson and other members of the Lawson family, Deena and John Leaf, Angela and Ken Legood, Mark Litchfield, Jean Jones, Bryan McCarthy, Madginford Women's Institute, Bruce Malcolm Fotosouvenirs, Marriott Tudor Park, Pat Marshall, Vic Matthews, Meresborough Books, John Mills, Pauline Moore, Margaret Morris, MPE football club, Richard Odell, the late Jessie Page, Roseacre School, Rosemary and Vince Pearce, Margaret Peat, Joan Perrin, Michael Perring, Margaret Plowright, Elisabeth Rackham, Ewin Rayner, Mick Rayner, Peter Rosevear, Linda Siems, Jack Smith, St Mary's church, Geoff Tester, William Thackwell, Margaret Tomalin (née Baker), Kenneth Trafford, Richard Tree, Thurnham Football Club, Liz Vickers, Graham Walkling, Brendan Walton, Peter Warland, Martin Weeks, Len White, Barbara Wickens (née Penney) Mary Wigan, Lorraine Wilkins, Keith Willson, Peter Willson, Bill Woolven and Roger Vidler.

We thank our fellow contributors – Alan, Angela, Richard, Rosemary, Michael and Roger, for all their hard work. We thank also all of our families, children and friends for their generous forbearance and tolerance of thoroughgoing distraction whilst this book was being researched and written.

Thanks, once more must also be expressed to Malcolm Kersey for seemingly boundless technological knowledge and Mary Lambert for unstinting hospitality, and without both of whom, publication would not have occurred.

Editorial Note

Where there is a particularly helpful description of events or an explanation of circumstances, it has been incorporated into the main body of the text for reasons of greater clarity and ease of reading. Any inclusions are subject to a note to indicate that the source used and that the words should not be regarded as written by one of the contributors - by this means it is hoped to avoid all accusations of that particular horror of all writers: inadvertent plagiarism.

Where an original document has been used, or transcribed, the original spelling is given. So, although the current spelling of Thurnham is now more or less regularised, many sources refer to Thornham. Likewise, Detling is sometimes written as Debtling in the text. For ease of reading, the spelling given is that given in the original document.

Addresses given are all in Bearsted or Thurnham and place names are in Kent, unless otherwise stated. St Mary's church, Thurnham is referred to as St Mary's church. Holy Cross church, Bearsted is referred to as Holy Cross church.

The subject of sport and the varying performances of teams and sportsmen can provoke strong sentiments and opinions. The editor wishes to draw attention to the fact that she is not answerable for opinions which contributors may express in their signed articles; each author is alone responsible for the contents and substance of their work.

Abbreviations Used

CCRC	Medway Archives Centre, Civic Centre, Strood
CKS	Centre for Kentish Studies, County Hall, Maidstone
KAS	Kent Archaeological Society, library located in Maidstone Museum
NA	National Archives, Kew, London (previously known as the Public Record Office)

<u>Latin</u>

ibid.	In the same place and refers to the previously named publication.
op.cit.	In the publication already named.
passim	Wording used that is dispersed through the text rather than a direct quotation.

It should be noted that children at play are not playing about; their games should be seen as their most serious minded activity

Michel de Montaigne
(1533-1592)

Contents

	Introduction	xi
1.	A Variety of Amusements on Bearsted Green	1
2.	Occasional Holidays and Celebrations (for children of all ages)	7
3.	Coronations and Jubilees	21
4.	Introduction to Cricket in Bearsted and Thurnham	34
5.	Bearsted Cricket Club: The First Two Hundred Years	35
6.	Bearsted Cricket Club: Into More Modern Times	47
7.	Thurnham Cricket Club	58
8.	Milgate Park Cricket Club	72
9.	Cricket in Bearsted and Thurnham: an envoi	76
10.	Bearsted Football Club	77
11.	Thurnham United Football Club	92
12.	MPE Football Club	97
13.	Bearsted Golf Club: People and Personalities	105
14.	Bearsted Golf Club: Around and About the Course	119
15.	The Tudor Park Hotel and Country Club	129
16.	Bearsted and Thurnham Bowling Club	133
17.	Tennis in Bearsted and Thurnham	143
18.	From Boer to Bulls Eye: Bearsted Rifle Club	155
19.	Rights of Way and Footpath Walking around Bearsted and Thurnham	165
20.	Roll Up! Roll Up! The Circus comes to Bearsted and Thurnham	170
21.	Drama in Bearsted and Thurnham	175
22.	Scouting and Guiding in Bearsted and Thurnham	184
23.	Traditional pub games and other miscellaneous pastimes	196
24.	Bearsted and District Local History Society	204
25.	Bearsted and Thurnham Fayre and Carnival	213
	Notes to the text	226

Introduction

Since I first began to write and publish books about Bearsted and Thurnham, it has become obvious that the villages have long enjoyed a wide variety of leisure pursuits. As these began to be mentioned in reminiscences, it did not take long to conclude that to give these subjects the attention which they demanded; a further, but separate, publication was required.

During the nineteenth century, the villages were relatively small. Before Queen Victoria's reign, there are few records of opportunities for ordinary people to enjoy a day off other than traditional or religious festivals such as May Day, Easter, or Christmas. If there was a nearby fair though, many employers released their staff for the day as an anticipated absence was easier to manage. Sporting events were sometimes included in those activities.

The village and religious festivals that marked the year's round in a small community were all celebrated, but it was the arrival of the railway and charabancs which made cheap and swift travel widely available. Further opportunities for leisure were opened up by the 1871 Bank Holiday Act which provided six bank holidays throughout the year: Good Friday, Easter Monday, Monday in Whitsun Week, the first Monday in August, Christmas Day, and if it fell on a weekday, 26 December. The act ensured that there would be set days in the year when banks were closed and no financial transactions involving bank staff would take place, hence 'holiday'. The passage of the legislation was shepherded through parliament by Sir John Lubbock, (later Lord Avebury) who was the Member of Parliament for Maidstone.

In these pages will be found details of how members of the local communities took the opportunities of commemoration and celebrations as they were presented. Sometimes they were combined with sports. Whatever the reason for a day off from the usual round of work, the opportunity for relaxation was just as appreciated then as it is today.

Ian Lambert, a local man, but above all, a dedicated and enthusiastic sportsman of long-standing, has been pivotal in the dedicated research needed to uncover some of the facts about sport and leisure in Bearsted and Thurnham which is presented here. It did not take him long to discover that there is rather more information about some sports and pastimes than others, so for this reason, it is not a comprehensive list. We have been joined in the quest for research by fellow enthusiasts Alan Ferrell, Angela Legood, Rosemary Pearce, Michael Perring and Roger Vidler. It is our hope that the most attractive watercolour by local artist, Richard Odell, on the cover of this book, also reflects a good impression of the villages at play.

It has been both a joy and a privilege to act as editor and a fellow contributor to the contents of this book, but above all, in assisting it to form a shape and then evolve into the publication now before you. However, we remain conscious that this book will inevitably contain some errors and omissions, and I will be pleased to receive further information and corrections.

Kathryn Kersey

A Variety of Amusements on Bearsted Green

Between 1817 and 1821, a series of one-day fairs and races took place on the Green at Bearsted. There is little is known about the reasons why these were held and who organised them, but they were obviously sufficiently popular to merit the expense of advertising them in the local newspapers. There is no evidence to suggest the origins of the event lay in a Charter Fair, although it is interesting to note that all the stall holders in 1820 had to possess a licence.

This is a transcript of an advertisement which appeared in the Maidstone Gazette, 15 July 1817:

BEARSTED RACES AND FAIR

WILL commence on MONDAY the 21st of JULY, 1817, on BEARSTED GREEN, when a variety of Amusements will be exhibited, calculated to promote harmless mirth, and banish those troublesome companions, *Ennui* and the *Blue Devils*.

STEWARDS
Mr. JOHN BUDDS,   MR. JOHN BARNES,
RICHARD WEBB,   RICHARD CORDELL

Among the diversions of the day will be

A MATCH OF CRICKET between Gentlemen of Bearsted and Thurnham, for one Guinea a man. Wickets to be pitched at eleven o'clock.

DONKEY RACES for a Cheshire Cheese. The Donkies to be entered for running on or before Saturday the 19th instant, at the house of Robert Clifford, Bearsted, or they will not be permitted to start. Their *pedigrees* to be produced if required.

JUMPING IN SACKS for half a pound note.

GINGLING MATCHES for half a guinea, to be paid to the person who bears away the *Bell*.

A FOOT RACE by men for a Pound Note.

SMOAKING for a Pound of Pigtail–Wax and pipe lights included.

CATCHING A LIVE PIG BY THE TAIL The person catching him to have the Porker for his pains.

GRINNING THROUGH A HORSE COLLAR for a *gimcrack and trimmings*. The Candidates to come with clean faces, and close shaved, to prevent and *advantages* being taken beyond those bestowed by *Nature*.

The Stewards in compliance with ancient custom, and by particular desire, are induced to have the usual FEMALE FOOT RACE, for a prize, which though not quite so valuable as the golden apple, by which Atalanta *lost* her race, may not be unacceptable to those who can make a *shift* to win it.

There will be a variety of other amusements, as will be expressed in Bills.

A BAND OF MUSIC will attend in the evening, and accommodation will be produced for those Youths and Lasses who may feel inclined to whirl in the maze of a country dance, or display their skill in the more fashionable waltz, or quadrille.

A brilliant display of FIRE WORKS will be exhibited at Ten o'clock.

A GOOD ORDINARY by Robert Clifford at the White Horse, at Two o'clock.

The beauty of the spot selected for the exhibition of the various sports, and its vicinity to Maidstone, give the Stewards reason to hope that their exertions will procure them the pleasure of a numerous company. And they beg to say that neither pains or expense shall be wanting to combine respectability with amusement, and to render the pleasures of the day complete.

Reproduced courtesy of Kent Messenger newspaper group

The notices for each event yield some fascinating details. All of the named stewards for the events were local people and both public houses facing the Green were involved in the races. Robert Clifford was the licensee of the White Horse and was well known for his love of sport. He took over the running of the White Horse in the 1780s, and by 1785 he was participating in teams playing cricket matches for Kent and

All England. Robert had many talents; in addition to being the licensee, he was also a wheelwright and, evidently a very successful sportsman.[1]

The following year, the event had expanded: this is a transcript of the advertisement which appeared in the Maidstone Gazette, 14 July 1818.

BEARSTED AND THURNHAM RACES AND FAIR

Will take place on Monday the 20th July, 1818,

ON BEARSTED GREEN

When a variety of Amusements will be exhibited, calculated to promote harmless mirth, and banish those troublesome companions, *Ennui* and the *Blue Devils*

STEWARDS

Mr JOHN BUDDS,   Mr. EDW. BUDDS,
RICHD. WEBB,   JOHN JOY

Among the diversions of the day will be:

A MATCH OF CRICKET

Between Gentlemen of Bearsted and Thurnham, for one Guinea a man. Wickets to be pitched at Ten o'clock.

DONKEY RACES, for a Cheshire Cheese. The second best will receive 5s and the third best 2s 6d. The Donkies to be entered for running on or before Saturday the 18th inst. at the house of Robert Clifford, Bearsted, or they will not be permitted to start. Their *Pedigrees* to be produced if required. Caps will be prepared for the riders.

JUMPING IN SACKS for Ten Shillings.
JINGLING MATCHES for half a guinea: to be paid to the person who bears away the *Bell*.

A FOOT RACE by Men, for a Pound Note.

Smoking for a Pound of Pig Tail,
Wax and Pipe Lights found for the Smoakers.

GRINNING THROUGH A HORSE COLLAR, for a Gimcrack and Trimmings. The Candidates to come with clean Faces, and close Shaved, to prevent any *advantages* being taken beyond those derived from native Beauty.

CLIMBING A POLE FOR A GLOCESTER CHEESE.

Old Women to Drink Tea,
For a Quart of the best Maidstone Hollands, and pair of Spectacles. The tea to be the best *Gun Powder*, but no *blowing up* allowed: wooden spoons to be provided, if required, for the Candidates. Not the *Ghost* of a bit of Bread and Butter to be eaten during the tea drinking.

WHEELING WHEELBARROWS BLINDFOLDED FOR SEVEN SHILLINGS

The Stewards in compliance with ancient custom, and by particular desire, are induced to have the usual

FEMALE FOOT RACE,

for a prize, which though not quite so valuable as the golden apple, by which Atalanta *lost* her race, may not be unacceptable to those who can make a *shift* to win it.

With a variety of other sports.

A BAND OF MUSIC will attend in the evening, and accommodation will be produced for those Youths and Lasses who may feel inclined to whirl in the maze of a Country Dance, or display their skill in the more fashionable Waltz, or Quadrille.

A BRILLIANT DISPLAY OF FIRE WORKS,

Which will be exhibited at Nine o'clock by Mr THOMAS HULBURD, whose taste and skill as a pyrotechnist has given universal satisfaction.

A GOOD ORDINARY by George Wilson. At the *Royal Oak Inn*, at Two o'Clock.

The beauty of the spot selected for the exhibition of the various sports, and its vicinity to Maidstone, give the Stewards reason to hope that their exertions will procure them the pleasure of a numerous company. And they beg to say that neither pains nor expense shall be wanting to combine respectability with amusement, and to render the pleasures of the day complete.

As much confusion generally prevails at the exhibition of rural sports, for the want of a due arrangement, it is intended that every species of amusement shall commence by ring of Bell.

Reproduced courtesy of Kent Messenger newspaper group

George Wilson, who is mentioned in the advertisement, was the licensee of the Royal Oak. In 1826, he was recorded as the receiver of letters and postmaster for Bearsted and Thurnham. Unfortunately there are very few images available of the Royal Oak before a major fire in the late nineteenth century destroyed a great deal of the original premises. They were later re-built.[2] However, there is a sketch from around 1860 and also an undated photograph (both of which are shown below) and these give a good idea of how the public house may have appeared at the time of the fair and race meetings:

Reproduced courtesy of Maidstone Museum and Bentlif Art Gallery, Pretty Bequest 1865

Reproduced courtesy of Alex Bensley

Some of the competitions that were held seem rather obscure today. A Gingling Match was a race in which all the participants, apart from the Gingler, were blindfolded. The Gingler had a small bell which he had to ring constantly for an agreed time. During this time he tried to avoid being captured by the blindfolded competitors. The prize was won by the Gingler if he was uncaught when the match ended.[3]

Grinning through a horse collar was a contest but its origins are now lost. In other parts of Britain, these were known as 'Gurning' competitions. One such event is still held in the Lake District and can be traced back to 1266. The prize is awarded to the person considered to have made the most hideous face. In the twenty first century, it is difficult to ascertain what the prize of a 'gim-crack and trimmings' may have been, but it is reasonable to surmise that it may have been some sort of cheap ornament.[4]

By the early years of the nineteenth century, local firework displays were no longer confined to Bonfire Night and became popular. Several manuals had been published on the subject and were readily available. Unfortunately, nothing is known about Mr Thomas Hulburd, who organised the displays.

A Variety of Amusements on Bearsted Green

This is a transcript of the advertisement which appeared in the Maidstone Gazette, 1819:

BEARSTED and THURNHAM RACES AND FAIR

Will commence on TUESDAY the 20th of July 1819, on BEARSTED GREEN, when such Ladies and Gentlemen in the neighbourhood as have a taste for philosophical experiments will be gratified by the exhibition of a

SPLENDID AIR BALLOON

With an ELEGANT PARACHUTE attached, which will be disengaged from the Balloon when it shall have attained a suitable elevation. The process of filling the Balloon by means of the apparatus, prepared for that purpose, will commence at half past three o'clock, and the balloon will ascend at five o'clock precisely. A small PILOT BALLOON will be previously launched in order to ascertain the prevailing currents in the atmosphere

A MATCH OF CRICKET

Between Gentlemen of Bearsted and Thurnham, for one Guinea a man. Wickets to be pitched at ten o'clock.

DONKEY RACES

for a Cheshire Cheese. The second will receive 5s, and the third best, 2s 6d. The Donkies to be entered for running on or before Saturday the 18th instant, at the house of Robert Clifford, Bearsted, or they will not be permitted to start. Their *pedigrees* to be *produced* if required. Caps will be prepared for the riders.

DANDY HOBBIES

Now in training for the sport. It is requested that the spectators will not get in the way, as the Racers being *high mettled*, are very likely to *kick*

JUMPING IN SACKS
FOR SEVEN SHILLINGS AND SIXPENCE

Climbing a Pole for a Gloucester Cheese

GINGLING MATCHES for half a guinea

WHEELING WHEELBARROWS BLINDFOLDED
For Seven Shillings

The Stewards in compliance with ancient custom, and by particular desire, are induced to have the usual
FEMALE FOOT RACE
For a PRIZE, which though not quite so valuable as the golden apple, by which Atalanta lost her race, may not be unacceptable to those who can make a Shift to win it.

WITH A VARIETY OF OTHER SPORTS

A BAND OF MUSIC will attend in the evening, and accommodation will be produced for those Youths and Lasses who may feel inclined to whirl in the maze of a County Dance, or display their skill in the more fashionable Waltz, or Quadrille.

A BRILLIANT DISPLAY OF FIRE WORKS

Which will be exhibited at ten o'clock. By Mr THOMAS HULBUND, whose taste and skills as Pyrotechnist, have given universal satisfaction

A GOOD ORDINARY by Robert Clifford at the White Horse Inn, at two o'clock.

The beauty of the spot selected for the exhibition of the various sports, and its vicinity to Maidstone, give the Stewards reason to hope that their exertions will procure them the pleasure of a numerous company. And they beg to say that neither pains nor expense shall be wanting to combine respectability with amusement, and to render the pleasures of the day complete.

Reproduced courtesy of Kent Messenger newspaper group

A Variety of Amusements on Bearsted Green

The most elaborate event took place in 1820, as this advertisement which appeared in the Maidstone Gazette, shows:

BEARSTED RACES AND FAIR

Will take place on Monday, the 17th July 1820, on Bearsted Green

When a variety of Amusements will be exhibited, calculated to promote harmless mirth and banish those troublesome companions Ennui and the Blue Devils.

Among the diversions of the day will be

A GRAND MATCH OF CRICKET, between the Gentlemen of Bearsted and Maidstone, at which much science it is expected will be displayed. Wickets to be pitched at nine o'clock, and the game to begin without delay.

RACES OF PONIES (not exceeding 13 hands high). The best two in three Races for a Bridle. The Ponies to be named to one of the Stewards of the Day, at Mr Wilson's, Royal Oak Inn, on or before Saturday, the 15th inst. To start at four o'clock.

DONKEY RACES FOR A Cheshire Cheese. The second best will receive 5s and third best 2s 6d. The Donkies to be named on or before Saturday the 15th instant, or they will not be permitted to start. Their *Pedigrees to be produced* if required. Caps will be prepared for the riders.

FOOT RACES of an extraordinary kind.

The celebrated RAINER will run a match against another excellent pedestrian. Besides this match there will be other Foot Racing for men.

JINGLING MATCHES for Half a Guinea. To be paid to the person who bears away the *Bell*.

CLIMBING A POLE for a Gloucester Cheese.

WHEELING WHEELBARROWS BLINDFOLDED for 7s.

FEMALE FOOT RACE, for a prize which though not quite so valuable as the Golden Apple by which Atlanta *lost* her race, may not be unacceptable to those who may make a *Shift* to win it.

Bands of Music will attend the Ground.

A brilliant display of FIREWORKS will be exhibited at Nine o' Clock, by Mr THOS. HULBURD, whose taste and skill as a Pyrotechnist have on former occasions given universal satisfaction.

A GOOD ORDINARY, at Mr WILSON's, the Royal Oak Inn, at Two o'clock.

The beauty of the Spot selected for the Exhibition of the various Sports, and its vicinity to Maidstone, give the Stewards reason to hope that their exertions will procure them the pleasure of a numerous Company, and they beg to say that neither pains nor expense shall be wanting to combine respectability with amusement, and to render the pleasures of the day complete.

As much confusion generally prevails at the exhibition of Rural Sports for the want of due arrangement, it is intended that every species of amusement shall commence by ring of Bell.

To prevent accidents it is particularly requested that no squibs or crackers be let off previous to the display of Mr Hulbard's fire-works.

All Persons desirous of fixing Stalls or Stands of any other description, are desired to apply to Mr WILLIAM RICHARDS, Constable, for the day, without which they will not be permitted to set up any stall, &c. Marquees will be provided.

Reproduced courtesy of Kent Messenger newspaper group

A Variety of Amusements on Bearsted Green

In 1821, the lavish advertising that had been previously undertaken for the Fair and Races, changed. This is a transcript of the notice which appeared in the Maidstone Gazette, 10 July 1821:

BEARSTED RACES AND FAIR

Will take place on Tuesday, 24th July, 1821

The Amusements will consist of

A CRICKET MATCH

DONKEY RACES

FOOT RACING

JINGLING MATCH

CLIMBING A POLE

JUMPING IN SACKS, &c. &c.

A Brilliant display of FIRE-WORKS will be exhibited at nine o'clock.

Marquees will be provided. Bands of Music will attend.

A Good Ordinary at MR CLIFFORD'S, the White Horse Inn, at two o'clock.

The utmost attention will be paid by the Stewards to the accommodation and amusement of the company.

Reproduced courtesy of Kent Messenger newspaper group

The event in 1821 was the last fair and set of formal races to be held on the Green in the nineteenth century. The idea of a fair in Bearsted then seemingly lay in abeyance until the late 1920s, and the attention of another generation.

It is not known why the Fair and Races ceased to be held, but perhaps it is significant that there were other distractions becoming available. Horse race meetings were held in Tunbridge Wells and a further series of meetings began in Chatham around 1821. These were both advertised in the Maidstone Gazette. It is possible that it was felt that it was no longer appropriate to hold such an event at Bearsted.

Perhaps, for a few years, at least, the event served its advertised purpose of banishing boredom. It would be good to think that many ordinary families in Bearsted and Thurnham were left with memories of a day in which they forgot their troubles for a time and went to the fair.

Roger Vidler

Occasional Holidays and Celebrations
(for Children of All Ages)

Until the middle of the twentieth century, holidays for most people were largely associated with the festivals of Easter, May Day, Ascension Day, Whitsun or Christmas. Nevertheless, if an opportunity arose, all members of the community in Bearsted and Thurnham appreciated the chance to enjoy an occasional day off.

The local festivals and holidays which marked the year's round were celebrated in the villages, and frequently took place on the Green; it was an ideal and central location. At the heart of many of the events were the younger generations. Some of these occasions were decidedly informal or associated with local agricultural practices such as hop stringing or hop picking.

As with many rural communities, May Day celebrations always seemed to be very popular, although there is little information formally recorded. It was not until the twentieth century that folk and maypole dancing were introduced at Bearsted School but garlands of flowers and leaves were certainly manufactured and displayed by the children. It is likely that the garlands would have been taken around the villages, stopping at every door to display it and chant a special May Day verse: [1]

> The first of May is Garland Day
> So please remember the Garland
> We don't come here but once a year
> So please remember the garland.

After the verse, if a penny or two could be spared from the household, the children received payment. In 1876, Elizabeth Vincent, the Mistress of the school, certainly recorded in the log book that there had been absentees: [2]

> 5 May
> Monday being "May Day", several children were permitted by their parents to carry garlands about the parish.

During the middle years of the nineteenth century, there was a branch of the Ancient Order of Foresters friendly society operating in Bearsted and Thurnham. A friendly society was a group of people who had joined together for a common financial or social purpose. Before national insurance and the welfare state, these societies provided a form of social services to ordinary people and some provided free access to a doctor. Members made regular payments into a common fund so if they became ill and unable to work, they could receive an allowance or grant for financial assistance, even extending to funerals. Many of the friendly societies ran annual programmes of social events such as fetes and dances, developed sporting teams and contests. The Foresters regularly held fetes and other events on the Green prior to the First World War.

Entries in the school log books from 1865 onwards faithfully record days off awarded in order for the children to attend this type of annual event:[3]

> 25 June 1866
> Foresters Fete on Green - half holiday.
>
> 24 July 1867
> Harvesters Fete in Bearsted - very thin attendance.
>
> 22 July 1868
> Fete in Vinters Park: scarcely any school, so half day holiday.

Both reproduced courtesy of Roseacre School

Occasional Holidays and Celebrations (for Children of All Ages)

There were occasions when events in Maidstone also affected the life of the school and attendance as these two typical entries from the log book show.

> <u>18 October 1878</u>
> Thursday and Friday being the days on which Maidstone Fair is held, a great number of the children were taken there by their parents either on one day or the other, this has again reduced the average attendance to eighty four.

> <u>6 August 1879</u>
> Holiday given in the afternoon: the New Maidstone Bridge being opened.

Both reproduced courtesy of Roseacre School

The new Maidstone bridge was designed by the engineer Sir Joseph Bazalgette. It was reported that the opening ceremony was witnessed by a great assemblage of people, estimated to include five thousand school children, each wearing a medal which had been struck in honour of the occasion.[4]

Margaret Tomalin, (née Baker), remembered her father (who was born in 1888) describing the occasional arrival of a German band in the village. This was usually on a Monday, so the women of the village had a musical accompaniment to their laundry routines. Sometimes the band also brought with them a dancing bear which was a great spectacle for the children.

This photograph of a band on the Green is undated. It is possible that it was taken during the coronation celebrations for King George V in 1911:

Reproduced courtesy of Margaret Tomalin

Occasional Holidays and Celebrations (for Children of All Ages)

In this undated photograph another band are playing behind Smarts Cottages on the Green. In later years, the cricket pavilion was built upon this site:

Reproduced courtesy of Bearsted and District Local History Society

The demands of agriculture frequently intruded into the school year and resulted in children taking unauthorised days off. These are some typical entries from the school log book: [5]

> <u>14 July 1876</u>
> Many of the children have gone "Currant-picking". The average attendance for the week reduced to 94.
>
> <u>4 August</u>
> Harvesting having early begun in the neighbourhood, many of the elder children are absent assisting their parents in the fields.
>
> <u>11 August</u>
> Great falling off of attendance in the Upper Standards owing to "Gleaning" having commenced.
>
> <u>18 August</u>
> Several children have asked leave of absence for the next few weeks as hop picking to commence early next week.
>
> <u>24 August</u>
> Closed school today for hop picking holiday.

Reproduced courtesy of Roseacre School

Absence through working in the fields alongside other family members might not sound too much of a holiday to modern reader. However, it was a break for the normal round and an opportunity to earn some extra money for financially-pressed families.

9

Occasional Holidays and Celebrations (for Children of All Ages)

Guy Fawkes and Bonfire Night celebrations held on the Green were always popular and the children sometimes paraded a guy figure around the area, earning some pennies for the fireworks. As the Mistress, Miss Love Jones, recorded in the school log book: [6]

> 5 November 1872
>
> Guy Faux day. Order interrupted by bringing guys to the school door.

Harry Hodges, who was born in 1898, passed on a memory to his daughter, Jean, of tar barrels being rolled onto the Green before they were set alight as another part of the Bonfire Night festivities.

Mr Walkling also once recalled details of some of the local celebrations which were recorded by Robert Skinner, the Headmaster of Bearsted School. Although undated, the details indicate that these took place before the coming of the railway in 1884. This is a slighted edited transcript: [7]

> ...On Guy Fawkes' day, the Green was the centre of activities. A huge combustible stack was built in the middle of the Green, whilst fireworks had been in construction for weeks in the place where the railway station now stands.
>
> A procession would march from The Bell public house to the White Horse along Ware Street. People joined in from all directions and dressed in all kinds of appropriate costumes for the occasion.
>
> The central part of the procession would be a wagon bearing an effigy. The people that made it would add a touch of humour to the proceedings by making the effigy into a likeness of a local figure that seemed appropriate in that particular year. Mr Knowles, a local builder, once figured on the wagon as Tiger Knowles and once even the vicar provided the centre piece under the name of Holy Joe!
>
> Once on the Green, the fun started. With the effigy set well alight and the fireworks spluttering, flaming tar barrels would be set going. On one occasion one resident spent all night ensuring that the tar barrels did not collide with his faggot fence...but the excitement for everyone else was immense...

Both reproduced courtesy of Roseacre School

The arrival of midwinter in the countryside was frequently marked by the performance, at a local inn, of a Mummers Play known in Kent as the Plays of the Seven Champions. The stories are performed to this day by men wearing traditional costumes. The characters include a Father Christmas, two champions who fight, a Doctor and some begging characters usually called Johnny Jack and Beelzebub. Some of the dramatic origins are now lost but it is believed that they lie in pagan annual fertility rituals which include a death and resurrection to reflect winter and spring. Later, the ritual adopted many Christian elements and figures such as St George.[8]

Many different texts for Mummers Plays survive but amongst the most well known are those called The Seven Champions, thought to be based upon the Famous Historie of the Seavearn Champions of Christendom, published by Richard Johnson in 1596.[8] The Bearsted Play is one in that series. The origins for the play are again, obscure. It is included in a list of texts for folk plays published in 1933 compiled by Sir Edmund Chambers, but this states it was found in a manuscript once owned by a Miss Coombes.[9]

There is also a reference to earlier performances of a Mummers play around 1880 included in the Centenary booklet for Bearsted School. It is not clear, though, if it took place at the school or at another location in Bearsted and some of Jack Sweep's lines quoted in the account differ from the surviving text.[10]

Occasional Holidays and Celebrations (for Children of All Ages)

The original version is one which was performed between the First and Second World Wars at the School, although there is no specific record of this in the log books. Fran and Geoff Doel, authorities on Mumming, have commented that parts of this version are rather unusual as it begins with figures sweeping and includes Rock the gardener: [11]

> Open the door and let me in.
> I beg your pardon, I'm sure to win.
> Whether we rise or whether we fall
> Room, room, room, I require,
> Step in guard and show your face like fire.

Jack Sweep makes an entrance near the end:

> In comes I Jack Sweep
> All the men I have to keep
> Whether they're little or whether they're tall,
> It takes a lot o'money to keep them all.

Father Christmas concludes the play:

> In come I old Father Christmas,
> Am I welcome or am I not?
> Hope Father Christmas is not forgot.

The Bearsted Play includes the characters Father Christmas, Guard, King George, Turkish Knight or Little Slasher, The Doctor, Jack Sweep and Beelzebub. However, if the character Rock is counted, this makes rather more than Seven Champions! [12] It is notable that Father Christmas is particularly depicted as a 'green' character; wearing the colour to reflect the evergreen foliage of trees and shrubs, thus alluding to the constancy of nature during winter.[13] The play was most recently performed in Bearsted in November 2006 by the Tonbridge Mummers, led by Geoff and Fran Doel, at a meeting of the Bearsted and District Local History Society.

The photograph below shows a postcard from America, sent in 1907. Most unusually, it incorporates the nature elements of the Father Christmas figure in the Bearsted Play, including a green robe and a fir tree.

Reproduced courtesy of Malcolm Kersey

Occasional Holidays and Celebrations (for Children of All Ages)

At Christmas, during the first two decades of the twentieth century, Holy Cross church and the Methodist Chapel began to hold separate celebrations for the children through their Sunday Schools. Both events were arranged around a decorated Christmas tree which had small presents tied to it. There was a substantial tea for everyone and the afternoon concluded with the distribution of the presents. Understandably, it was popular with the children, although Margaret Tomalin's father, Richard Baker, never received the toys he longed-for as a small boy, such as a top or a ball: his present always contained socks! Margaret recalled that he also spoke about occasions, possibly around Christmas, when a cart used to be drawn into Bearsted, and hot farthings were thrown from it for the children to catch. In some parts of the country this was called Snap Dragon, but the tradition has many variations.

Ellen Hodson (née Byam), usually called Nell, also recalled a special Sunday School Christmas party. When she was small she hated the dark. As her family lived at Howe Court in Crismill Lane, it was a long walk back from the middle of the village after playing with her friends by the Green or attending commitments such as a confirmation class. In the winter, the journey home was nearly always in the dark.

As Nell was growing up, Mr Beale lived in the village for a time. He was a commercial traveller for a firm that sold prams and toys for children. One year, his company donated a Meccano set for a boy and a doll's pram for a girl to the party organisers on the condition that they were given to poor children in Bearsted. The organisers found this much too difficult so they decided to raffle them instead. Nell wanted the pram so much that it hurt; she prayed very hard about it. To her surprise and delight she did win the pram but she also realised at the end of the party that night had fallen. Despite this, Nell walked all the way home with her prize, discovering, she felt, that perhaps God really had answered her prayers: not only had she won the pram but also, for the first time, was unafraid of the dark.

The annual School Treats were highly popular events but there were no fixed dates for them in the year. In February 1875, this report appeared in the parish magazine: [14]

Our School Treat

The annual treat to the children of our National and Sunday Schools was given on the 23rd of last month in the usual place of meeting - the beautifully situated paddock of Henry Tasker Esq. They mustered at the schoolroom upwards of 150 in number and proceeded in procession to the Church, singing as they went hymns 366 and 164 and preceded by the parish banner made last year by Mrs Tasker.

After a short and hearty service of praise, the procession reformed and proceeded to the meadow where many flag-bearers were relieved of their burdens. A general rush was made to the swings, and very soon the whole number was engaged in various games, enjoying themselves to their hearts' content; - the numerous amusements being promoted and shared in by their teachers and other active friends.

An excellent tea was provided for them at 5pm enhanced by sieves of cherries and gooseberries kindly presented by Messrs Bridgland and Larking; and after the contents of a brawn pie had been distributed, the sports were resumed and carried on till sunset. We were glad to see so many parents of the children, and other parishioners, present on the ground.

In the course of the day, rewards of handsome books and texts were distributed to every regular attendant at the Sunday School. The proceedings were brought to a close by hearty cheers from the children for Miss Vincent and their Sunday School teachers; for Mr and Mrs Tasker and other promoters of the treat, and for the Vicar, and by their singing the beautiful hymn for children, No. 368 beginning:

>   Now the day is over
>   Night is drawing nigh –
>   Shadows of the evening
>   Steal across the sky.

Reproduced courtesy of Holy Cross church

Occasional Holidays and Celebrations (for Children of All Ages)

In 1878, the treat also included a religious service before the celebrations: [15]

> Our School Treat took place on June 28th, too late to be notified in our issue for July. We were favoured this year with a fine day, very hot, but tempered by a cool breeze from the north. The children assembled as usual at the school at 1.30pm and then proceeded to the church in procession, headed for the first time by the Juvenile Drum and Fife Band, which gave much satisfaction and which will, we hope, ripen into a permanent village band. They greatly need better instruments and we hope that as winter comes on, with its dark evenings, giving opportunity for practice, some effort may be made to supply them with what they need.
>
> The service in church consisted as usual of an abbreviated evensong, with some hymns, which were well sung by the children, and after that they proceeded in procession to Mr Tasker's meadow, being joined at his gate by the Infants, who swelled the total number to about 150.
>
> As soon as their ranks were broken up, there was a rush made for the swings, while the bigger boys enjoyed a cricket match. Much regret was felt at the absence of the Mistress, Miss Vincent, not so much on account of the children, who were well amused and cared for, as for her own sake - being prostrated by illness. We must hope that she will return after the holidays quite renovated in health and able to take charge of the school again.
>
> As we have implied, there were plenty of friends able and willing to promote the enjoyment of the children and to assist in the distribution of their tea, which took place at 4.30. At 6pm Mrs Tasker gave a present of some toy to every child in the school and then they re-engaged in their various games until dusk. We were glad to see several of the parents come up to the meadow and hope to see their number increased another year. The thanks of the parish are due to Mr Tasker, not only for the loan of his meadow - without which we should have difficulty in finding a suitable place - but also for the heartiness with which he promoted the amusement of the children.

Reproduced courtesy of Holy Cross church

The inhabitants of Bearsted and Thurnham were not slow to venture further afield, if an opportunity was provided. Children were at the forefront of exploring a wider world.

One of the first excursions recorded as undertaken from Bearsted took place on 21 July 1864. Children from the School, who had passed the government examination, or who were about to leave, visited Rosherville Gardens in Gravesend. These had been developed from twenty acres of disused chalk pits by Jeremiah Rosher of Crete Hall. He had planned to create a zoological garden but the pleasure aspect soon overcame any philanthropic or educational ideas.[16]

Such was the popular attraction of the gardens that one of the houses in Bearsted is still called Rosherville. At the height of its success, there was a dedicated station on the London, Chatham and Dover railway line. The garden employed professional acts for a limited period during the summer season together with a resident drama group, the Bijou Theatre Company. Music and dancing, led by Mr W T Williams and Mr J Willis, took place in a Baronial Hall. The attractions that the children would have seen included a bear pit, monkey cages, a maze and some side-shows.[17]

A transcript of a report in the Maidstone Telegraph about the excursion:

> <u>23 July 1864</u>
>
> **BEARSTED SCHOOL CHILDREN'S HOLIDAY**
>
> On Thursday last, the Children connected with the Bearsted schools were treated to a journey to Rosherville Gardens. No less than six vans full passed through Maidstone to the station, where a train was in readiness to take them to their destination. They returned in the evening highly delighted with their day's recreation.

Reproduced courtesy of Kent Messenger newspaper group

Occasional Holidays and Celebrations (for Children of All Ages)

This photograph shows the café at Rosherville taken around 1900:

Reproduced courtesy of George Frampton and Meresborough Books

It is not recorded whether anyone from Bearsted or Thurnham visited the Great Exhibition at Hyde Park in 1851 but it was a popular attraction. However, the centrepiece of the exhibition was later moved to Sydenham. Once again, children went to see it from the school as Samuel Taylor, the Master, briefly recorded in the log book: [18]

> 9 August 1865
>
> Fifty children were taken to see the Crystal Palace.

Reproduced courtesy of Roseacre School

Empire Day was normally commemorated. 24 May 1921, was marked by an address given to the children by Mrs Dibble on 'Responsibility', and this was followed by patriotic songs and recitations. In the afternoon, a guest speaker from the Temperance Society talked to the children on 'The Food We Eat'.

This undated photograph shows Mr Whitehead addressing the children on the Green during Empire Day. Note the figure of Britannia and that the members of the Scouts and Guides are wearing their uniforms:

Reproduced courtesy of Roger Vidler

Occasional Holidays and Celebrations (for Children of All Ages)

In 1924, the Empire Exhibition at Wembley opened and was tremendously popular. Some of the children from Bearsted School paid a visit to the exhibition as Mr Goodman, the Headmaster, recorded: [19]

> <u>17 July 1924</u>
>
> As I shall be visiting Wembley Exhibition tomorrow, with ten of the children, the school will be in the charge of Mrs Dibble.

Reproduced courtesy of Roseacre School

Although the travel arrangements were not described, most people that visited the exhibition travelled by train up to London and then used the Underground to arrive at Wembley.

The Official Guide to the Exhibition described the event as:

> ...a Family Party of the British Empire...

on a site of 216 acres. Each colony of the empire was represented by its own building which was called a 'pavilion'.[20] Other buildings showed the achievements of the Empire in the fields of Engineering, Industry and the Arts as well as the work of HM Government. The exhibition was a popular attraction.

This is a typical advertisement for part of the exhibition produced in 1925 for Sharp's Toffees. The confectionary company had a large factory in Maidstone which employed many local people.

Reproduced courtesy of Malcolm Kersey

In later years, before the Second World War, the Empire Day commemorations were expanded into a small concert or entertainment in the early evening at one of the halls in the village. Norah Giles recalled that there were pageants and other events on the Green during the day. On one occasion it was decided that there would be a different type of pageant, highlighting different countries of the Empire. Norah was chosen to represent Wales so her mother made her a special dress and she carried a bunch of daffodils.

Occasional Holidays and Celebrations (for Children of All Ages)

This photograph was taken of Bearsted School Empire Day celebrations on 24 May 1927, on the Green outside Mote Villas:

Reproduced courtesy of Jenni Hudson

Back row includes: Nora Pettipiere (South Africa), Phyllis Baker (New Zealand), ---- (Canada), Fanny Tree (England), Ada White (Northern Ireland), Violet Foster (Britannia), ---- (Wales), Eileen Blandford (Scotland), Hilda Shorter (Newfoundland), ---- (Australia)
Middle row includes: Peggy Foreman and Winifred Gravel
Front row includes: Alfred Croucher, George Wilkinson, Stanley Forward, Bernard Hirst, and Reginald Guest.

One of the major events which took place regularly in both parishes was the Beating of the Bounds, held until relatively recently. The next two photographs show the elements of the Bearsted ceremony. They are not specifically dated but they were taken before the Second World War. The participants assembled outside the shops in Chestnut Place.

Reproduced courtesy of Margaret Morris

Occasional Holidays and Celebrations (for Children of All Ages)

Everyone carried hazel wands which were used to beat the boundary stones or parish markers as this undated photograph shows:

Reproduced courtesy of Jessie Page

The photograph below dates from around 1955, and shows the 'bumping' part of the ceremony in which someone was chosen to receive a physical reminder of the boundaries. It was taken where the Ashford Road crosses over the Lilk stream opposite Major's Lake and close by to Otham Lane; the boundaries of Bearsted, Thurnham and Otham wriggle around in this area in a fairly erratic fashion.

Reproduced courtesy of David J Elliott

Occasional Holidays and Celebrations (for Children of All Ages)

The Beating of the Bounds for Thurnham parish was slightly more complicated in that the wide extent of the Thurnham boundaries meant that the ceremony took place over two days. The photograph below shows the enormous map of the parish which accompanied the ceremony in 1911 and was probably taken during the lunch break. Note the man behind the top of the map; to hold it, he has had to stand on the top of a haystack!

Reproduced courtesy of Chris and Sue Hunt

Norah Giles recalled that on one occasion she was able to have some time off school along with Fred Martin as they were chosen to witness the beating-of-the-bounds in Thurnham. On the second day Norah walked a great deal of the distance with the vicar of Thurnham, the Rev Arthur Scutt, and Mr Scott, who lived in a house in Thurnham called The Friars. At the end the day, tea was taken at The Tudor House tea room and Norah went along too; a great treat!

In this undated photograph, the Thurnham boundary marker on the tree has just been renewed:

Reproduced courtesy of Margaret Peat

Occasional Holidays and Celebrations (for Children of All Ages)

Day excursions and outings grew in popularity in the late nineteenth and twentieth centuries. Groups and societies in the two villages arranged them, using horse drawn vehicles and then, as technology developed, motorised vehicles. For the outing shown below, the ladies are clearly dressed in their finery and there is a definite air of celebration evident. However, the outing certainly took place after 1906 as the corner of the Men's Institute building is just visible on the right hand side of the photograph. Note the solid rims to the wheels; the ride may not have been particularly comfortable!

Reproduced courtesy of Brenda Donn

Excursions and visits by the choirs for Holy Cross and St Mary's churches were greatly anticipated. The venues for these included Margate, Folkestone and Dover. This is an undated photograph of one outing. The lettering just visible on the side of the coach indicates it was owned by the Maidstone and District Motor Services Limited.

Reproduced courtesy of Margaret Tomalin

During 1949, Bearsted parish council decided to mark the Festival of Britain, due to take place in 1951, by erecting a village sign. A competition was held with a £5 prize. There were nineteen competitors and twenty four designs.[21] The competition winner was Alan Warland, an architect and talented artist who lived in Otham Lane. His work regularly featured in the exhibitions of the Maidstone Art Club. Alan's son, Peter, recalled that his father thoroughly discussed the matter with his family around the dining table. Alan was a particularly keen cricket follower, and thought it appropriate that Alfred Mynn should be the centre piece of the sign, flanked by oast houses and Holy Cross church, complete with its beasts. As the design took shape in the studio, several versions were produced before Alan was satisfied.

The sign, mounted on a nine feet high oak post, cost £69 and 17 shillings to make and was unveiled in 1951.[22] The photograph below was taken at the ceremony and as Peter has commented, captured the scene beautifully with the small group on the balcony of the White Horse, the flags, the infant in the pram and the dogs patiently waiting. Alan Warland is standing directly behind the flag on the left hand side of the photograph. It is understood that the homburg-hatted gentlemen are Messrs Grout and Monckton, the Chairman and Vice Chairman of the Parish Council. Also, just visible is the surplice worn by Walter Yeandle, vicar of Bearsted, who is standing behind the foremost figure in the draped-off area:

Reproduced courtesy of Peter Warland

As Peter recalled, Alan was always extremely proud of the village sign and took an interest in the way it has weathered on the green and the occasional need for its renovation. Since it was first erected, the sign has become one of the most familiar features of Bearsted situated on the green at the heart of the village.

Kathryn Kersey

Coronations and Jubilees

For any British monarch, accession is a solemn and unforgettable moment. On 20 June 1837, Victoria ascended the throne aged just eighteen, and at a time when the monarch held relatively little political power. Britain was a well-established constitutional monarchy. Few of her subjects would have hazarded a guess as to how long she would be queen or what enormous social, economic and technological progress the nation would achieve during her reign.

By 1887 Victoria had been queen for fifty years, and the official commemoration of this achievement was known as a 'Jubilee'. Although there is little recorded in the local press about the 1887 celebrations, Bearsted School log book mentions: [1]

> 20 June 1887
> Monday - all day holiday on account of the Jubilee.
>
> 8 July
> A very good attendance this week, the Jubilee School Treat having been announced for Friday 8th.
> The vicar visited and informed the children of the arrangements for the tea.
> Half holiday in the afternoon for the Treat.

It is probable that there were several commemorative photographs taken, but only one image seems to have survived: this was a group of children at Bearsted School. There are no records as to the identity of anyone in the photograph, but John Day was Master between 1884 and 1897 and he was certainly assisted in his teaching duties by his wife, Emily. It is possible that they are included in the photograph which is shown below. Note the wording on the mount:

Reproduced courtesy of Roseacre School

21

Coronations and Jubilees

In 1897, Queen Victoria celebrated her Diamond Jubilee. The local festivities included the unveiling of a wooden pump cover by the White Horse, shown in this later photograph. The pump cover has been restored on several occasions and still stands by the Green.

Reproduced courtesy of Terry Clarke

This report of the local festivities appeared in the Bearsted parish magazine: [2]

The Queen's Jubilee

The Jubilee Festivities on June 22 for the joint parishes of Bearsted and Thurnham passed off without a hitch, owing to the energy and forethought of the Committee, aided by the active labours of a large number of volunteer helpers.

There was to have been a Church Parade but owing to the very serious illness of the Vicar of Bearsted, this part of the programme was perforce abandoned. At 1.30pm the actual proceedings began with the singing of the National Anthem and a procession of about 250 children round the Green, headed by the Sutton Valence Band. During the afternoon, various races were run, the sack-races perhaps evoking the greatest interest. A large fire-balloon was let off with great success at each hour except at 5pm (when everyone was busily occupied elsewhere). The Schoolrooms had been placed in the hands of the Committee by the School Managers and the Parish Hall by Mr Marley, and free teas were given to all ticket-holders of the two parishes, young and old. The tables were most tastefully decorated with beautiful flowers and a bountiful meal was provided and we may further say was thoroughly appreciated by about 370 children and about 550 adults.

In the evening 252 Diamond Jubilee mugs were presented to the School Children and oranges and buns to all the children on the Green. At half-past 9 the whole Green was lit up with coloured fires, which made our picturesque village appear more picturesque than ever, and showed up the decorations which some had taken the trouble to put up, to great advantage. This was followed by a display of fireworks, which lasted until 10, when the Thurnham bonfire and the bonfires all round the country were lighted. From Thurnham Hill, nearly 60 bonfires could be counted, the effect being fine indeed.

Reproduced courtesy of Holy Cross church

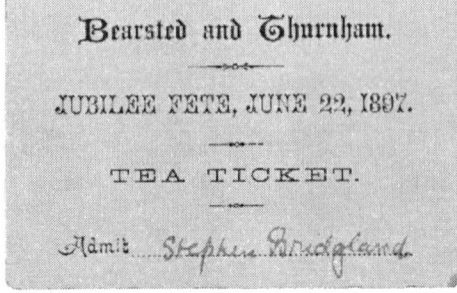

It was agreed by the organisers of the celebrations that tickets would be issued and then surrendered before participation in the events. As Stephen Bridgland had a ticket, but did not attend the tea, the ticket shown here, is an astonishingly rare survival.

Reproduced courtesy of Norah Giles

Coronations and Jubilees

The next two photographs were taken to commemorate the Diamond Jubilee. The children are standing in front of The White Horse by a door that is now blocked up, situated on the corner of Yeoman Lane and The Street.

Both reproduced courtesy of Roseacre School

Coronations and Jubilees

In 1902 King Edward VII acceded to the throne. However, the preparations for the coronation were disrupted as he became unwell and needed an operation. The coronation was postponed and a nation offered prayers for a swift recovery. The July edition of the Bearsted parish magazine carried details of the situation and the decisions made about the celebration: [3]

> The Coronation Festivities which had been so greatly looked forward to, had to take place in a very different spirit to what we anticipated. Owing to the sudden and dangerous illness of our King, which postponed his coronation so abruptly and unexpectedly most of the national rejoicings, especially those in London, had of course, to be put off, but with his usual forethought and consideration for his people so as to avoid inconvenience or disappointment, the King expressed his earnest desire that all Celebrations which had been arranged in the Country, should still be carried through.
>
> A Special Committee Meeting was therefore called here, with the result that the Public Dinner and Children's Tea took place on what should have been Coronation Day and the Sports Programme was carried out on a modified scale, much to the joy of the children who took part. In the morning, there was a Special Service of Intercession for the King, at which many people were present.
>
> After the Children's Tea in the School, Mr Tasker kindly invited them up to *Snowfield*, where Mrs Tasker presented each child with a book, descriptive of the Realm of our King, and Mrs Whitehead gave away over 100 mugs commemorative of the occasion. Three cheers were given for the donors and Miss Barclay, but perhaps the heartiest were those which Mr Tasker called for the King. It was a hard day for the Committee who all helped so well, and the best thanks of all are due to Mr Whitehead, upon whom as Secretary fell the chief share of organisation.
>
> The day passed off very quietly, indeed no one seemed to forget under what anxious circumstances they were gathered together. The cloud of suspense that hung so darkly over us that day seems now, by God's mercy to be dispersing as we read day by day of the King's remarkable progress towards recovery.

Reproduced courtesy of Holy Cross church

By the time George V's coronation took place on 22 June 1911, the villages were in the grip of measles epidemic. Both schools were closed but the communities still celebrated. It is possible that the large photograph featured on the next page, showing the children in front of the school, was taken on this occasion.

It is likely that the next three small photographs, showing sports events on the Green, were also taken at the 1911 coronation celebrations:

Reproduced courtesy of Margaret Tomalin

Coronations and Jubilees

Reproduced courtesy of Roseacre School

Reproduced courtesy of Margaret Tomalin

Reproduced courtesy of Jean Jones

For the celebrations of the 1935 Silver Jubilee of George V's accession, the parishes of Bearsted and Thurnham combined. On 6 May, there was a Thanksgiving service at Holy Cross church and in the afternoon, sports were held on the Green. A tea was held at the Women's Institute hall for children aged between five and fourteen. Violet Hale remembered that her cup of tea was served in a Jubilee mug. The parish council accounts reveal the total cost of the mugs came to £7 10s and the refreshments cost £10.[4]

Coronations and Jubilees

This is one of the many designs available for the commemorative mugs:

Reproduced courtesy of Malcolm Kersey

Later in the day there was dancing on the Green, a beacon was lit at Thurnham castle and there was a display of fireworks. As part of the Jubilee celebrations, children were given free rides at a fair held in Mote Park. There was also a Jubilee Essay competition set by the Member of Parliament for Maidstone, Mr A C Bossom. The winners were presented with Jubilee Medals.

For the coronation of George VI on 12 May 1937 Bearsted and Thurnham combined once more for the celebrations, as was reported in the parish magazine: [5]

Coronation Celebrations

Coronation Day was both a Holy Day and a holiday. The religious significance of the occasion was not lost on Bearsted, nor did we fail to rejoice at the crowning of our King. Our celebrations were combined with those of Thurnham and a committee representing both parishes planned the various events for the day. Bearsted bells, rung on many Coronation days, heralded the proceedings at 6.45am and were heard again in the afternoon.

Holy Communion was celebrated at 7.15am and at 8am at Bearsted church and the morning was free for listening to the broadcast from Westminster Abbey. The broadcast and the inclement weather combined to keep most people indoors until the sports commenced in the afternoon.

In the Fancy Dress parade, the standard of entries was high and in spite of the discouraging weather, the numbers were good. After dusk a bonfire was lit on Thurnham Hill and so despite the poor weather the two villages celebrated the Coronation of His Majesty King George VI.

The Green was gay with colour. Fluttering pennants strung between decorated and beflagged poles encircled the Green. There were two decorated arches whilst the houses round the Green, dressed with flags and bunting, lent colour to the scene. There were prizes for the best decorated houses. The persistent rain caused a postponement of the start of the sports but in spite of the weather, a start was made soon after 3pm and the whole programme completed. During the afternoon, many people sent off balloons. We have not yet heard of any that have gone prodigious distances but they have got to August Bank Holiday! About 200 Bearsted and Thurnham children had tea at the WI and were presented with Coronation mugs.

In the Fancy Dress parade, the standard of entries was high and in spite of the discouraging weather, the numbers were good. After dusk a bonfire was lit on Thurnham Hill and so despite the poor weather the two villages celebrated the Coronation of His Majesty King George VI.

Reproduced courtesy of Holy Cross church

Bearsted had a direct involvement during the coronation ceremony of Queen Elizabeth II in 1953 as the vicar of Bearsted, the Rev John Long, carried a cross before the Archbishop of Canterbury in Westminster Abbey. Before coming to Bearsted, he had been the Archbishop's chaplain.[6]

Coronations and Jubilees

Closer to home, Bearsted School was given the responsibility for supervising the village sports on the Green. Alas, the sports day was washed out by rain in a typically British fashion but there was a very successful carnival procession. The parish council gave the children china mugs as a souvenir and a street party was held at Cross Keys on 4 June as this photograph below shows:

Reproduced courtesy of Rosemary Pearce

This is part of the Coronation Souvenir Programme that was printed for the local festivities:

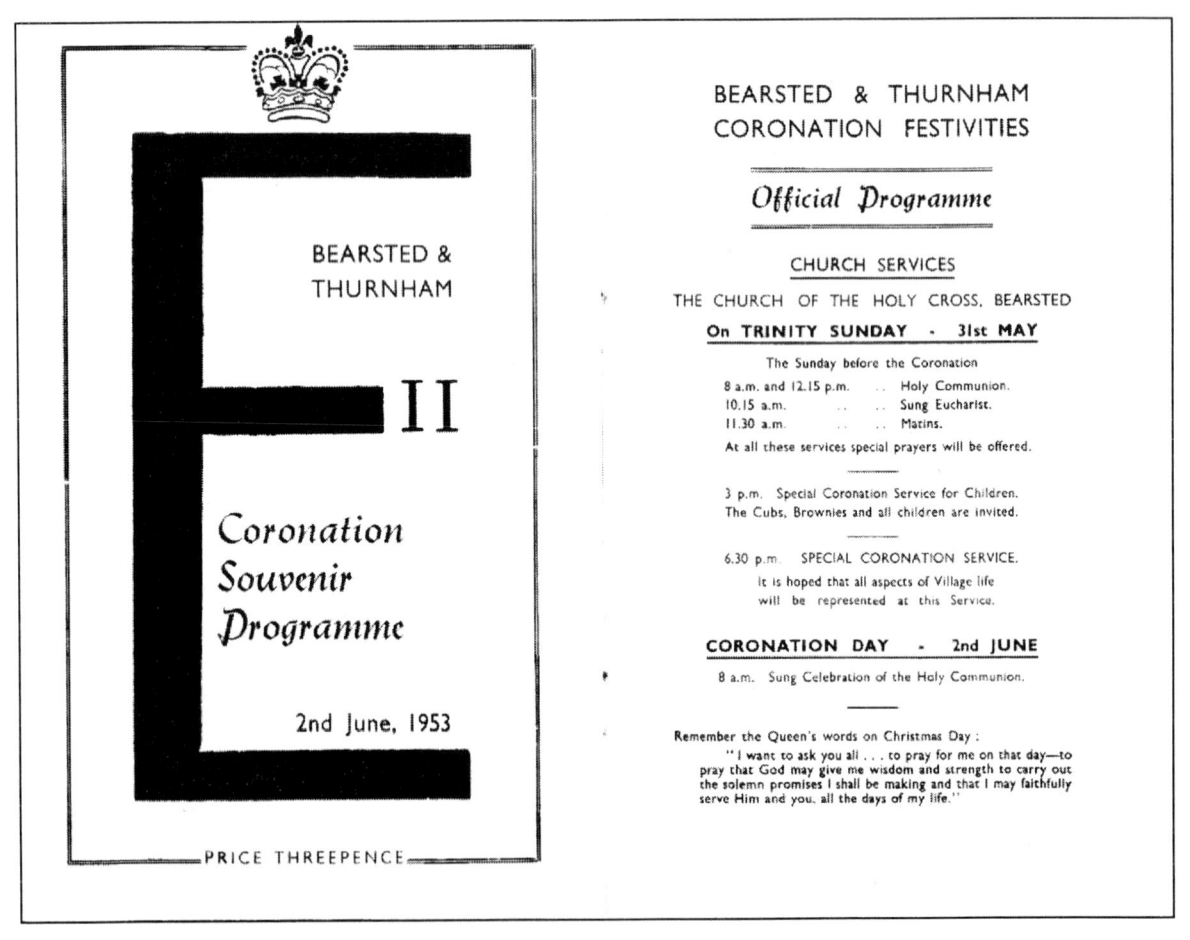

BEARSTED & THURNHAM

E II

Coronation Souvenir Programme

2nd June, 1953

PRICE THREEPENCE

BEARSTED & THURNHAM CORONATION FESTIVITIES

Official Programme

CHURCH SERVICES

THE CHURCH OF THE HOLY CROSS, BEARSTED

On TRINITY SUNDAY - 31st MAY

The Sunday before the Coronation

8 a.m. and 12.15 p.m. .. Holy Communion.
10.15 a.m. .. .. Sung Eucharist.
11.30 a.m. .. .. Matins.

At all these services special prayers will be offered.

3 p.m. Special Coronation Service for Children.
The Cubs, Brownies and all children are invited.

6.30 p.m. SPECIAL CORONATION SERVICE.
It is hoped that all aspects of Village life will be represented at this Service.

CORONATION DAY - 2nd JUNE

8 a.m. Sung Celebration of the Holy Communion.

Remember the Queen's words on Christmas Day:
"I want to ask you all . . . to pray for me on that day—to pray that God may give me wisdom and strength to carry out the solemn promises I shall be making and that I may faithfully serve Him and you, all the days of my life."

Reproduced courtesy of Norah Giles

On 12 June 1953 Robert Skinner, and several other members of Bearsted School staff, accompanied seventy-two children on a visit to London to see all the coronation decorations. British Railways ran an express train and the children arrived in time to see the Queen drive past to Guildhall in an open coach. In the afternoon they embarked upon a three-hour coach tour of the streets.

Eileen Jakes (née Young) was a teacher at Bearsted during this time, and recalled:

> In 1953, a week after the Coronation, a trip was arranged to see the London decorations. A special train from Folkestone picked us up at Bearsted station and took us to Charing Cross. I remember that we were responsible for ten children each. They were well drilled about safety and were extremely good. The crowds were enormous and quite terrifying.
>
> At one point we managed to climb to a stand near Admiralty Arch and there we saw the Queen and the Duke ride by in an open carriage on one of their state drives. Some of the children were disappointed that the Queen was not wearing her crown but wore an ordinary coat and hat!
>
> Getting back to Charing Cross was truly a nightmare and as a young teacher I was quite frightened. I instructed my ten children to hold hands in a line and I took the hand of the first child and pulled him through the dense crowds. I warned them not to let go or they would be lost. As I pulled, I continually looked behind and saw their little white faces coming along.
>
> All went well and we arrived safely on the station platform where Mr Skinner counted everyone on to the train.

1977 marked the Silver Jubilee of the accession of Queen Elizabeth. The Bearsted and Thurnham Jubilee Committee was formed by Bearsted parish council. It was decided to revive the Bearsted and Thurnham Fayre, overseen by Pat Marshall, and proved so popular that it has been run ever since. The main celebrations for the Jubilee took place over several days.

The Fayre took place on 4 June and included a carnival procession which wound its way through the roads from Madginford Junior School, to Landway, past Roseacre School and arrived at the Green for the official opening at 2pm. The theme for the floats and procession was 'film or television cartoons'. There were sports and sideshows too on the Green. In the evening there was a dance and barbeque followed by fireworks.

On 5 June, a service of Thanksgiving was held at Holy Cross church and on the following day, several street parties were held. The bell ringers also performed a quarter peal to mark the event and concluded by ringing the bells in an order known as 'Queens' which was thought to be most appropriate. On 7 June, a beacon was lit at Thurnham castle which formed part of a chain of bonfires from Windsor to Dover.[7]

The majority of the Silver Jubilee celebrations were marked, by thoroughly traditional, and very mixed, British weather! Although it was dry for the Fayre, a great many of the street parties planned for 6 June were either abandoned or, if space permitted, moved indoors so there are few photographs available.

Coronations and Jubilees

These photographs below show some of the carnival procession floats. The official jubilee insignia can be sign on the side of the lorry cab in the first picture.

Both reproduced courtesy of Ian Lambert

The parish magazine carried the following report about the festivities: [8]

> **Bearsted & Thurnham Jubilee Carnival**
>
> Bearsted & Thurnham Jubilee Carnival and Fayre was held on Bearsted Green on 4 June, and the celebrations on that day will be remembered by many.
>
> A pre-requisite of a successful outdoor function is good weather and we were extremely fortunate in this respect and as a result, takings from all sources, Carnival, Fete, Barbeque and Disco exceeded £1,700. After deductions of expenses, a net profit will be £800 to be given to the Queen's Silver Jubilee Appeal.
>
> This is an exceptionally good result and all credit is due to the hard work and effort of the various organisations in both Bearsted & Thurnham parishes. Particular mention must be made of Madginford Residents' Association, Eylesden Court School, Thurnham Football Club, Bearsted Round Table, The WRVS, The WI's, Scouts, Guides, Cubs, Brownies, and the local political and church organisations.
>
> The parishes took part in the local downs bonfire chain and successfully linked with Hollingbourne and Detling on Monday night. The Bearsted & Thurnham beacon was lit by Farmer John Button at 10.17pm on his land at Cold Blow Farm. He provided labour, material and equipment to assist Thurnham Football Club in building a very adequate beacon at short notice.
>
> We would also like to extend our thanks to the few who attended early on Sunday morning to clear the Green and the school especially to the ladies who picked up all the litter.

Reproduced courtesy of Holy Cross and St Mary's churches

The parish councils also decided to mark the Jubilee. Thurnham Parish Council installed a seat in Sharsted Way, Ware Street and planted trees in the parish. Photographs of the trees were later presented to Thurnham Infant School. Bearsted Parish Council agreed to place a drinking fountain upon the Green. There were problems with the local water pressure which had to be resolved before it could be installed, so it was not until December that it was unveiled.

This photograph shows the fountain today:

Reproduced courtesy of Malcolm Kersey

Coronations and Jubilees

Twenty five years later, there was once again a great deal of debate about marking the Golden Jubilee of Queen Elizabeth II's accession. The Fayre programme carried details of the local celebrations and part of this is shown below:

Bearsted Parish Council
warmly invite you
to our Jubilee Celebrations
"June is Jubilee Month"

MAY 27TH – 30TH
'Jubilee Jolly Week'
Madginford Park Infants' School
Contact: 738351
(Linda Cann or Carol Denham)

SATURDAY JUNE 8TH
Bearsted Choral Society Concert
Holy Cross Church 7.30pm
FREE Entry
Mozart's Mass in C ~
The Coronation Mass plus
9.30am–11.30am Open Day Singing in
Holy Cross
An invitation to ALL to come and sing
Contact: Joan Simon 738649

WEDNESDAY JUNE 12TH
Pre-School Children's Party
10am–12 noon
at the Guides & Brownies Site,
Church Landway
Contact: June Wilkins 737773

FRIDAY JUNE 14TH
'Music on the Green'
Maidstone Winds and
Dicky Diamond's Traditional
Jazz Band
Go 'alfresco on the Green' for a summer
evening's entertainment
Refreshments and Barbecue available
Fireworks at 10.30pm
Car parking in the Elizabeth Harvey Field
(entrance via Cross Keys)
Admission a £3.00 donation to be
collected by the Scouts

SATURDAY JUNE 22ND
Bowls Club Open Day
10am–12noon Junior Coaching/Training
Fun Matches for Novices
(enter your team NOW)
Contact: Cliff Hill 739164

SATURDAY JUNE 22ND
Guides' Sausage Sizzle &
Treasure Hunt
Church Landway Site
Contact: Shan Lythgoe 738304
4.00pm–6.30pm
Food and drink at 5.00pm
Tickets £3.00 adults, £2.00 children
Join us on our Treasure Hunt in the
afternoon

SATURDAY JUNE 22ND
Round-Kent Veteran Car Rally
(Victorian/Edwardian Veteran cars)
The Village Green (by the pond)
2.00pm–4.30pm
Contact: Eileen Terry at the KM 717880
"The London–Brighton comes to
Bearsted"

SUNDAY JUNE 23RD
Churches Together in Bearsted
"Songs of Praise'
Holy Cross Church 3.30pm
Contact: Christine Tate 737183

TUESDAY JUNE 25TH
Roseacre Junior School Concert
Astley House
Contact: The School 737843

SATURDAY JUNE 29TH
Bearsted and Thurnham Carnival & Fayre
1.15 Procession and Opening Ceremony
Closes at 5.00pm

**MONDAY JULY 1ST –
THURSDAY JULY 4TH**
Roseacre School Jubilee Pageant
Contact: 737843

Reproduced courtesy of Bearsted and Thurnham Fayre Committee

Coronations and Jubilees

After hearing about the coronation in 1953, the children at Thurnham and Roseacre schools were keen to commemorate the Golden Jubilee. A summer concert and a pageant of children's literature were held. Part of the programme from the pageant is shown below:

"FIFTY GOLDEN YEARS OF CHILDREN'S LITERATURE"

Afternoon Performance - Monday 1st July
Evening Performance - Wednesday 3rd July

YEAR 3 - presents Tales from Enid Blyton

Introduction	
Song - "The Faraway Tree"	
Dance - Fairy Dance	
Five on a Treasure Island	
Song - "Row Row"	
Song - "A Policeman's Lot"	
Noddy	
Song - "The Faraway Tree"	

Interval

YEAR 5

5R	BFG by Roald Dahl
5W	The Church Mice by Graham Oakley
	Summer Holiday by Graham Oakley
5G	Charlie & The Chocolate Factory by Roald Dahl
5W	Rats by Graham Oakley
	The New Parson by Graham Oakley
5R	Matilda by Roald Dahl

Afternoon Performance - Tuesday 2nd July
Evening Performance - Thursday 4th July

YEAR 4 & YEAR 6

Year 6CA	The Bash Street Kids from The Beano
Year 4HC	Playground Poetry
Year 6DT	Chitty Chitty Bang Bang by Ian Fleming
Year 4BT	"When I grow up!" Aspirations for the future

Interval

Year 6CL	Harry Potter and The Philosopher's Stone by JK Rowling
Year 4HB	People, Poems & Pets
	Year 4 choir
Year 6GM	The Lottie Project by Jacqueline Wilson

There will also be refreshments provided, courtesy of the PTA. Tickets for the Grand Draw will be drawn after the performance on Thursday 4th July.

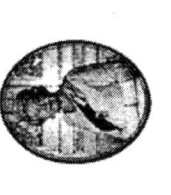

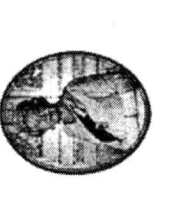

Reproduced courtesy of Roseacre School

Kathryn Kersey

Cricket – an introduction

The game of cricket developed in the Weald of Kent. Significant dates relative to the modern game are 1744 when the first known laws of cricket were issued; 1750, when the Hambledon Club was formed in Hampshire; 1760, the first reference to cricket played at Oxford; 1744; the first innings to reach a century was recorded, and 1788, when the Marylebone Cricket Club played their first match at the original Lords cricket ground.

The two parishes of Bearsted and Thurnham can therefore lay claim to being nurseries of the noble game of cricket as the earliest local references to cricket are 1749 at Bearsted, 1773 at Thurnham and 1789 at Milgate Park.

It is regrettable that it has not always been possible to show conclusively that cricket has been played on a continuous basis by the three clubs. This is not surprising, as newspaper reports were limited in the early days and generally confined to the County and major clubs, or those which involved well-known players of the day. Some clubs obviously preferred playing cricket to making a formal record of matches played, especially as they had to submit their own match reports for publication for which, in 1878, the Kent Messenger newspaper required payment of one shilling.

There were other factors which also influenced whether or not games were played. For example, in 1888 neither Detling or Boxley were able to field a full team, owing to the weather being favourable for making hay! [1]

Games were played at Maidstone relatively early in the history of the game too. Events and games at the county town, seem to have attracted more attention from artists than those which took place at the local villages. This picture is undated but is believed to depict a game in Maidstone around 1800 and that William Alexander may have been the artist. [2]

Reproduced courtesy of MCC

In the following pages there is information about cricket being played at Bearsted, Thurnham and Milgate Park. All three clubs had distinctly individual characteristics.

Ian Lambert

Bearsted Cricket Club: The First Two Hundred Years

The spectacle of a cricket match taking place on the Green at Bearsted; the players in white forming a background as leather meets willow, encapsulates an essential part of English country life. Even the village sign shows Alfred Mynn depicted forever at the crease:

Reproduced courtesy of Malcolm Kersey

Bearsted certainly has one of the earliest grounds in the country but the exact date that cricket was first played on the Green remains unknown. Barely five years after the laws of cricket were written down and published, an article appeared in the General Advertiser, 11 August 1749:

> In the Artillery Ground, Finsbury Square, London, Monday next at 1.00pm, Eleven Gentlemen of Bearsted, Kent, play against the Gentlemen of London, for one guinea per man of their own money exclusive of all other by-bets which may be considerable. The Gentlemen having beaten the neighbouring parishes and thereby themselves inferior to few induces them to come so far to play....

It is from this date that the club's origins are accepted, as the report provides conclusive evidence that Bearsted was part of the development of cricket.

E W Swanton, one of the most influential and authoritative commentators on cricket, wrote: [1]

> ...Cricket was born and first nurtured in the Weald, as all historians are well aware. The roots however lie deeper and stronger in some places than in others, and the credentials of Bearsted are unassailable, copper-bottomed and whatever phrase comes to mind...

During the first hundred years of cricket the game underwent an evolution to resemble the game played today. In the eighteenth century, there were few teams but no shortage of matches. It was therefore not uncommon for areas to amalgamate and there are references to Bearsted combining as a team with players from Charing, Leeds, Woodchurch and Harrietsham for matches. Other combinations included Bearsted, Thurnham, Detling and Boxley; also Bearsted, Thurnham and Leeds.[2]

Some games involved just a few players. In 1785 three men of Barming played Mr Thomas Taylor of Maidstone and Mr Robert Clifford, wheelwright and landlord of the White Horse at Bearsted, for twenty five guineas a side. As a young man, an accident had resulted in two of the fingers on Robert's right hand contracting into the palm of his hand. Despite this disability, he was evidently very successful at his chosen sport as he played for Kent and All England. He was buried in the churchyard at Bearsted, but not before he passed on a love of the game to his son and grandson who also played for the club.[3]

Many local people, including members of the Betts and Ellis families, played in matches in the early years of the nineteenth century. In 1829 it was recorded that George and Thomas Betts of Bearsted played against James and John Rayfield of Tovil; two people in each side. The Betts family were either butchers or farmers but devoted a considerable amount of their free time to cricket. Two members of the Ellis family, William and John, began to play in 1847. William kept the Royal Oak pub and John was a Collector of Rates. Thomas Knowles, a plumber, also started that year. Thomas was joined by his four sons and one of his brothers. Another member of the family, Henry Joseph Knowles, played until 1878 before retiring. He subsequently became the first named umpire for Bearsted. Henry ran the White Horse between 1899 and 1903.[4]

However the most famous cricketing name in Bearsted and Thurnham during the reign of Queen Victoria is that of Alfred Mynn. Although Alfred was born in Goudhurst, he spent a great deal of his life in and around Bearsted where he played cricket from 1831 until his death in 1861. Alfred and his family lived in various local properties including Snowfield Cottage, and then a house at Friningham in Thurnham before moving to Mount Pleasant in Ware Street It is not surprising that he quickly received the nickname of the 'mighty Mynn' as at the height of his career, Alfred stood over six feet tall and weighed over eighteen stone.[5]

This undated portrait of Alfred Mynn gives an indication of his physical appearance: [6]

Reproduced courtesy of Cambridge University Press

Alfred regularly played for Bearsted with his brother, Walter. He once played a single wicket competition on the Green. against Nicholas Wanostracht, who was usually known as Felix, another legendary figure of the era.

At the end of October in 1861, Alfred suddenly died whilst away from home. His funeral was held on 6 November, in atrocious weather conditions, and he was laid to rest in Thurnham churchyard, next to the grave of two of his daughters; Mary and Eliza. The report of his funeral referred to the cortege proceeding past the White Horse public house where Alfred had been the centre of many convivial evenings.[7]

Between 1872 and 1895 there were two other cricket organisations which briefly flourished and played on the Green: Bearsted Camomile Club and Bearsted Chestnut Place. The Camomile Club took its name from the plant which grew on the Green. They reputedly opened the season at Bearsted on Good Fridays. The Chestnut Place Club took its name from the area at the bottom of Thurnham Lane.[8] It is not clear why these two clubs were not part of Bearsted Cricket Club. Games were not played on the same day by the various clubs and it known that some players appeared for more than one of them. It is possible that they played under the umbrella of the main club but there is no evidence of an agreed formal arrangement.

The first surviving information about the structure of Bearsted Cricket Club dates from 1875. Presumably prior to this there had been some re-organisation and in November, a meeting was held. The following were elected: [9]

President:	J R Isherwood
Treasurer:	H Tasker
Secretary:	W E Balston
Committee:	Messrs Stoneham, Meredith, Turley, Warman, Carberry, Knowles and the vicar of Bearsted, Frederic Mayne.

Just as the team and match arrangements for the game have evolved, so has the location of the cricket square at Bearsted. It is not known where the first square was placed. The schedule which accompanies the 1842 tithe map for Bearsted recorded the Green cultivated as 'pasture' but it was also described as a cricketing ground.[10]

This photograph is undated but is believed to have been taken in the early 1900s. It shows a cricket match taking place at a different location on the Green near to the pond:

Reproduced courtesy of Irene Hales

In 1876 there was a successful application to close the public footway running across the Green in a diagonal direction from Yeoman Lane towards the Royal Oak public house. The application was successful and the path was closed up and turfed over.[11]

In 1896, local residents supported the formation of a boys cricket club. The details are sparse, and it is not clear if it was part of the main cricket club, or how long it operated. The boys played under the name of Bearsted Star. The parish magazine in June recorded: [12]

The Rev A L Brine begs to acknowledge with many thanks the following kind subscriptions to his boys cricket club:			
Rev J Scarth	5s	Mr H Tasker	5s
General Talbot	5s	Mr E Green	5s
Mr W Fremlin	5s	Mr J Wood	5s
Mr A'Vard	5s	Dr Adams	2s 6d
Mr E Procketer	2s 6d	Mr J Jewell	2s 6d
Mr H Bensted	2s 6d	Mrs Topley	2s 6d
Mr C Tubb	2s 6d	Rev A L Brine	2s 6d
Total £2 12s 6d			

Reproduced courtesy of Holy Cross church, Bearsted

Games played in the first year included one at Milgate Park, and in the following year, against Mr Perrin's XI on the Green.[13]

This undated photograph is the oldest known in Bearsted to show two cricket teams. From the background details it was certainly taken before 1906, because there is a glimpse of the original forge on the left hand side which was replaced by the Men's Club building in that year. The men are standing by Raggetts butchers premises on the Green. It is not clear whether all the players are from Bearsted and nothing is known about their identities:

Reproduced courtesy of Richard Tree

38

The only known person to have been lived in Bearsted and to have played First Class cricket in the 1900s was Eric Jesser Fulcher. He was born 12 March 1890 but sadly died at the age of 32 in Llandogo, Monmouth, as the result of a gun accident. He was recorded on the 1891 census as living at Milgate Park. He attended school at Radley. In 1911 to 1912 he toured Argentina with the MCC under Lord Hawke but was then playing for Norfolk.

Eric's first class debut was in 1913 and he played four matches for Kent in 1919 before playing his tenth and final First Class game for the MCC in 1921. Eric probably inherited his talent for cricket from his father, Arthur William Jesser Fulcher, who had played seven matches for Kent between 1878 and 1887. [14]

During the early years of the twentieth century, Sir Pelham Warner lived at Caring House. Pelham was born in Trinidad, where his father had been Attorney-General. During his distinguished career, he scored nearly 30,000 runs and received virtually every honour that the game could offer, both on and off the field. He captained Middlesex and England between 1894 and 1920.[15]

On 20 April 1907 a match was played on the Green between Warner's XI and Bearsted. This souvenir photograph is notable because it is one of the few images from this time to have all the players named:

Reproduced courtesy of Bearsted Cricket Club

<u>Back Row (left to right)</u>: A Whitehead, J Douglas, Aviss, G Rivierre, B W Haynes, G G Napier, B D Bannon, W Betts, R A Kent, J J Ellis, J A Gibb
<u>Middle Row (left to right)</u>: M W Payne, B J T Bosanquet, W H Whitehead, P F Warner, Canon Scarth, H Tasker, C H B Marsham, J R Mason
<u>Front Row (left to right)</u>: B Tillman, J Walkling, S Gibbons, (blank), F Ballard, E Smith, F Murray.

In 1909, a match was played between Bearsted and HMS Dominion. It is believed that this is one of the few references to Pelham playing for Bearsted rather than Warner's XI. The following scorecard and photograph featured in the Kent Messenger. Some of the players may have participated at the invitation of Sir Pelham.

```
BEARSTED v. H.M.S. DOMINION.
Played at Bearsted on Saturday, resulting in
a win for the village by 53 runs. Score:—
            BEARSTED.
F. L. Fane st Godfrey b Syfret....      20
L. H. W. Troughton c de Roebeck b
    do ...............................   8
B. D. Bannon st Godfrey b Morna-
    ment ............................   14
B. J. T. Bosanquet c Brooke b Syfret   12
P. F. Warner c Brooke b Elstob....     73
Rear Ad. Sir F. Jellicoe c Bigg-
    Wither b Mornament .............    6
K. G. MacLeod b Elstob .............   19
W. H. Whitehead lbw b Mornament         7
A. Brownscombe b Dutton ............   45
G. C. Mercer not out ...............   20
J. J. Ellis b Brooke ...............    1
                    Extras......  23—248
         H.M.S. DOMINION.
Capt. de Roebeck b Bosanquet......     18
Lieut.-Surg. Jones b do ............    7
Mornament b MacLeod ................    1
Bigg-Wither b Bosanquet ............    6
Godfrey c Brownscombe b MacLeod         0
Elstob b Bosanquet .................   13
Syfret b Bosanquet .................    4
Forbes b do ........................    0
Morgan not out .....................   84
Dutton c Brownscombe b do ..........    6
Brooke b Ellis .....................   33
                    Extras......  23—195
```

Both reproduced courtesy of Kent Messenger newspaper group

THE MATCH ON BEARSTED GREEN

<u>Standing top row (left to right)</u>: Lieutenant E N Syvret RN, G C Mercer, J Ellis, Captain Godfrey, Lieutenant Bigg-Wither RA, Forbes, Morgan, B J T Bosanquet, A Brownscombe
<u>Sitting middle row (left to right)</u>: Rear Admiral Sir J Rushworth Jellicoe KCVO, Captain De Roebeck, P F Warner, Lieutenant Dutton RN, W H Whitehead, B D Bannon
<u>Front Row (left to right)</u>: K G MacLeod, M P Jones, F L Fane, L H Troughton, R H Mornament RN, Brook, E B Elstob
<u>Umpires</u> (left) Mr Underdown (Lenham) and (right) Lieutenant D Blair HMS Dominion.

Sir Pelham was instrumental in bringing many famous cricketers of the era to play on the Green with the most notable team being the South African tourists in 1929. Maidstone Cricket Week always reduced the attendance figures at Bearsted School but the children were given a special holiday on 29 April 1929 in order to attend the match by kind permission of the School Managers.[16] This photograph was taken of the two teams:

Reproduced courtesy of Chris and Sue Hunt

Roger Vidler was able to supply the details of some of the leading figures in this photograph:

Back Row (left to right): Mr R T Stanyforth, (Captain of England whilst in South Africa between 1927 and 1928), (next four men are unknown), 'Patsy' Hendren (of Middlesex and England) and Greville Stevens, (of Middlesex and England).
Middle Row (left to right): The Honourable Lionel Tennyson who is wearing cricket sweater with a distinctive v pattern, (next two men are unknown), A J Evans, (a former Captain of Kent is wearing a vertically striped blazer), Frank Woolley of Kent and England, (the rest of the row are unknown).
Front Row (left to right): Mr C Frelinghaus (Manager of South African Tourists), Plum Warner, Mr Whitehead, Lord Harris, H G Deane (Captain of South African Tourists), H G Owen Smith is crouching at the end of the row.

This press cutting is unsourced, but contains details of the match:

CRICKET ON THE VILLAGE GREEN: SOUTH AFRICANS BRIGHT BATTING

"Plum" Warner (second from right) leading out his team against the South Africans on the village green at Bearsted, near Maidstone, yesterday. On the left is R. T. Stanyforth, who captained the last M.C.C. team to tour South Africa.

R. H. Catterall (South Africa) makes a big hit. A feature of the game was the bright hitting of the tourists.

Reproduced courtesy of Norah Giles

Bearsted Cricket Club: The First Two Hundred Years

This undated caricature of Pelham was issued as one of a series of cigarette cards by John Player and Sons. At the time he was playing for Middlesex and on the reverse of the card he was described as:

...the best known and most popular player in the cricketing world...

Reproduced courtesy of Roger Vidler

From 1932 to 1933 Pelham was joint manager of the MCC team to Australia during the controversial Bodyline tour, and in 1937 he was knighted for his services to cricket. For many years, Sir Pelham was also editor of The Cricketer magazine. This is an advertisement for the magazine from 1937:

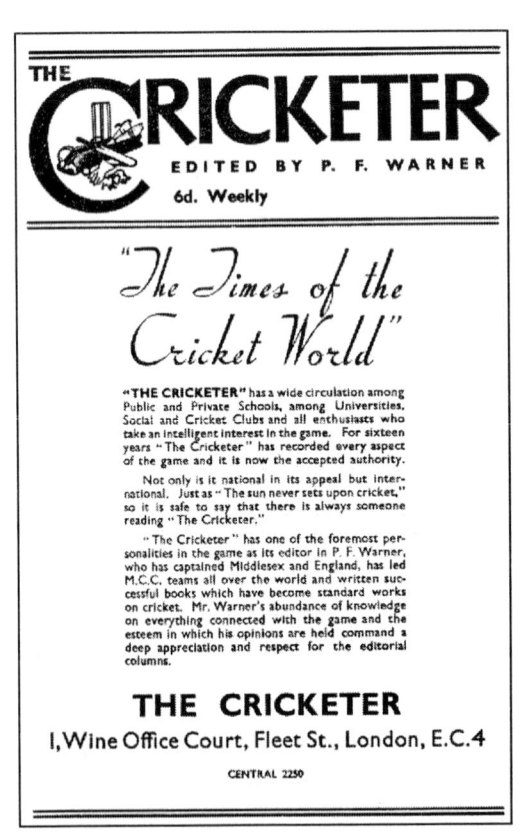

Reproduced courtesy of Ian Lambert

After his retirement, Pelham led MCC teams abroad, was Chairman of Selectors and wrote extensively on cricket. From 1950 to 1951, he was President of the MCC, and after he died in 1963, his ashes were scattered at Lords.[17]

Between 1922 and 1937, the cricket club was part of the Bearsted Sports Club which combined cricket, football and tennis. Despite this, the cricket section appears to have been largely independent, with separate details appearing for each sport in the parish magazine for Bearsted. The sports club was disbanded in 1937. [18]

This photograph shows a Bearsted XI from the 1930s. The gentleman at the rear on the extreme right is the Secretary, Mr George Dibble, who held office from 1902 to 1935. There are several photographs in which George appears but none have captured him looking directly at the camera. Seated on the extreme right is William White. His son, Len, is at the rear without a cap.

Reproduced courtesy of Len White

The Second World War interrupted normal club activities but cricket continued on the Green, albeit with enforced breaks during air raids.. Teams were often drawn from the armed forces stationed locally.

In 1944, a match was played between teams of Ladies and Gentlemen, captained by Mrs Margaret Litchfield from Snowfield and Mr Whitehead. During play, a V1 rocket was spotted coming over the Green but fortunately, did not stop. This photograph was taken to commemorate the match. Mr Whitehead is in the front row and Mrs Litchfield is next to him, second from the right:

Reproduced courtesy of Mark Litchfield

By the middle of the twentieth century, it is remarkable to note that no less than three former Kent and England cricketers lived in Bearsted! It is perhaps fitting to conclude this article about cricket in the village by taking a look at these players.

Alfred 'Tich' Freeman gained his nickname from his height of five feet, two inches. He lived at 'Dunbolyn', a bungalow on the Ashford Road, and after retirement from first class cricket, played for Bearsted. Alfred was the only cricketer to capture 300 wickets in a single season of the County Championship. His final tally was 3,766 wickets in his career but despite his success, made only twelve Test appearances for England.[19] The undated portrait photograph and cartoon of Tich Freeman bowling, shown below, appeared on cigarette cards produced by R J Hill Limited and John Player and Sons respectively. The reverse side of the former described Tich as 'a useful batsman who shows great promise.'

Whilst resident in Bearsted, Thomas Godfrey Evans lived at The Wickets, which was on The Landway. He later moved to a house in Tower Lane, before then re-locating out of the county. Godfrey was a wicket keeper, playing 258 games for Kent and making 91 Test appearances. Godfrey, however, had to overcome divided loyalties to achieve these statistics as prior to his debut in 1939 he had obtained a professional boxing licence. A broken nose in his third fight led the Kent Committee to offer him the choice of boxing or cricket![20] This portrait photograph of Godfrey is undated, but shows him wearing an MCC blazer gained for a tour against the West Indies and bears a badge dated 1948:

All reproduced courtesy of Roger Vidler

Godfrey was an extrovert character, with a flair for spectacular fielding manoeuvres. In his first match as wicket keeper, he took a catch at full stretch and this set the pattern for hundreds of similar predatory leaps and dives. Opinions vary as to where precisely Godfrey Evans ranks in the pantheon of Kent wicket keepers stretching back to Ned Wenman in the 1820s. Brilliant, acrobatic, always entertaining and regularly achieving the near impossible, he possibly lacked the consistency of Les Ames or Alan Knott. He was very much the man for the big occasion, but by some accounts there could be the odd lapse of concentration when the crowds were sparse, usually in away matches.[21]

Leslie Ames moved to Bearsted in 1951. He was a close neighbour of Tich Freeman. At the time of the move, the Kent Messenger expressed a hope that the change of air and atmosphere from Gillingham would be beneficial in his recovery from lumbago.[22] Leslie was associated with the Kent County Cricket Club for over sixty six years and was a true servant of county cricket. He made his debut for the First XI in 1926 and retired in 1952.

Between 1957 and 1974 Leslie was Manager and then combined duties of this post with that of Secretary. In 1975 he was the first former professional to be appointed President. He appeared on forty seven occasions for England. He was a Test Selector for eight years and was Manager of three MCC teams on tours abroad.[23] His name is commemorated in Bearsted as one of the roads on the Landway estate bears the title Ames Avenue.

This cartoon of Leslie was issued as one of a series of cigarette cards by John Player and Sons during 1938:

Reproduced courtesy of Roger Vidler

At the time he was playing for Kent and England and on the reverse of the card he was described as:

...a stylish, hard-hitting batsman...

Despite the presence of these distinguished cricketers, in the middle of the twentieth century, Bearsted remained a thoroughly village team. During the past two hundred years, the Green had indeed proved to be the nursery of cricket. Local residents Alfred Mynn and Pelham Warner had made significant national contributions to the development of the game. Matches on the Green had become so firmly established that foot paths had been diverted around the pitch.

These photographs show how the main area of the Green had developed. This first was taken around 1900. Part of the Royal Oak public house is just visible behind the large oak tree in the background. Note also the original route of the footpath: [24]

Reproduced courtesy of Centre for Kentish Studies

This picture shows roughly the same area of the Green during a match in 1947 - quite a contrast! [25]

Reproduced courtesy of Kent Messenger newspaper group

As the twentieth century continued, fresh chances, challenges and changes would be encountered by both the national and village game played in and around Bearsted.

Ian Lambert

Bearsted Cricket Club: Into More Modern Times

By the middle of the twentieth century, the game of cricket had been played on the Green at Bearsted for at least two hundred years. This photograph was taken during a match between Bearsted First XI and Gore Court Second XI, 2 June 1957. For many years this scene represented part of typical village life and, seemingly, unchanged.

Reproduced courtesy of Kent Messenger newspaper group

As the century advanced, however, changes began to occur around the Green as some local businesses closed and new ones opened. The large oak tree in front of the Royal Oak public house was lost in the great storm of 1987. Happily, a replacement was planted and continues to flourish. Changes would also occur in the organisation of the sport, the facilities offered by the club and the matches played.

The pavilion, shown on the left hand side of this photograph was located on the verge between Bell House and Church Lane. Graham Walkling recalled that the building resembled an old summer house. It was removed soon after the Second World War.

Reproduced courtesy of Roger Vidler

Bearsted Cricket Club: Into More Modern Times

This undated photograph shows Frank Harnett and Bill Moss standing in front of the pavilion:

Following several years of fund-raising, in 1957 the original pavilion was dismantled and a permanent replacement was erected at the current location on the Green ready for the 1958 season. This programme was produced for the official opening:

BEARSTED CRICKET CLUB

A Souvenir

TO COMMEMORATE THE

OFFICIAL OPENING

OF THE

NEW PAVILION

BY

THE RIGHT HON. THE LORD CORNWALLIS, K.B.E., M.C.,

ON

SATURDAY   :   APRIL 26TH   :   1958

AT 4.0 PM

Both reproduced courtesy of Bearsted Cricket Club

This illustration is taken from the fixture list of 1958 and provides a good indication of how many local people were involved in the cricket club in addition to the players:

President:
W. H. WHITEHEAD, Esq., M.A.

Vice-Presidents:

Mrs. F. L. Blehr	Mr. A. E. Graves
Mrs. Ben Brook	Mr. G. G. Green
Mrs. L Brook	Mr. R. C. Gregory
Mrs. M. R. Ireland-Blackburne	Mr. F. W. Grout
Mrs. D. Whitehead	Mr. R. Holworthy
Mr. J. W. R. Adams, O.B.E.	Cpt. M. R. Ireland-Blackburne
Mr. L. E. G. Ames	Mr. A. D. Johnson
Mr. A. E. Andrews	Mr. J. G. Laidler
Mr. R. J. Angel	Mr. F. P. Litchfield
Mr. J. D. Awde	Cpt. J. Litchfield, O.B.E., R.N., (RTD.)
Mr. R. F. Baker	Rev. J. Long, M.A.
Mr. L. F. Bassom	Mr. W. Lutener
Mr. G. Bishop	Mr. H. G. Matthews
Mr. J. D. Buckingham	Mr. F. G. E. May
Mr. E. P. Bungay, J.P.	Mr. S. Mendel
Mr. F. Cooper	Mr. L. R. S .Monckton
Mr. M. W. J. G. Corps	Mr. W. J. Moss
Mr. A. E. Cox	Mr. F. Naylor
Mr. L. Datson	Mr. J. Nicholson
Mr. F. Davey	Mr. C Peach
Mr. A. N. Dearing	Mr. W. H. Richardson
Mr. J. Dulson	Mr. A. Rowe
Mr. C. Fleetwood	Mr. L. J. Sargeant
Mr. K. F. Forknall	Mr. F. A. Simmonds
Mr. A. P. Freeman	Mr. G. Smith
Mr. J. S. French	Rev. J. Fortescue Thomas, B.A.
Mr. E. L. Fuller	Lt. Col. A. C. Wilson
Mr. E. A. George	Mr. F. W. Wright, O.B.E., F.A.I.
Mr. J. T. Goodwin, M.B.E.	Mr. D. C. P. Wylde

General Secretary:
MR. D. B. LISTER
"Rusaker," Roseacre Lane, Bearsted
(Tel.: Maidstone 87636)

Hon. Treasurer:
MR. L. J. SARGEANT
95 Chase Road, Southgate, N.14

Fixture Secretary:
MR. L. E. AUSTIN
"Rockies," Yeoman Lane, Bearsted
(Tel.: Maidstone 87891)

Match Secretary:
MR. G. L. W. LAMBELL
"White Gates," Roseacre Lane, Bearsted

Captain 1st IX:
MR. A J. SNOOK

Vice-Captain 1st IX:
MR. G. A. HAWKINS

Captain 2nd XI:
MR. H. C. WOOD

Vice-Captain 2nd XI:
MR. K. BOORMAN

Committee:

MR. F. H. BAYLEY	MR. J. MARSHALL
MR. A. GIBSON	MR. S. MENDEL (Chairman)
MR. P. KING	MR. J. W. T. PRINCE

Hon. Asst. Treasurer:
MR. N. TILEY

Hon. Auditor:
MR. E. P. BUNGAY

Reproduced courtesy of Bearsted Cricket Club

Other key players during the 1950s and 1960s were George Smith (the local police sergeant), Vic Pound, the Gibson family (father Alan, and his sons Neville, Mick and Tony), Gordon Hawkins, Tony Snook, brothers Bert and George Wood, Bryan Ellswood, Colin Fleetwood, Ted White and many more.

During 1958 the parish magazine featured the progress of a team from Holy Cross church in Maidstone Choirs League. Unfortunately they only managed to win a single game to finish bottom of the league. Other teams were from St Philip's, St Andrew's, St Martin's, Holy Trinity, St Michael's, St Paul's and All Saints churches.

In 1962, Sunday Cricket was played on the Green for the first time since before the Second World War. Previous applications by Bearsted Cricket Club to the parish council to permit play on Sundays had been rejected although some away fixtures had been played under the name of the Infidels!

1962 was one of the most successful seasons that the club has ever achieved as the First XI lost only one game and remained unbeaten until September. An outstanding feature was the batting of Dave Andrews, who scored over a thousand runs: unique in the history of the club for any First XI. Peter Longley also distinguished himself by being the only post war player to take all ten wickets against Headcorn for the Second XI.[1]

This photograph shows a typical cricket match taking place on the Green in 1972:

Reproduced courtesy of the Gibson family

A scheme for junior players known as 'Colts' was set up in 1972. The policy of junior members acquiring valuable match experience through Colt team games before progressing to the Senior teams continues today. It is a credit to Robin Cunningham who, with great skill, ran the junior section for twenty one years.

In 1990, the Colt of the Year Award was awarded by Bearsted Cricket Club to Stephen Pearce, with the comment by Robin Cunningham:

> ...with any luck he will be turning out for the Senior team for years to come...

This photograph below shows Stephen being congratulated on winning the award by Pam Gibson, First XI Scorer for Bearsted. Stephen has fulfilled his promise with great success as in 2001 he became the only player to have scored a double century for the club.

Reproduced courtesy of Rosemary Pearce

Bearsted Cricket Club: Into More Modern Times

This is a transcript of the report about Stephen's double century from the Kent Messenger:

Pearce in record 201

Bearsted opener Steve Pearce set a club record with an unbeaten 201 in the 174 run victory over West Farleigh. It beat the previous best of 178 not out, set 18 years ago by Mike Read. Pearce smashed four sixes and 32 fours in his 152 ball stay and shared in partnerships of 79 with Noel Johnston (33), 96 with Ian Sandwell (29) and 87 with Peter Clark (19 not out). Farleigh were immediately in trouble against Doug Reid (five for 27) and Andy Dampier (two for 25). They were four for four at one stage and finally dismissed for 125. P Baines was top scorer with an unbeaten 52.

Reproduced courtesy of Kent Messenger newspaper group

On 10 June 2006, there were further high scores when Bearsted achieved a mammoth 336-1 against Willesborough in a league match on the Green. In that total, both Steve Pearce (127 not out) and Steve Heap (159 not out) scored centuries. This is only the fourth occasion since the Second World War that this feat has been achieved.

Today, the Colts Section is as strong as ever, but it is run on a far more formal basis. Accreditation has been obtained which affects all aspects of the planning and structure of all levels of the club including management, cricket development, first aid and risk assessment. Child protection and welfare are also important for the Colts; the qualified coaches and all persons working with them have to undergo a Criminal Records Bureau check. Colt players are required to wear helmets when fielding close to the wicket or batting and there are restrictions on the number of overs delivered by fast bowlers. The Colts have teams of different ages and entry into League cricket was undertaken for the first time in 2006.

The present Colts manager, David Bracey has commented: 'Youth is the future of any club and the section provides the opportunity for individuals to progress in a structured competitive environment.' Bearsted Cricket Club has a history of family connections with many having played together in the same teams.

This photograph shows some of the Colts and their fathers, who are all club members, taken at a club day in June 2006. It bodes well that the family tradition will continue for years to come.

Reproduced courtesy of Bruce Malcolm Fotosouvenirs

Back Row (left to right):
K de Silva, John Haggart, A Haggart, T Lush, N Jefferies, D Bracey, N Johnston, R Luxton, D Vant and C Norris
Front Row (left to right): Nimal de Silva, Robert Haggart, Ben Lush, Alex Lush, Daniel Jefferies, Adam Bracey, Madeline Bracey, Benjamin Johnston, Charlie Luxton, and Nicholas Vant.

(George Norris and Alexander Lush both missing from picture).

Bearsted Cricket Club: Into More Modern Times

League cricket was introduced in 1981 and today forms the basis of Saturday cricket with leagues of both First and Second XI teams. The First XI won their league in 1987 and 2002 whilst the Second XI won their league in 1991, 1993 and 2003.

Financial sponsorship of Bearsted Cricket Club began during the 1980s, and like many sports today, has become an accepted part of village and national clubs. The sponsorship has come in a variety of ways including raffle prizes, equipment, and advertising in fixture cards and on sight screens. These are just a few examples, and the generous support of local companies, individuals and vice presidents is vital to the running of the club.

The 1980s saw the new advances in ground preparation. The days of the hand operated grass mowers were long since over, abandoned in favour of petrol driven models, although this undated photograph shows an early, but rather charming, mechanised form of preparing the ground:

This decade saw further changes with the departure of what had become a fixture on the Green: the heavy hand-pulled roller was replaced by a mechanical one. The original had been assembled from a large drum used in the printing industry and before the Second World War had been horse-drawn. After the war it was propelled by at least six members of the club, with the original shafts being replaced by a bow assembly. This undated photograph gives an indication of the number of small boys that were willing to pull the heavy roller:

Both reproduced courtesy of Roger Vidler

1999 was a significant year for the club as it marked two hundred and fifty years of cricket in Bearsted. A commemorative book and painting were produced and a dinner dance was held at the Great Danes Hotel. The special guest was Lord Cowdrey of Tonbridge, former Kent and England captain. This is part of the menu card:

BEARSTED
CRICKET CLUB
1749 - 1999

250th ANNIVERSARY
DINNER & DANCE

**GREAT DANES HOTEL
HOLLINGBOURNE
FRIDAY 30th APRIL 1999**

Reproduced courtesy of Bearsted Cricket Club

Special games were arranged throughout this anniversary year. The club played an exhibition match in authentic clothing and according to the laws of 1749 in the arena at the Bearsted Fayre. This photograph of some of the team gives an indication of the scenes witnessed during the match on the Green:

Reproduced courtesy of Kent Messenger newspaper group

The opposition were Ripley from Surrey (also celebrating their two hundred and fiftieth anniversary), local rivals Linton Park, Hadlow, Sevenoaks Vine and the MCC. There was a visit to Lords to play the Cross Arrows on the Nursery Ground and a further match against the Honourable Artillery Company at the Artillery Ground where it all began.

Bearsted Cricket Club: Into More Modern Times

The Bearsted players were able to use the England dressing room at Lords and this photograph was taken on the balcony:

The photograph was a distant echo of the occasion when in July 1952, a former Bearsted Cricket Club President, chairman, Secretary and First XI Captain, Colin Fleetwood, also changed in the Lords dressing rooms when he appeared for Tonbridge in the annual match against Clifton. On that occasion Tonbridge won by seven wickets and Wisden recorded a hard hitting 55 from opener C S Fleetwood.[2]

This photograph below was taken of the Honourable Artillery Company and Bearsted:

Both reproduced courtesy of Bearsted Cricket Club

Back row: Honourable Artillery Company (HAC), Graham Walkling (umpire), Stephen Pearce, HAC, Richard Luxton, Pam Gibson (scorer)
Centre row: Michael Clifton, HAC, HAC, Mick Filmer, HAC, HAC, Peter Court, HAC, Stephen Heap
Front Row: Robin Cross, HAC, Geoff Chapman, HAC, Steve Horrocks, HAC, Andrew Naish, HAC, Rod Maloney.

In 2002, Bearsted achieved a 'double' with the First and Second XIs winning their leagues. This is a transcript of an undated report about this achievement from the Kent Messenger:

Title double has Bears beaming

The ability to field settled sides was the main reason behind Bearsted Cricket Club's championship double in the Invicta League. The first team carried off the Division 1 title for the first time in 15 years while the seconds were Division 2 champions. Both only lost one game, the first to Meopham and the seconds in the last fixture of the season against Horton Kirby.

"Almost everyone has been available every week and that has made a big difference," said the first team skipper Steve Pearce. "We only used 15 players all season and two of them only played one game." We also had a good age range in the side with the youngest just 17 and only one player in his 50s. With the average age 32, it meant that we were quite young and athletic in the field." A welcome addition was Darren Breame, from Rumwood, who batted and fielded well. Twenty six year old Pearce led the way in prolific fashion, scoring 501 runs in the league at a Don Bradman like average of 100.2. Ian Sandwell scored 383 runs at a highly respectable 42.5 while wicket keeper Noel Johnston contributed 335 runs at 33.5. Douglas Reid led the bowling averages with 17 wickets at a cost of 16.35 whilst 17 year old John Lee made a big impression with 21 wickets at 6.5. Andy Dampier and Steve Horrocks both claimed 20. Sarath Chandrasekera took 18.

Winning the Division 2 title was a fitting end to Mick Filmer's three years as skipper. "Because the first team didn't call on many of our players were able to put out much the same side," he said. He said the bowlers had played a major part in the success. Off spinner Robin Cross took 33 wickets, 22 year old Richard Filmer, Mick's son, claimed 30, Thomas Judges 26 and Jason Reeves 210. Another member of the Filmer family, Mick's nephew Chris, was one of the mainstays of the batting with Uncle Mick, who scored 100 against Staplehurst and Mick Clifton, who made a successful return after injury.

Reproduced courtesy of Kent Messenger newspaper group

The photograph on the next page shows the club after this remarkable double achievement. The Second XI retained the league trophy in the following year and the First XI league was divided into two divisions: Premier and First. In the short period of change, the club has experienced both relegation and promotion, with the highlight being champions of the First Division in the 2006 season, having won all their games.

An important part of any cricket match is the tea provided by the home team. The role of the tea ladies was recognised in 2004 with the provision of a bench supplied by English Courtyard, a sponsor of the cricket club. This photograph of the tea ladies on their dedicated seat, with Ted White, (a stalwart with bat and ball who also has a separate dedicated seat) was taken in September 2004.

Reproduced courtesy of Rosemary Pearce

Back Row, left to right:
Pam Gibson (First XI scorer), Rosemary Pearce (Honorary Secretary),
Carol Geddes (English Courtyard), Caroline Filmer, Helen Head
Front Row, left to right
Babs Hewson, Ted White, Mary Lambert, Tracey Johnston.

Bearsted Cricket Club: Into More Modern Times

Reproduced courtesy of Bruce Malcolm and Fotosouvenirs

Front Row: Helen Turner (2nd XI scorer), Robin Cross, Mick Clifton, Ali Mills, Chris Filmer (2nd XI vice captain), Mick Filmer (2nd XI captain), Steve Pearce (1st XI captain), Rod Maloney (Chairman, Sunday captain), Andy Dampier (1st XI vice captain), Peter Court, John Lee, Sarath Chandrasekera, Pam Gibson (1st XI scorer).

Middle Row: Babs Hewson (tea lady), Rosemary Pearce (tea lady), Dan Dawson, Jason Reeves, Richard Luxton, Gareth Oakland, Ian Sandwell, Leroy Bradley, Peter Clark, Doug Reid, Noel Johnston, Helen Head (tea lady), Sheila Humphrey (tea lady), Bob Humphrey (vice president).

Back Row: Peter Judges (treasurer, groundsman and 1st XI umpire), Ramulka da Silva (tea lady), Adrian Dawson, Geoff Chapman, Ted White (vice president), Kishan de Silva, David Bracey, Steve Horrocks, Tim Lush (fixture secretary), Ann Reid (tea lady), Bernard Head (vice president), Sue Horrocks (tea lady), Jane Court (tea lady), Mary Lambert (tea lady), Ian Lambert (player and groundsman), Rod Hewson (2nd XI scorer and groundsman).

The club has now embarked upon two very successful ventures which have become annual events. There is a Family Day which brings together all sections to show their talents, and a charity game against the Mens Club which attracts a large attendance of good humoured spectators.

Sadly, the club lost two popular members in recent years. Sarath Chandrasekera was tragically killed in 2005. He hailed from Sri Lanka and joined in 1988. Primarily, a spin bowler, he took 725 wickets with a best analysis of 8-55 and also scored 3841 runs with a top score of 101. He won the league bowling award in 1996 and was club captain in 1997-1998. This photograph below goes some way to convey Sarath's authoritative confidence, which was an inspiration to many local players:

Sarath Chandrasekera 1948-2005

Reproduced courtesy of Bearsted Cricket Club

Pam Gibson died the following year. She was part of a Bearsted cricketing family as her husband Alan, and their sons Neville, Mick and Tony all played for the club. She was secretary for nine years.

One of the most recent additions to the pavilion was made in October 2007: a lovely new weather vane with two figures depicting a cricketer at the wicket and a wicket keeper was installed on the roof. The vane was donated by the Maidstone branch of the Council to Protect Rural England in memory of local resident Bob Humphrey who died in 2005. Bob chaired the Council for twelve years.

Many years have passed since cricket was first played upon the Green at Bearsted. The ground has witnessed the beginning and ending of many players' innings and activities. As the twenty first century begins, it is a tribute to the many supporters of the game that it retains a widespread popularity within the community and a constant presence in Bearsted and Thurnham.

Ian Lambert

Thurnham Cricket Club

Although Bearsted enjoys a great dominance in the story of cricket in Kent, Thurnham also has a place in the history of the game.

As detailed in a previous chapter, both Bearsted and Thurnham regularly supplied members for joint teams against other villages when the sport was in its infancy, but Thurnham had its own cricket club. There are few records from the early years, so it is difficult to say much about these games, but in 1773, Leeds played Bearsted, Thornham, Debtling and Boxley. In 1789 Bearsted and Thurnham played Lenham and Harrietsham.[1]

Further records show annual matches between the Gentleman of Bearsted and Thurnham, played on Bearsted Green as part of the Bearsted Races and Fair in the years 1817 to 1821. Advertisements for the early matches indicated prize money of one guinea per man.

Further positive confirmation about cricket being played in Thurnham is found in sales particulars which were drawn up for Sir Edward Dering in 1834 concerning the Thurnham Court Farm estate. The land holdings included Parsonage Farm and the schedule mentions:

| Old Cricketing Field | 3 acres | 2 rods | 34 perches |

On the 1840 tithe map, a field of a similar size is shown, located across several fields behind the main buildings for the farm.[2] The sale did not proceed as Sir Edward could not prove that he had the freehold title. Perhaps he, along with later owners of the estate, was fond of cricket.[3]

This sketch map shows the location of the cricket ground at Thurnham, based on an Ordnance Survey map from 1966. It is not to scale.

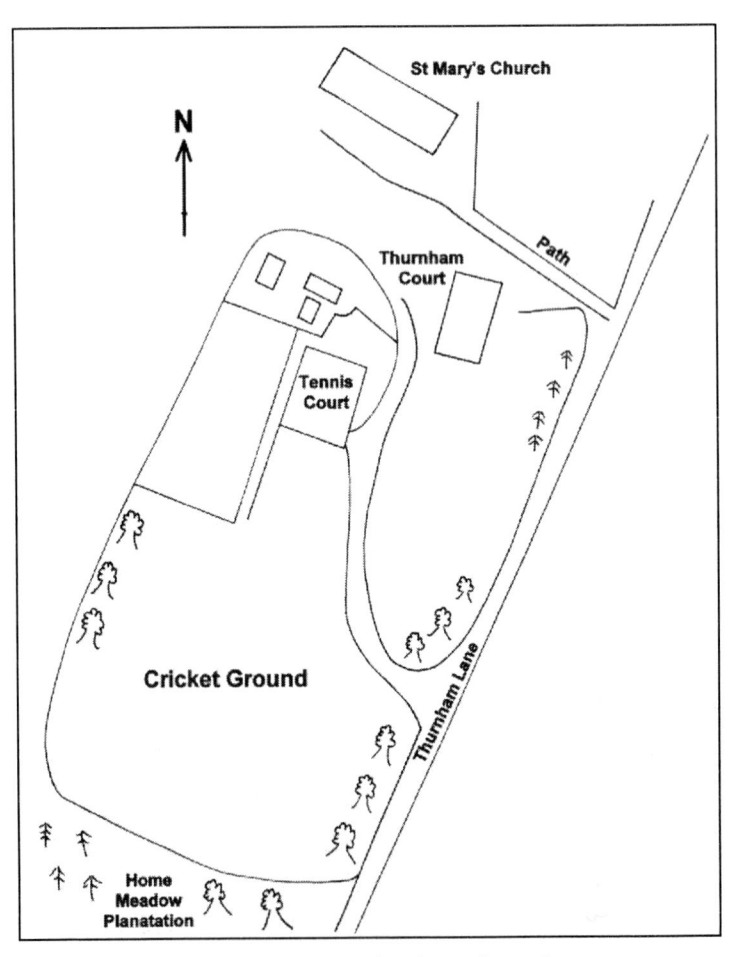

Diagram by Kathryn Kersey based on Ordnance Survey

In 1878, Bearsted beat Thurnham by an innings and 8 runs. In the same year, Bearsted Rangers beat a team called Thurnham Star on the Green. The Thurnham team was: H Stamford, A Green, F Bolton, C Wells, L Cheeseman, S Rose, D Attwood, W Tolhurst, T Thomsett, W Thomsett and W Grant.[4] In view of the cricket being played in the area by other teams, it is almost certain that matches were held in Thurnham for a considerable time before these reports.

Cricket in Thurnham was played more or less continuously throughout the last two decades of the eighteenth century, throughout the nineteenth century, and apart from a gap during the First and Second World Wars, into the later half of the twentieth century.

The Kent Messenger carried this comment on 9 May 1896:

> The Bearsted and Thurnham Club is an unambitious organisation formed more for mutual enjoyment than for fierce competition for honours.

The combined Bearsted and Thurnham team away to Boughton Monchelsea in 1905 comprised: W Watcham, L Gibson, L Merral, J Walkling, F Knowles, J Datson, J Cheeseman, C Moon, T Walkling, A Hills and W Moon. It was also recorded that Bearsted played Thurnham and Harrietsham.[5]

In 1908 Bearsted and Thurnham intimated their willingness to complete for a Kent Messenger prize which was to be awarded for the best batting and bowling averages and winning the highest proportion of games.

In 1914 Thurnham beat Bearsted in an away match by one run.

There is no record of cricket being played during the First World War, but this is a transcript of an article which appeared in the Kent Messenger, 3 July 1915:

> **CRICKET & FOOTBALL OUTFITS**
> **Wanted For Kent Men**
>
> The boys of the 10th Service Battalion of the Royal West Kent Regiment badly want cricket bats, balls and stumps as well as a football or two and some boxing gloves; in fact, anything useful connected with sport. There must be quite a number of old bats in the County of Kent which are not seeing much of the turf this summer - there must be several footballs which are certainly not being used at the present time and which perhaps have no great prospect of being used in the coming winter. Now is the time to turn them to really good account by sending them to the offices of the 'Kent Messenger' for the boys from Maidstone and the County who are devoting themselves to the service of King and Country. Sport is an essential part of their training for braving damages and perhaps death itself on behalf of those of us who stay at home.

Both reproduced courtesy of Kent Messenger newspaper group

After the war, in 1919, the Thurnham score of 28 during a game proved insufficient against Bearsted's score of 110.[6]

In 1921, A Ayres and G Flood gave all round performances with bat and ball. S Mankelow scored 25 out of the Thurnham total of 66 against Hollingbourne Second XI.

In 1922 Thurnham lost at home to Boxley by 63 runs and their total of 39 was considerably assisted by 'extras' with the ball rising badly on the hard wicket. In a low scoring match against Tovil, Thurnham could only manage 26 runs but J Wisdom and H Ayres bowled well before the opponents finally won by 4 wickets.

In that year, Lenview Cricket Club also used the Thurnham ground for home games. In their win against Hollingbourne Second XI during Maidstone Cricket week, they could only initially raise seven men. Through the generosity of the opposition by providing two supporters and one player, a 10-a-side match was played.[7]

From 1923 to 1928 it does not appear that a formal Thurnham Cricket Club existed. However, the ground, occasionally referred to in match reports as Court Farm, was regularly used by Lenview CC, West Borough Adult School and Lower Brewery, Maidstone. It is not clear whether there was any direct link between the three teams and the village.

In 1923 Lenview CC played Bearsted and West Borough Ladies played Ashford Ladies. The 1924 match between West Borough and Lower Brewery resulted in a tie with scores of 29 each side.[8] In one game played by the Lower Brewery in 1925, the following team was fielded: A J Staplehurst, L Tuffield, W Tucker, J Daveney, S Bernard, D Veale, D Attwood, F Epps, S E Tucker, S Ring and F W Cope.[9]

Although Broad Street is located in the parish of Hollingbourne, during the 1920s and 1930s they fielded a team described separately as Broad Street, Thurnham, and Broad Street, Hollingbourne. In 1928 the team against Hollingbourne was Dr J Small, H Markham, D Hope, E Smith, J Pollard, F Whiddett, J Whiddett, H Matthews, A Attwood, S Lampard and T Apps.

By 1929, results for Thurnham were beginning to appear in local newspapers. The team against Maidstone Gas Works were: R Dawes, S Boorman, E Flood, S Daniels, W Fox, R Hitchen, A Hunt, J Richards, J Hunt, S Hunt and R Penney. A match against Broad Street ended in a 24 run defeat.

This photograph of a Thurnham cricket team was taken in June, 1930. Sadly, nothing further is known about the occasion:

Reproduced courtesy of Norah Giles

<u>Standing (left to right)</u>: Bert Hanford, Ted Lee, Jack Flood, Harry Chawner, Jack Vidgeon, Ron Hickmott, Frank Swift
<u>Seated</u>: Frank Gatland, Frank Grant, Ted Flood, Bunny Ayres, Edgar Pettipiere.

In 1930, the team was known as St Mary's, Thurnham, but it is not clear whether there was a formal link with Thurnham church. Some of the players reported as representing the club in matches during the season were: E Flood, J Richards, A Ayres, R Hitchen, G Smith, J Grant, M Grant, J Flood, G Flood, E Pettipiere, W Giles, R Richards, F Grant, W Hallett, S Betts, G Lee, G Betts and J Hood. Opposing teams included Maidstone Technical School, Maidstone Corporation Employees, Cox Brothers of Maidstone, Maidstone Corporation Transport and Batchellors of Maidstone. In a game against the Technical School, the venue for the match was listed as Thurnham School.[10]

An unusual incident was described in a report included in the Kent Messenger newspaper, 9 August 1930:

> During a match between Maidstone Corporation Transport and St Mary's, Thurnham, held at Thurnham on Saturday, a swarm of bees invaded the pitch. An umpire and several of the players were stung and the game had to be suspended until the bees dispersed...

Reproduced courtesy of Kent Messenger newspaper group

A tie was recorded in 1931 against Stockbury with each side scoring 33. E Flood took 7 for 16 versus Maidstone Corporation and J Richards scored 52 against Batchellors. Richards went in first and was next to last out, finding the boundary on ten occasions.[11]

Matches involving Broad Street continued to be reported. The Kent Messenger were regular opponents and the team against them in 1931 was: F Whiddett, T Minter, G Hawkins, K Jordan, G Brown, H Brown, F Stevenson, E Pollard, F Panthony, R Woodger and J Panthony Junior.

There were several good bowling performances for Thurnham in 1932. W Chawner took 6 wickets for 8 runs (including a hat trick) against Leeds and Broomfield Second XI. G Flood achieved 5 for 7 and H Chawner 5 for 5 for Thurnham St Mary's XI against Maidstone Corporation Transport. The full team was: G Flood, P Filmer, H Chawner, W Hallett, J Richards, A Ayres, R Hickmott, E Flood, J Vidgeon, F Martin and J Flood. The opposition were bowled out for 17.[12]

In 1933 reports included in the Kent Messenger newspaper referred to teams from both Thurnham and St Mary's, Thurnham. Matches played were against Leeds Broomfield II, Lenview and Rumwood A. Players for that year included F Martin, W Grant, S Betts, W Howard, G Cleaver, J Flood, G Flood, W Cox, R Filmer, R Hickmott, J Richards, T Grant, D Filmer, J Vidgeon, E Flood, B Grant and I Howard.

St Mary's, Thurnham, won by 14 runs against Etceteras in 1934. The team comprised: F Martin, J Flood, W Howard, J Vidgeon, G Tolhurst, D Filmer, E Flood, W Cox, J Merrill, W Filmer, and G Grant. Fortunes were reversed in the return fixture with St Mary's only scoring 15 in reply to Etceteras 112.

There was a very similar game in 1935 with St Mary's scoring 17 in reply to Etceteras 128. The Etceteras bowler, L Fagle, took 7 for 7 in each game: a remarkable statistic. The team against Addington comprised: E Shorter, J Flood, J Richards, J Hyland, C Harnett, B Hirst, E Martin, D Filmer, J Vidgeon, W Fox and E Flood.

In 1936 St Mary's played Astra Sports at Otham.[13]

There is no evidence that a Thurnham XI played in either 1937 or 1938. Games were played in 1939 and the team name was just recorded as Thurnham; perhaps the link with the church had been broken. Significant defeats were recorded that year against Ulcombe by 168 and East Sutton by 142 runs. The team against Ulcombe comprised C Tolhurst, C Cox, P Harman, J Vidgeon, F Walkling, R King, F Grant, S Penney, E Costin, J Flood and C Hood.[14]

The club continued after the Second World War and in 1949, the names of R Penney and C Palmer regularly appeared in match reports which recorded solid all-round performances. In a game against Stockbury Second XI, Thurnham scored 50 (R Penney 21) against a reply of 27 (C Palmer 4 for 9 and R Penney 5 for 18). R Penney took 5 for 28 in a win against Blue Bell Hill and although the team lost against Detling, C Palmer achieved bowling figures of 8 for 27 which included a hat trick. Games were also recorded against Trottiscliffe and King Street Church, Maidstone.[15]

As the 1950s began, Ron Penney continued to be a major performer for Thurnham, ably assisted by his son, Brian. Ron took a number of five wicket hauls in 1950, including 6 for 18 against King Street Church. They scored 53 but Thurnham could only manage 39 runs in reply. In the return fixture Ron took 7 for 16 and the result was reversed: King Street Church scoring 28 and Thurnham 58 runs. Other matches played were against Ryarsh, Offham, Howard de Walden and the Maidstone Electricity Works.[16]

Low scores appeared in 1951 with only 48 runs against Ryarsh, 26 runs versus A R Tongs XI, 50 versus Old Williamsonians A and 88 against Charles Arkoll's Second XI. All were defeats. Teams from the British Legion Village and Rumwood II were bowled out for 39 and 31 runs respectively in games which Thurnham won. Notably, Colin Palmer took 8 for 10 in the Rumwood game.[17]

The situation continued in 1952. Chasing a score of 81 by Expenses Accounts in which R Gould took 3 for 5, Thurnham were dismissed for 55 and John Avard, with 19, was the only batsman to achieve double figures. Other low scores were 64 against a total of 115 by King Street Church (who had recovered from 29 for 5) and 63 against Maidstone Working Mens Club. A score of 108 (in which K Howes reached 32) was sufficient to beat Old Williamsonians A by 12 runs.[18]

A transcript from the original 1952 scorebook of an innings by Weavering is shown below. In this record of a local derby there are many well-known names. Thurnham scored 106, thereby winning by 84 runs.

Reproduced courtesy of Ian Lambert

In 1953, Colin Palmer 64, not out, and Ron Penney 49, not out, shone with the bat in a total of 158 for 5 declared in a game against Gravesend Wanderers that was drawn. Ron Penney then went one better with a score of 50 not out in a 20 run victory against Odd Fellows. Despite scoring only 51, Thurnham beat Maidstone Waterworks as they could only manage 14 runs. R Penney took 5 for 5 and Colin Palmer 4 for 9. [19]

This undated photograph of Ron Penney was probably taken at a cricket match, and gives an indication of the form of transport used to attend matches!

Reproduced courtesy of Barbara Wickens

Despite these performances, there were losses against St Francis and against local rivals, Weavering, by 75 runs. A satisfying win was achieved by 7 runs against Leeds with K Coulter taking 6 for 35 in the Leeds total of 67. Thurnham then lost at home to Bearsted A, scoring 70 in reply to a total of 89.

The following year Thurnham could only manage 26 with Graham Walking scoring 17 runs in reply to the total by Townsend Hook of 128 for 9. [20]

One game that Thurnham would probably wish to forget took place in 1955. They were bowled out for a score of 19 and Barming proceeded to win by 10 wickets.[21] There were however many good performances during the year, and the picture below, which appeared in the South Eastern Gazette, shows club captain Colin Palmer receiving the cup for the season's best batting average from Mrs Ben Brook, at a social held at the White Horse public house. On the left of the photograph is Ron Penney, winner of the cup for the most wickets taken during the season. Vice captain Graham Walking and Vera Seager are on the right:

Reproduced courtesy of Kent Messenger newspaper group

Ron Penney had another good season in 1956 with Jim Peat and Graham Walkling also putting in notable performances. The latter took 4 for 9 against Alabaster Passmore. There was a close game against Chatham Suburban who were to win by three runs with Ted White scoring 38 of Thurnham's total of 60. He also scored 49 of a total of 78 in a 12 run win against Corinthians. Leeds were bowled out for 30 with Jim Peat taking 6 for 16. Ron Penney taking 4 for 1, helped to restrict Rootes Social to 31 runs. Thurnham however could only manage 31 runs in the return match against Corinthians and the same score against Barming.[22]

1957 was a mixed year with a low point undoubtedly being the defeat by 10 wickets to Alabaster Passmore; Thurnham were dismissed for 12 runs. Scores of below 50 were also recorded against Corinthians: 32, in losing by 8 wickets and 46 against Detling whilst chasing a total of 166 for 8 declared.[23] Despite this, honours were shared against neighbours Weavering, with more than 200 runs being scored in each game. Other victories were recorded against Welders & Burners, by 8 runs and against Chatham Suburban in a very close match, by a single run.[24]

A sample of the games played in 1958:[25]

Thurnham 89 B Chapman 47 not out	v	**Chart Sutton** 61 B Penney 6 for 22	Won by 28 runs
Barming 81 J Peat 3 for 16 R Penney 4 for 16	v	**Thurnham** 49 J Peat 23	Lost by 32 runs
Thurnham 118 E White 50	v	**Corinthians** 33 R Penney 4 for 5	Won by 85 runs

In 1958, the Honorary Secretary, Mr J Flood, was presented with a barometer in recognition of his thirty years service to the club by the chairman, Mr E Seager. This photograph of the occasion appeared in the South Eastern Gazette, 14 October:

Reproduced courtesy of Kent Messenger newspaper group

Graham Walkling will remember 1959 as during the game against Chatham POM he achieved a hat trick. His bowling analysis was 4 for 6. The opposition could only manage 38 and were beaten by 8 wickets. During this season, Staplehurst were beaten but Birling were made to work for their win, scoring the 58 runs needed with only two wickets in hand.

Throughout the 1960s, there were regular home and away fixtures against Bearsted Second XI. A total of fifteen games were played but Thurnham only managed one win and three draws. There were local connections in these games with Bearsted stalwart, Ted White, who had previously played for Thurnham, showing no favours with scores of 121 not out and 68, with the bat, 5 for 40 and 5 for 1 with the ball. Brothers Mick and Keith Filmer who both later played for Bearsted also appeared for Thurnham, following the example of their father, Dick Filmer.[26]

Thurnham Cricket Club

In 1960, Bearsted's total against Thurnham was 154 runs (R Penney 6 for 52) and they won by 72 runs.

The following year saw a high scoring draw: Thurnham 193 for 8 declared (A Plant 47, C Filmer 49) and Bearsted 174 for 8 (B Penney 5 for 45). In the return match, Bearsted won by 44 runs: Bearsted 101 (R Penney 7 for 23) and Thurnham 57 (K Filmer 23).[27] Other games in the season had a range of scores, significant individual performances and even a tie! A summary of the season's results is shown below.

Main matches and results for 1961 [28]

Nettlestead 78 J Peat 6 for 29 B Penney 3 for 10	v **Thurnham** 66 K Filmer 28 T Plant 25	Lost 12 runs
Leeds & Broomfield 89 B Penney 4 for 18	v **Thurnham** 90 for 5 B Penney 41 not out	Won by 5 wickets
Inland Revenue Chatham 148 J Peat 6 for 41	v **Thurnham** 149 for 7 J Peat 65, K Filmer 37	Won by 3 wickets
East Sutton 151 for 7 dec.	v **Thurnham** 104 J Peat 41	Lost by 47 runs
Thurnham 87	v **Weavering** 88 for 5	Lost by 5 wickets
Thurnham 151 for 4 K Filmer 66 J Peat 38 not out	v **Detling** 113 for 7 B Penney 4 for 49	Draw
Thurnham 129 K Filmer 71	v **William Hobbs** 129 R Penney 5 for 51	Tie
Thurnham 87 J Peat 23	v **Inland Revenue Chatham** 81 J Peat 7 for 25	Won by 6 runs
Thurnham 45	v **Reeds Corrugated Cases** 46 for 7	Lost by 3 wickets
Barming 166 for 8 dec. G Walkling 3 for 30	v **Thurnham** 87	Lost by 79 runs
Beltring 85 J Peat 6 for 33 A Plant 3 for 13	v **Thurnham** 88 for 9 R Chapman 40	Won by 1 wicket
Reeds Corrugated Cases 119 A Plant 4 for 27	v **Thurnham** 120 for 6 R Chapman 57 not out E Fremlin 33	Won by 4 wickets
Thurnham 63	v **Barming YC** 64 for 6 A Plant 4 for 19	Lost by 4 wickets
Thurnham 96 R Chapman 45	v **Detling** 76	Won by 20 runs
Thurnham 40	v **Barming** 41 for 5	Lost by 5 wickets
Thurnham 86 N Colegate 26	v **GPO** 36 J Peat 7 for 24	Won by 50 runs
Thurnham 111 K Filmer 41	v **Saracens** 112 for 6	Lost by 4 wickets
East Suttons 48 B Penney 8 for 14	v **Thurnham** 50 for 9 B Penney 27 not out	Won by 1 wicket
Maidstone Post Office 97 G Walkling 6 for 20	v **Thurnham** 23	Lost by 74 runs
Thurnham 103 R Chapman 81	v **Leeds** 87	Won by 16 runs
Weavering 125 R Penney 5 for 25	v **Thurnham** 103 C Filmer 32 B Penney 22	Lost by 22 runs

1961 also saw a bout of 'cup fever' through entry into the Maidstone District Knock Out Competition. In the first round, East Malling Research could only manage to score 31 (J Peat 5 for 8, B Penney 5 for 23) in reply to Thurnham's score of 91 for 7 (B Penney 35). The second round was against Primrose and Len but Thurnham's score of 70 (C Filmer 24) was insufficient and they lost by 4 wickets despite Brian Penney taking 5 for 21.[29]

This is a transcript of a report on the following season's cup competition, taken from the Kent Messenger, 18 May 1962:

> **SHARPS SHATTERED BY THURNHAM'S PENNEY**
>
> Thurnham skipper Ron Penney was his side's match winner in their surprise 19 run success against Sharps at the Kreemy Works ground in the first round of the David Clark cup in Wednesday evening.
>
> Needing only 80 to win, Sharps were demoralised by Penney's excellent bowling - he took 7 for 34 - and none of the first seven batsman reached double figures.
>
> Praise too for the fine wicket keeping of Roger Chapman. He made two stumpings, helped in a run out and did not concede an extra. Chapman had been Thurnham's star turn with the bat: the 40 he scored was over half the side's total. Brian Penney contributed a valuable 23 and together, their partnership was virtually the whole of the Thurnham innings.

Reproduced courtesy of Kent Messenger newspaper group

The draw for the second round determined that the formidable Mote First XI would visit Thurnham in a classic 'David and Goliath' match. In the event, there was to be no upset as Thurnham lost by 85 runs. The Mote total of 138 for 6 included John Pocock's contribution of 83. John has also played several games for Kent and so is possibly the only person who has played first class cricket and to have appeared on the Thurnham ground.[30]

During that season, Thurnham lost both games against Bearsted, each by over 100 runs. However, there was a 115 run win against Stockbury, scoring 207 for 7 (R Chapman 89, M Webb 39). Stockbury were dismissed for 68 (R Penney 5 for 31).

The winning team against Anstey & Miles comprised R Chapman, C Martin, N Colegate, J Peat, B Varney, G Walkling, C Filmer, D Ralph, M Munn, R Penney and A Gibson.

The losing team against Maidstone Working Mens Club was R Giles, G Tutteman, G Walkling, E White, J Peat, D Ralph, T Gibson, C Filmer, R Penney, J Offard and J Shepherd.

Barming Heath lost their last 4 wickets for only 2 runs, going from 102 for 6 to 104 all out. R Penney claimed 3 of the last 4 wickets to finish with 5 for 48. J Peat took 4 for 31. Thurnham passed the total for the loss of 8 wickets with openers Chapman (34) and Ralph (20) given them a good start.

Other fixtures included Inland Revenue Chatham, East Sutton, King Street, Boughton Malherbe, Barming, Staplehurst, Saracens, Nettlestead, Leeds & Broomfield, Maidstone Post Office and Weavering.[31]

In 1963, the local derby at Weavering produced outstanding bowling performances with B Naylor finishing with 10 for 33 from 11 overs for Weavering, in Thurnham's score of 79. Weavering were dismissed at 55 runs with the wickets shared between J Peat (6 for 25) and R Penney (4 for 26).[32] In another match, Roger Chapman scored 105 not out in a total of 157 for 4 in reply to 208 for 9 declared by Jackson & Smith. Both games against Bearsted were lost in reply to totals of over 200; Thurnham could only manage 103 and 41.[33]

The opposition included Loose Amenities, Boughton Monchelsea, Corinthians, King Street, Weavering, Buckhurst, Barming Heath YC, Headcorn Second XI, Staplehurst, Egerton, Belnor Sports (Sittingbourne), East Sutton, Inland Revenue (Chatham) and GPO.

The following year, Thurnham also played Hanwell, Ryarsh, Nettlestead, Milton Regis Conservatives, Leeds & Broomfield and Stockbury. Both games against Bearsted were lost.

A match against King Street was lost by 8 wickets with the scores being 39 and 42 for 2. The Thurnham team was: R Chapman, R Tree, D Cleggett, B Penney, G Walkling, C Filmer, J Offard, C Miles, K Willson, M Munn and R Penney. [34]

For 1965, Thurnham maintained the same fixtures. The team which lost to Hanwell comprised: J Peat, D Cleggett, G Walkling, B Penney, D Filmer, M Filmer, B Hale, M Munn, N Colebrook, K Willson and R Penney.

Only one game was played in the season against Bearsted and this was at home. It resulted in a comprehensive win for Thurnham, who scored 120 and bowled Bearsted out for 67.

Participation in a local team and pursuing an active sporting life can bring it with it many successes and disappointments, but it can also impinge upon other areas of a player's life. However, there can be few 'sporting widows' who have felt sufficiently emboldened to write to the national press about it. Nevertheless, Ron Penney's wife, Doris, wrote to the Daily Express newspaper expressing her thoughts, which were published 30 July 1965:

> **Never on Saturday…**
>
> We didn't have a party on our silver wedding day, so I said to my husband: 'Never mind, we will make up for it by having a lovely party on our golden wedding day.' He looked across at me and said: 'well, don't arrange it for a Saturday because I shall be playing cricket.'
>
> He is now in his 50th year and can still show the young ones how to bowl each week. He would be 72 on our golden wedding day.

Reproduced courtesy of Daily Express newspapers and Barbara Wickens

The 1966 season included new fixtures with Beltinge and Gillingham British Legion. The first game at Bearsted was drawn but the return match at home was lost by 202 runs with Thurnham being bowled out for 27 with Tony Webb taking 7 for 9.

The team against Hanwell showed a few changes and comprised: G Walkling, D Avard, K Hysted, B Penney, R Patey, D Jenkins, C Filmer, M Munn, R Penney, J Offard and J Sheppard. [35]

In June 1967, the home game against Tunbridge Wells Gas Board was delayed by one and half hours of rain, so the skippers decided to play on a knock-out basis of sixteen eight-ball overs each. Thurnham's 85 looked like being more than enough until Prebble hit a rapid 38, including three sixes but when he was caught, Thurnham quickly gained advantage of the match to win by 11 runs.

In other matches, several good performances with the ball were recorded and this included J Peat's 8 for 37, and 7 for 15, R Patey's 6 for 23 and D Cleggett 6 for 26. Dennis Cleggett showed his all round ability against the Inland Revenue side by scoring a century followed by his bowling figures of 5 for 16. [36]

Both of the matches against Bearsted were lost: the second showed Bearsted scoring 220 for 4 with the Gibson brothers, Neville and Mick scoring 85 not out and 56 respectively. Ken Boorman took 5 for 45 in Thurnham's total of 101 all out. [37]

Thurnham Cricket Club

This photograph of Thurnham Cricket team was taken during the 1960s:

Reproduced courtesy of Keith Willson and Kent Messenger newspaper group

Back Row (left to right): Bryant Hale (umpire), Ryan Delves, Ainsley Clark, Graham Walkling, Malcolm Miller, Neville Colebrook, -----, Susan Delves (scorer)
Front Row (left to right): Rev Dudley Tizzard, Bob Patey, Jim Peat, Keith Willson, Phil Pickering.

Thurnham Cricket Club

It is fair to say that the cricket pavilions of many village clubs in the post-war years were relatively basic by today's standards. It was not unusual for teams to share the same dressing room. The provision of washing facilities was sometimes regarded as a luxury. In 1967, following fund-raising and hard physical work by the members of Thurnham Cricket Club, separate accommodation was provided for each team.

These photographs show some of the early stages of construction of the buildings and laying out of the ground. Given the lack of formal records and photographs that exist of Thurnham Cricket Club; these are an astonishingly rare survival. The first photograph features Graham Walkling, who is standing on some of the concrete supports for the building:

In this photograph, Malcolm Munn and Ernie Seager are looking at the ground plan:

Both reproduced courtesy of Jack Smith

This photograph shows Graham, Malcolm and Ernie. The building on the left is a garage which was used to store equipment:

Reproduced courtesy of Jack Smith

At the start of the 1968 season, there was no indication that it was to be the last played by Thurnham Cricket Club. S Beg and Brian Penney were in good form batting and bowling, and A Clark also had the remarkable figures of 5.5 overs, 4 maidens, 5 runs and 6 wickets in the dismissal of the team from Singlewell for 53. The players representing Thurnham against Tunbridge Wells Gas Board and Singlewell were: W Beg, P Pickering, B Penney, A Clark, B Patey, G Carpenter, B Hale, C Miles, G Walkling, J Peat, K Willson, J Smith, M Miller and D Peachey.[38]

This undated photograph shows Brian Penney:

Reproduced courtesy of Barbara Wickens

The first game against Bearsted was lost by 2 wickets after being bowled out for 74. In the return game on 7 September, Thurnham had the better of a draw with scores of 190 for 5 declared (Mick Filmer 51 not out) and 137 for 5 (Mick Filmer 3 for 13).[39]

In the autumn, freak winds wrecked the buildings at the ground and parts were deposited on the motorway, more than 500 yards away. The practicalities of replacing the buildings proved too daunting and reluctantly the club decided that it could not continue. The last ball had been bowled at Thurnham Cricket Club.

Memories of the club remain and are recalled whenever old team mates meet. Such an occasion was at Ron Penney's seventieth birthday in 1985, where the following photographs were taken:

Brian Chapman (left) and Malcolm Munn:

Vera Seager (left) and Graham Walking:

All reproduced courtesy of Barbara Wickens

Ian Lambert

Milgate Park Cricket Club

The tradition of cricket being played at Milgate Park was probably begun during the 1700s when the estate was owned by the Cage family. Although there are no surviving written records about the games played, there is a portrait of Lewis Cage painted by Francis Cote in 1768. This photograph shows a copy of the portrait which hangs in the Members Pavilion at Lords cricket ground. Lewis is depicted as a small child, defending a wicket that had just two stumps, with a rather curved bat: [1]

Reproduced courtesy of MCC from a copy of the original painted by Katherine Lloyd

Nothing further was recorded about the game on the estate for well over a century.

Milgate Park Cricket Club

Walter Fremlin, from the brewing family had an interest in the estate and so he was able to use a section of the grounds to host events and cricket matches as part of his leisure pursuits. Thus on 13 August 1896, it was reported that W T Fremlin, Esq, had arranged for the Sunday School Treat to be held at Milgate Park and that cricket and the usual popular games were kept up with vigour. Later that year, Milgate played Bearsted Star, a youth side, and won by four runs. The Milgate team comprised: A Goodhew, C Apps, W Maxted, G Baker, W Attwood, C Rundle, W Warde, C Cucknow, G Stamp, E Pollard and J Watts.

A team from the brewery also played some matches at Milgate.[3] In 1898 the Kent Messenger reported that the Fremlin's Pale Ale Brewery commenced their season with a match at Milgate Park by kind permission of Mr W T Fremlin. In the previous year, Milgate had played both the Pale Ale Brewery and Bearsted & Thurnham. Cricket at Milgate was obviously thriving.

In 1902, Walter Fremlin bought Milgate Park.[2] Many long-established residents could recall that he had his own cricket pitch in the grounds and fielded his own team. There does not appear to be a surviving photograph of the cricket ground, but this one of the house was taken in the early years of the twentieth century:

Reproduced courtesy of Jean Jones

This photograph of Walter Fremlin accompanied his obituary in the Kent Messenger in February 1925:

Reproduced courtesy of Kent Messenger newspaper group

For the first decade of the 1900s, regular opponents of Milgate Park were teams from Leeds Castle, Boughton Monchelsea as well as the Pale Ale Brewery. Leeds Castle were the superior side over this period and results included wins by an innings and 97 runs; 136 runs (The Kent Messenger reported that Mr Lushington batted in capital style for 24 but that Mr E Moon was the only man he could get to stay with him); 44 runs (Milgate were dismissed for only 9); 128 runs (the Milgate team was A Gower, W Attwood, A Goodhew, E Waghorn, W Dixon, W Austen, E Moon, C Foster, J Hallenshoe, R Sears, B Rabjohn) and 294 runs (Leeds 325-6 in one and three quarter hours, Milgate 31).[4]

P F Warner ('Plum') played the occasional game for Milgate Park with scores of 47 in a drawn game against Leeds Castle; 140 versus Depot and a valuable 16 not out in a score of 31 to beat Pale Ale Brewery by 6 runs. Other teams played were Bearsted, Turkey Mill, Harrietsham, Maidstone Church Institute, Fremlin's, Sutton Valence School and Wye College. In 1909, W T Fremlin's XI lost to J Bazeley White's XI who scored 329-7 declared.[5]

Cricket at Milgate between 1909 and 1911 featured matches between Mr W T Fremlin's XI and Mr P F Warner's XI. The teams were a mixture of cricketing greats and local men. The following players had first class cricket experience:

'Plum' Warner	Middlesex and England
Frederick Fane	Essex and England
'Patsy' Hendren	Middlesex and England
Colin Blythe	Kent and England
Edward Litteljohn	Middlesex
Kenneth Macleod	Cambridge University and Lancashire
James Douglas	Middlesex
Frederick Levenson Gower	Oxford University and Hampshire
Fitzhardinge Liebenrood	MCC
F J V Hopley	Cambridge University

In the 1909 match, P F Warner's XI won an evenly matched game in which E Dadswell of Fremlin's XI took 8-40, 7 of which were clean bowled.

In 1911 P F Warner's XI could only muster 91 with Blythe taking 8-42. Fremlin's XI scored 335 in reply, with F B Leney scoring 119 not out. In their second innings Warner's XI scored 177-5 with K G Macleod scoring 125 not out.[6] In 1912, the Milgate team against Pale Ale Brewery comprised: G Fraser, Lieutenant Thompson, Rev S Wigan, A Paddle, F W Gosling, T Avis, L Pollard, R Gibbons, F Moon, W Attwood, and G Stern.[7]

It is known that the clergy were involved in local cricket and the Rev Stephen R Wigan, vicar of Thurnham, from 1901-1927 was no exception. Although Stephen mainly played for the Wigan Cricket Eleven, a team set up by Sir Frederick and James Wigan, two of the younger sons of John Wigan of Clare House, East Malling; he is known to have also played for Milgate Park, Bearsted, and Leeds Castle.[8] In 1895, he opened the batting for a game called Single versus Married at East Malling.

This undated photograph of Stephen was taken whilst an undergraduate at Cambridge:

Reproduced courtesy of Mary Wigan

The following year, W R Gosling scored 109 against Lancashire Fusiliers and E R Dadswell scored 116 for W Fremlin's XI versus Wye College.[9]

In the Kent Messenger on 27 August 1921, there was a report about a match at Milgate. This is a slightly edited transcript:

> There was jubilation at Milgate on Saturday afternoon, when the Estate XI won their first match of the eleven played to date. The visitors were Caring who scored 56. Milgate scored 72 in the first innings (Hughes 25 not out) and 64-9 in the second innings.
>
> Milgate have made a most acceptable acquisition in Mr Hughes, who played consistently, both at the wicket and in all positions in the field.

Reproduced courtesy of Kent Messenger newspaper group

The following week, they recorded their second win of the season with a victory over Fremlin's Brewery with scores of 123-5 and 54.[10]

The next year, Milgate Park were more consistent, with the highlight being a 158 run win against Bearsted Division Police. Milgate scored 242-8 declared with M Key scoring 151 not out including ten 6s and fifteen 4s.[11] A number of two innings games were played, and Leeds & Broomfield were defeated by an innings and 32 runs. Lieutenant H Thompson took 6-0 in the Leeds first innings of 22. F Gatland scored 68 for Milgate.[12] Bearsted Church XI were beaten by 81 runs with Major Gosling scoring 60 and W Hawkins taking 9-29.[13]

Other opposition teams in 1922 included Boxley, Boughton Monchelsea, Kreemy Works, Maidstone Corporation Tramways Cricket Club and Pale Ale Brewery. In 1923, Milgate Park beat Pale Ale Brewery with J Thornby scoring 53. The team comprised: G Fraser, J Thornby, A Gilbert, M Filmer, L Wright, A Dear, F Gilbert, E Pollard, W Bodiam, W Hawkins and A Tree.[14] Dr Lucy scored 20 in a defeat by Otham. L Wright scored 88 in a total of 176 with W Hawkins taking 5-54 and E Pollard 4-46 in Pale Ale Brewery's reply of 121. A low point in the season was a total of 19 against Boughton Monchelsea. Milgate Park also played Sutton Valence School.[15]

The highlight of 1924 was the match in which Mr W T Fremlin's XI unfortunately lost by 38 runs to St John's College, Cambridge.[16] It is not known if this was the last match played at Milgate. However, Walter Fremlin was now aged 80 and firmly in the twilight of his life. He died on 25 February 1925 and as he had no children, the estate was put up for sale.

Ian Lambert

Cricket in Bearsted and Thurnham: an envoi

Perhaps the final sentiment about the special role of cricket within the communities at Bearsted and Thurnham is best expressed in the following poem, which appeared in the Kent Messenger, 2 July 1927:

A Cricketers Sonnet

If I were told to choose the time and place

In which to end my little earthly day

My choice would be an afternoon in May

Upon some peaceful battlefield of Grace

There hope mounts high in all the human race

Inspiring clean-limbed men and youths at play

On emerald fields in spotless white array

While keen endeavour marks each sun kissed face

There is a spirit on the cricket ground

Which breathes the breath of friendship into man

Uplifting them from pettiness and then enriching and enlarging all around

Where willow bat makes music with the ball

There would I answer the eternal call.

'A Kentishman'

Reproduced courtesy of Kent Messenger newspaper group

Ian Lambert

considerable effort on the part of both teams and the officials of the Bearsted Club that the spectators left the field.

In the 1926/1927 season, the team against Wrotham Pilgrims comprised: [9]

> C Beale, A Ayres, F Cooper, S Gee, W Hodges, C Colegate, A Gilbert, C Earl, F Hooker, L White and H Gilbert.

This photograph but was taken between the First and Second World Wars. The team are standing by Raggetts butchers premises on the Green.

Back row (left to right): J Sent, B Hirst, S Earle, L White, E Raggett, C Colegate, S Gee
Front row (left to right): G Taylor, C Raggett, G Smith, T Gilbert, B Carr.

After many years without success, the First XI won Division IIB in the 1928/1929 season. The photograph below was taken of the team in front of Bearsted House. At the end of the season, Major Clarence Craig, President and Chairman of the Bearsted and District Sports Club, gave a copy of the photograph to each of the players and officials. Little is known about the team members but Ewart Cathcart is fifth from the left in the back row. Major Craig is third from the left on the back row and Jack Sent, the football club secretary from 1927 to 1939, is in the back row, second from the right.

Both reproduced courtesy of Chris and Sue Hunt

The return to Division I for 1929/1930 was fleeting. The team were relegated to Division II at the end of the season.

Bearsted Football Club

The 1930s was to be the decade of the cup with the First XI reaching the semi finals of the Hospital Cup on seven occasions. The team progressed to three finals, they were victorious in 1930/1931 and 1935/36 and runners-up in 1931/1932. This photograph is believed to be the winning 1930/1931 side in front of Bearsted House.[10]

Reproduced courtesy of Bearsted Football Club

Back row (left to right): Sent, Bromfield, Cathcart, Henley, Gee
Middle row (left to right): Gilbert, Hodges, Colegate
Front row (left to right): Smith, Earle, White, Westover, Ames.

A rare occurrence took place in April 1930 as in a home game against Marden, the result was 20-0. Every member of the Bearsted side scored!

During the summer of 1932 the Sports Club was one the beneficiaries of the Fayre, receiving £15. The Football section was described in the parish magazine as an important part of the life of Bearsted.[11]

The parish magazine in 1934 recorded 139 consecutive league and cup appearances by the club captain and goalkeeper, Ewart Cathcart. This was a remarkable achievement which was only broken when he had arranged to attend an International match at Wembley. Ewart had not anticipated that the club would have a fixture![12]

The officers for the 1934/1935 season were:[13]

Chairman:	Mr G Marsh
Vice Chairman:	Mr T Swain
Treasurer:	Mr G Goodman
Honorary Secretary:	Mr J Sent
Honorary Assistant Secretary:	Mr W Fairbrass
Committee Members:	D Walking, A Ayres, Lee
Captain First XI:	Mr S Gee
Vice Captain:	Mr C Colegate
Captain Second XI:	Mr S Betts
Vice Captain:	Mr R Wellard

In 1937/1938 Bearsted had another successful season, becoming the League Champions of Division II.

Bearsted Football Club

The football club did not continue to function during the Second World War but in 1949 the parish magazine carried the following report: [14]

> It was unanimously agreed at the meeting on July 7th to reform the Bearsted Sports Football Club disbanded in 1939 owing to the war. Mr A C Bossom MP was elected as President and Mr Stanley Johnson is vice-president. The committee comprises:
>
> | | |
> |---|---|
> | Chairman: | Mr W Giles |
> | Vice Chairman: | Mr E Thwaites |
> | Secretary: | Mr W W Gorham |
> | Treasurer: | Mr K Baker |
> | Committee: | Messrs J Brooks, R Filmer, B Hunt, G Walkling |
> | Captain: | Mr B Hirst |
> | Vice Captain: | G Walkling |
> | Groundsman: | Mr A Martin |

Reproduced courtesy of Holy Cross and St Mary's churches

This photograph shows the team, 1949/1950:

Reproduced courtesy of Bearsted Football Club

Standing (left to right): Referee, R Gould, T White, Ewin Rayner, The Avard Boys, 'Punch' Palmer, Billy Giles, W Gorman
Seated (left to right): Pat Amos, Ted Jones, B Hirst, C Raggett, S Colgate, (in front) Master Colegate.

The first success came in 1955/1956 when the First XI won the Group B Challenge Trophy. The opposition was Holoplast and the first game at the Athletic Ground ended in a 2-2 draw. The replay at Aylesford was won 4-2. [15]

During the 1956/1957 season the Reserves withdrew from Division IIIC and re-entered in 1958/1959. There was an air of crisis within the club prior to the start of the 1957/1958 season. The report of the Annual General Meeting held at the Royal Oak on 1 July referred to the fate of the club hanging in the balance through lack of support. However, it was decided to try again, hoping for more support in the future. Mr D Plant was elected Chairman.[16]

In 1960/1961 the club entered the indoor evening 5-a-side league played at the Agricultural Hall in Lockmeadow, Maidstone.

Bearsted Football Club

In 1961/1962 the Reserves were Champions of Division IV with a record of:

Played	Won	Drawn	Lost	Goals for	Goals against	Points
24	21	3	0	157	33	45

An 8-0 victory against Reeds Corrugated Cases with goals by Brian Beavis (4), Peter Mannering (2), David Wyatt and Colin Smith saw them reach a hundred goals in the season. In another match, the Reserves beat Collier Street 18-0 with Brian Beavis and David Wyatt each scoring six goals. The goalkeeper, Keith Willson, barely touched the ball but managed to miss a penalty for Bearsted! [17] On the same day the First XI defeated Mangravet 10-4 with Jim Bonner scoring six goals. How many clubs can boast two games on the same day, scoring twenty eight goals with three separate double hat-tricks?

At that time, the club had a cut-out Yogi Bear mascot which was displayed on match days. On their way to play at Aylesford, members of Ashford Rugby Club decided that Yogi would be a suitable trophy and he found a new home on a rugby touchline. With all the skill of Huckleberry Hound, Yogi was tracked down and returned to his rightful home. His return may have been influential as Bearsted and Ashford were losing their respective games but both of them went on to win.

In 1962/1963 the Reserves finished bottom of Division IIIA and so returned to Division IV. In the following season they showed their resolve by finishing runners-up and gaining promotion again.

In 1964/1965 the First XI came tantalisingly close to achieving a league and cup double. After a 2-0 victory in the Group B semi-final on a snow-covered pitch against Mote Reserves, Bearsted played Frittenden in the final at the Athletics Ground on 8 April. Bearsted won 1-0 with the only goal scored by Ian Lambert. The winning team comprised: [18]

D Andrews, R Tree, E Fremlin, K Filmer, T Plant, B Patey, I Lambert, M Harvey, B Brigden, J Parker and N Fisher.

The next year the First XI were runners up in the League. Bearsted again reached the final of the Group B Challenge Cup but lost 1-0 to Alabaster Passmore. The score belied the play in the match though as the team included Dave Cowie, who was aged sixteen, and centre half Derek Filmer, who gave an outstanding performance. Goalkeeper Danny Wiltshire was in fine form.[19]

In 1967/1968 the First XI were to finish runners up to Medway Brewery and were promoted to Division I. There was a recorded win of 15-3 against Staplehurst with goals by Frankie King (6), Trevor Perkins (4), Bob Patey (2), Ricky Carcary, Malcolm Harvey and Dave Cowie.[20] The same day, the Reserves beat Ulcombe 13-3. Once again the club scored 28 goals on the same day.

In 1969/1970 the League was re-organised into a Premier and five other Divisions. The First XI remained in Division I and the Reserves entered Division III. Bearsted benefited from an influx of new players who had come from some of the new housing estates that were being built in the village.

1971/1972 saw promotion to the Premier Division and the start of a period when Bearsted was a dominant force in local football. This achievement was largely due to Richard Filmer who was involved with the reformation of the club after the war. His sudden death on 15 November 1971 was a great loss to the club which he had served with diligence, enthusiasm and integrity. Whether as a Committee member, spectator or linesman his involvement was total. His three sons all shared his love of football and have played for the club. The association is continued through his grandson Richard. As a tribute to his memory, a club trophy is now known as the Richard Filmer Sportsman of the Year award.[21]

For the next ten seasons the First XI was to stay with the Maidstone and District League and enjoying phenomenal success. A report of a league match against Eccles in 1972/1973 in the Kent Messenger newspaper was perhaps indicative of things to come: [22]

> Bearsted are proving one of the most exciting teams to arrive in the Premier Division for a long time…they are a major force to be reckoned with…

Bearsted Football Club

Bearsted's early years in the League were dominated by Rangers and Eccles but in the five seasons from 1973/1974 to 1977/1978, Bearsted reached the final of the Group A Challenge Cup on four occasions, being winners twice and runners up twice. The semi-final during the 1973/1974 season was described as 'epic' in the match report. The first game ended in a draw with both sides scoring, before the Mote Wanderers missed two penalties. Even after extra time, the replay resulted in neither side scoring any goals, but in the second replay, Mote were crushed 6-1. After this excitement, the final against Rangers was an anti-climax and Bearsted lost 3-1. [23]

However, there was revenge in 1975/1976 when Bearsted played Rangers in a semi-final. Bearsted won 3-2 but not before a total of ten players were booked and one sent off! In the final, Bearsted beat Eccles 3-1 with goals from Ian Dyke, Alan Cunningham and Keith Emberley. The team comprised: [24]

>M Filmer, M Harvey, P Whittell, O Nicholls, J Mace, D Mason, T O'Grady, A Cunningham, K Lambert, K Emberley, I Dyke   Substitute: D McDougall or P Rudd.

In 1976/1977, Bearsted again beat Eccles 3-1, this time in a semi-final replay but went on to lose 2-1 to Rangers after extra time in the final. In 1977/1978, Bearsted met Eccles in the final but after extra time the scores were level at 2-2. The Bearsted team comprised: [25]

>Filmer, Mason, Evans, McAllister, Nicholls, Hutchins, Ryall, MacDougall, Rogers, Hefferon, (Everest), Bryan.

In the replay at Oakwood Hospital, Bearsted won 2-0 with goals by Bill Ryall and Captain, Ray Hutchins. Bearsted again reached the final in 1981/1982 when they lost 1-0 to The Rose.

In the Premier League there was a remarkable run between 1976/1977 and 1981/1982. Three consecutive seasons as runners up was followed by three Championships.

This photograph shows both the First and Reserve teams from 1978:

Reproduced courtesy of Bearsted Football Club

<u>Back Row (left to right)</u>: Paul Everest, Keith McKay, Dennis Lloyd, Mick Filmer, Mick Redman, Mick Everest, Richard Campion, Pernel Rogers
<u>Middle Row (left to right)</u>: Russ May, Percy Elmers, Andy Bryan, Steve Ellmer, Bobby Evans, Keith Lambert, John Mace, Tony Sowerby, Aldy Holden, Jeff Rogers, Tim Rust, John Young, Mike Anthony
<u>Front Row (left to right)</u>: Martin Nicholls, Alan Hefferon, Alan Cunningham, Paul Rudd, Ray Hutchins, Roger King, Dick Mason, Steve Talbot, Ricky Carcary.

During 1979/1980, Bearsted won the Championship of the Premier Division for the first time and applied to join the Kent Amateur League. The following year, the First XI again won the Premier Division title. For the first time the club negotiated sponsorship with a Maidstone sports shop which included a new set of shirts with advertising upon them. At the end of the season the club made a successful trip to France to take part in a tournament at Acheres, near Paris. Bearsted won the tournament and it was the start of many successful fixtures playing similar games in France; an arrangement which continues to this day.

The final top positions for the two seasons were: [26]

	1979/1980				
	P	W	D	L	Pts
Bearsted	20	13	4	3	30
Maidstone Rangers	20	11	4	5	26
Alabaster Passmore	20	10	3	7	23
Eccles	20	11	1	8	23
Snodland	20	10	2	8	22
	1980/1981				
	P	W	D	L	Pts
Bearsted	24	18	5	1	41
The Rose	24	17	2	5	36
Snodland	24	15	4	5	34
MALGO	24	13	8	3	34
Maidstone Rangers	24	12	6	6	30

Reproduced courtesy of Kent Messenger newspaper group

This photograph of the First Team Squad was taken in 1980:

Reproduced courtesy of Bearsted Football Club

Back Row left to right): John Young, Tony Sowerby, Steve Bailey, Ashley Mitchell, Dennis Lloyd, Mick Filmer, Paul Rudd, Franny Stevens, Percy Elmers
Middle Row (left to right): Russ May, Alan Cunningham, Malcolm Harvey, Jeff Rogers, Steve Elmore, Martin Abbott, Mike Anthony
Front Row (left to right): Peter Whittell, Ray Hutchins, Allan Hefferon, Pernel Rogers, John Mace, Keith Lambert, Jerry Osborne.

The final match of the 1981/1982 saw the First XI achieve a hat trick of Premier Division titles. For the second season running, only one league game was lost. There was no shortage of competitive action with

Steve Breeds, Mick Everest and Marty Abbott scoring a total of 73 goals between them in all the competitions.[27] The final league table was as shown below:[28]

	P	W	D	L	F	A	Pts
Bearsted	22	17	4	1	70	15	38
MALGO	22	17	3	2	68	20	37
Maidstone Rangers	22	14	4	4	64	34	32
Snodland	22	12	3	7	52	29	27
The Rose	22	10	6	6	48	35	20
Headcorn	22	9	2	11	35	46	20
Eccles	22	7	6	9	26	38	20
East Malling	22	6	7	9	38	44	19
Tovil & Bridge	22	8	3	11	41	48	19
Alabaster Passmore	22	8	1	13	41	44	17
Castle Sports	22	1	3	18	14	76	5
Coombe Estate	22	1	2	19	27	96	4

Reproduced courtesy of Kent Messenger newspaper group

Over the same decade, the Reserves team was similarly successful. In 1973/1974 they won the Division III title. The following season they achieved the Division II title at the first attempt, then the double by beating Yalding in the final of the Group B Challenge Cup. The league was clinched with a win in the final game of the season, achieving wins in sixteen matches out of twenty two played. Division I was won in the 1977/1978 season, taking the title by one point. In 1980, during Ricky Carcary's first year as Manager, the Reserves finished runners up in Division I.[29]

During the decade, Doug Avard retired as Treasurer after holding the position for twenty five years. The work of dedicated supporter Tom Jones with the collection box on match days was also recognised. Russ May retired as a player and then took over the post of Manager. He held this post with great distinction for many years.

The 1982/1983 season was a milestone in the club's history. For the first time, a team from Bearsted entered the Kent Amateur League (Division II). The Reserves played in the Premier Division of the Maidstone and District League while a third XI (the A team) was formed and played in Division I.

The First XI made an immediate impact by winning the Division II title at the first attempt. They were also runners up in the Kent Junior Cup losing 2-0 to Charlton Town and in the Sevenoaks Charity Senior Section, losing 4-1 to Sevenoaks. The team comprised:[30]

> Ricky Wiles, Keith Lambert, Ray Tripp, John Charman, Jeff Rogers, Ray Hutchins,
> Kevin Latham, Alan Cunningham, Steve Breeds, Martin Abbott, Steve Elmers
> Substitutes: Jim Needham and Mick Everest.

In the summer of 1983 the Football Club lost a true friend when Bill Giles died. Along with Richard Filmer he was instrumental in regenerating football in Bearsted after the Second World War. He had held office with both the football club and the Maidstone and District League and was a qualified referee.

The following year, the club succeeded in taking the First Division title and went into the Premier League, finishing as runners up for each of the next two seasons. 1985/1986 also saw Borough Green defeated in the final of the Sevenoaks Charity Cup. Bearsted took the Premier League title in 1986/87 and, in the Kent Junior Cup, recorded a 14-0 win against Sevenoaks Weald with ten different players scoring, including an own goal.[31]

1987/1988 was a triumphant season for the club, gaining a long-awaited place in the Senior Section. The First XI won both the League Championship at the first attempt and the League Senior Cup against Rusthall. The season also marked Keith Lambert's five hundredth game.

The Reserves entered the Kent County League in 1988/1989 finishing third and followed this success by beating Wilmington Reserves 2-0 to win the Sevenoaks Junior Charity Cup. At the end of the season,

Russ May resigned as Manager of the First XI after twenty five years service to the club. The next season saw an unfortunate incident in the game against Swanscombe. A Swanscombe player, who had committed a variety of offences and received a second yellow card, returned to the field of play with the team water bucket. The referee indicated that if the contents were thrown at him, the game would be abandoned, which it was!

The A team withdrew from the Maidstone and District League during 1991/1992 due to a lack of players. It was a sad move as the club had a long association with the League. The team struggled for a while but the younger players gained valuable experience. Nevertheless the side were joint runners up in 1982/1983 under manager Alan Heffron and won Division II in 1990/1991. They were also the losing finalists to APM Third XI in the Group B Challenge Cup.

A quiet period followed over the next seven seasons but the club still managed to win the Inter-League Trophy and the Division I Cup and were runners-up in the Division I and Inter-Regional Cups. During this time, the Kent County League was re-organised and Bearsted did not play in the new Premier League in 1992/1993 as their playing and changing facilities were not of a sufficiently high standard. An alternative ground was sought but hire could not be arranged within the timescale allowed.

1995/1996 was a special season as it marked the Centenary of the football club. A celebratory dinner was held in the Great Danes Hotel. The whole club was successful in the centenary season as the First XI were runners up in the League and winners of the West Kent Challenge Shield against Phoenix. The Reserves won their league and were winners of the Weald of Kent Junior Charity Cup against Iden. The Sunday XI won the Presidents Cup (Group A). The junior sides took four Maidstone League trophies and three from Invicta Primary League.[32] In the following three years, the First XI took the Division I League Championship, won the Inter Regional Cup against Milton and the Kent Intermediate Cup against New Romney.

This is the front of the souvenir menu for the celebratory dinner:

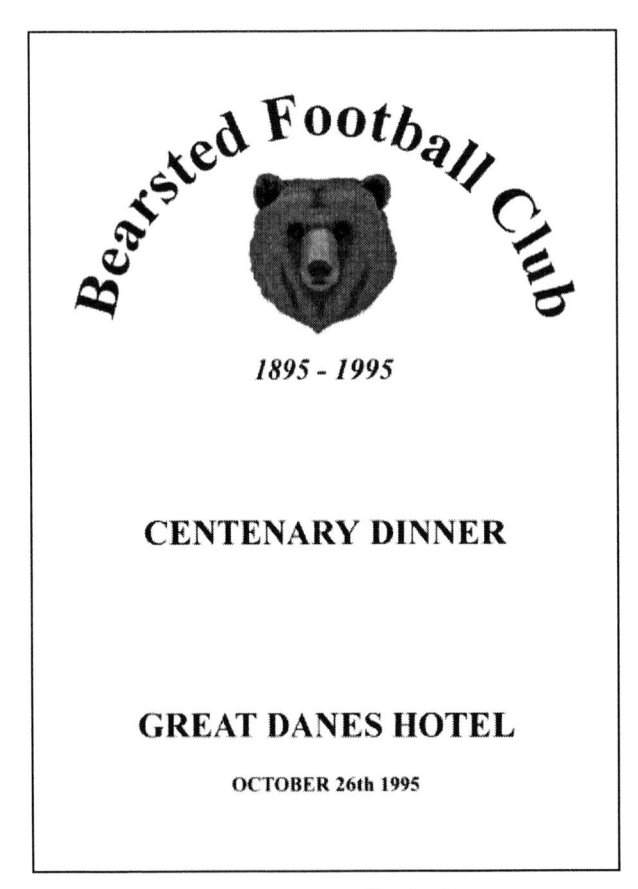

Bearsted Football Club

1895 - 1995

CENTENARY DINNER

GREAT DANES HOTEL

OCTOBER 26th 1995

Reproduced courtesy of Ian Lambert

Bearsted Football Club

One score that the club will not need reminding about was Sevenoaks 15, Bearsted 0 on 25 April 1998. How did it happen? This slighted edited report from the May edition of the Downs Mail, included Ian Hamer's explanation:

> …We had a depleted side due to injuries, sickness and players having to work. We arrived with only eleven men, so we didn't have any substitutes, and it didn't help when I was sent off after ten minutes for deliberate hand ball! We struggled on with ten men and then our goalkeeper Jamie Britt went for a 50/50 ball and was injured and had to go off, so we were down to nine men and no goalkeeper. The result speaks for itself…

Reproduced courtesy of Downs Mail

The 1999 season saw Bearsted firmly established as a major force in Kent Senior Football but ironically, no trophy was forthcoming. They were to finish runners up to Snodland in the league and losing semi-finalists in the Inter Regional Challenge Cup. It was, however, the Kent Senior Trophy that was the icing on the cake. Kent League teams Herne Bay, Sheppey and VCD[33] were all beaten, before losing in the semi final to Deal Town who were to win the FA Vase at Wembley.

The second round tie against Sheppey was played in the shadow of the sudden death of Ray Hutchins. The following tribute was included in the match programme:

> It is with deep regret that we inform you of the sudden death of Ray Hutchins. Ray died of heart failure on Wednesday, 1st December 1999, aged 54. In his youth he played for the top Amateur Clubs in the country and was awarded an England International Youth Cap. For many years he played for Bearsted FC and was a very successful Manager of our First team. Ray was a gentleman in the true sense of the word and will be greatly missed by all his family and friends. Our sincere condolences to all his family. Please observe the one minute silence before today's game.

Reproduced courtesy of Bearsted Football Club

This is the front of the match programme:

> **OFFICIAL PROGRAMME**
>
> **Bearsted v Sheppey Utd**
>
> Saturday 4th December
>
> K.O. 1.30 pm
>
> Honey Lane, Otham, Kent.
>
> **Kent Senior Trophy**
>
> Price - 50p

Reproduced courtesy of Ian Lambert

In 2000/2001 the First XI were awarded the championship in controversial circumstances. Snodland had failed to play a fixture against Bearsted at the end of the season, which would have been the championship's decider. In the following season Bearsted became the first club in the history of the League to win the League title in consecutive years. They were also runners up in the Inter Regional Cup losing 6-5 on penalties to Stansfeld.

One highlight of the 2004/2005 season was a 1-0 victory against second placed Kent League side Hythe Town. The goal scorer was Jason Batt. This photograph was taken during the match and appeared in the Kent Messenger, 8 October 2004. The Bearsted player is on the right.

Reproduced courtesy of Kent Messenger newspaper group

The 2005/2006 season started in an unusual manner with the commission of a poem about Bearsted football club by Peter Goulding from the Republic of Ireland who writes football-related poetry. This is the first verse from the finished eight-verse work: [34]

> As I roved out upon a glum
> And chilling winter's day
> I chanced upon a stadium
> Along down Maidstone Way
> Though tempted by a cosy pub
> I plumped for Bearsted Football Club

Reproduced courtesy of Bearsted Football Club

Early in the season, manager Murray Carcary came out of retirement to play in goal as a late replacement for the injured Jason Reeves. Sadly, there was not a happy ending as Bearsted lost 2-1 against Lewisham Borough.[35] This photograph of Murray accompanied the match report in Adscene, 1 September 2005.

Reproduced courtesy of Adscene newspapers

Early in 2006, the Shadow Sports and Olympics Minister, Hugh Robertson, MP for Mid Kent, presented the club chairman, Duncan Andrews with a grant for £6,000 from the Football Foundation for club development work. This photograph accompanied the Kent Messenger report, 3 February: [36]

Reproduced courtesy of John Westhrop and Kent Messenger newspaper group

In the summer of 2006, a Silver anniversary was achieved, twenty five years of sporting exchanges between Bearsted and Acheres. The main game was won 7-2 and there were other games between Veteran and Junior sides. The Acheres representatives were entertained with a reception at the Town Hall in Maidstone. [37]

This photograph shows Duncan Andrews with the Acheres Trophy:

2006/2007 was a fine cup season, but was preceded by two important presentations:

The National Charter Standard, denoting the standard of coaching, administration and child protection for clubs working with young people, was formally awarded by Sir Trevor Brooking before the England versus Macedonia game at Old Trafford in October. Duncan Andrews and youth development manager Colin Whitfield were guests of the Football Association. They also received a £300 cheque, a plaque and VIP tickets for the game.

A second presentation was to Keith Willson, by the Football Association and British Energy Kent County League in recognition of fifty five years service to the club. This photograph of Keith appeared in the club newsletter: [38]

Both reproduced courtesy of Bearsted Football Club

In the prestigious Kent Senior Trophy competition, Bearsted reached the quarter finals with a comprehensive 3-0 victory against Crockenhill. Goals were scored by Smith, Brown and Chaplain. The prize was a home tie against Kent League side Slade Green. The match was initially postponed due to a waterlogged pitch. In the re-arranged tie, Slade Green were defeated 2-1 in front of crowd of more than a hundred people. After going behind on the stoke of half time, Bearsted equalised after an hour with a goal by Russell McCleish and Alan Swift's volley clinched the game with just twelve minutes left. The team comprised: [39]

S Andrews, Hogg, Broadway, G Andrews, Stevens, Brown, Venamore (Sub. Swift), Lye, Radford, McCleish and Smith.

Bearsted had equalled their previous best achievement in the competition but then drew another home tie against Kent League opposition: Sevenoaks Town. Bearsted totally dominated the match and won 5-1 with a hat trick from Steve Smith and goals from Captain Danny Lye and Lee Radford.[40]

This photograph accompanied the match report in Kent Messenger, 9 March 2007, and shows several Bearsted players celebrating a goal against Sevenoaks:

Reproduced courtesy of David Antony Hunt and Kent Messenger newspaper group

15 April 2007 saw the biggest game in the club's history, against Whitstable Town, in the Trophy final at Princes Park, Dartford. Sadly, Bearsted were narrowly beaten 1-0 but can be proud of their performance against a side at the top of the Kent League Premier Division.

The season 2007/2008 was to prove something of an anti-climax with the First XI spending most of the season in the wrong half of table.[41] This photograph was taken during the season in a match against Lewisham Borough:

Reproduced courtesy of Steve Crispe and Kent Messenger newspaper group

The beginning of the twenty first century was to prove highly successful for the Reserves. The first five years of the decade have witnessed continued achievement in final matches; winning the league and the Weald of Kent Junior and Senior Charity Cups. The second successive League win was achieved in 2004/2005 in which Steve Bailey won two Manager of the Month Awards by the end of November and despite the team fielding eight different goalkeepers.

This was followed by further success in 2006/2007 with a record of P24 W19 D1 L4 F67 A23 Pts58. Hat tricks were recorded by Nick Taylor and Stuart Brockman. Division I side Kennington were beaten 3-2 in a thrilling end to end encounter in the Weald of Kent Cup.

The main senior football club section has now moved premises to Honey Lane in Otham from the Green. The move was not without its controversies, but as the club spokesman Rod Palmer said, better facilities were required in order to make progress.[42]

The club has now been running for over a century and has come a long way from its beginnings as a Saturday team. It has grown to include teams for veterans playing on Sundays, and youth teams starting with Under 7s. All age ranges make a valuable contribution to the club.

Although the main achievements have been through matches on the field, it would not have happened without the dedication of the managers. The club continues to hold social and fund-raising events, maintaining a family atmosphere and has enjoyed sustained success.

This is the current club badge:

Reproduced courtesy of Bearsted Football Club

Ian Lambert

Thurnham United Football Club

Even the most ardent supporter of Thurnham United Football Club would be hard pressed to describe its achievements during one-third of a century as anything but unspectacular! The club was formed in the early 1970s and the first venture into competitive football was the season 1973/1974 when they joined the Maidstone and District Football League.[1] Since that time, they have not progressed beyond the third tier of local football, have had limited success in cup competitions and only been league champions on one occasion. Furthermore, they have never played in the parish of Thurnham.

The club owes its existence to the new occupants of Hill Brow on the Landway estate. The area was then in Thurnham parish. The first secretary was Roger O'Brian and the original members comprised local residents, followed by Roger's colleagues in the police force - Ray Hutchins, well-known in local footballing circles, was among the original players. This photograph shows Hill Brow, where it all started:

The home pitch was a site on the Detling Showground near the top of Detling Hill. This diagram below provides an indication of the location of the ground:

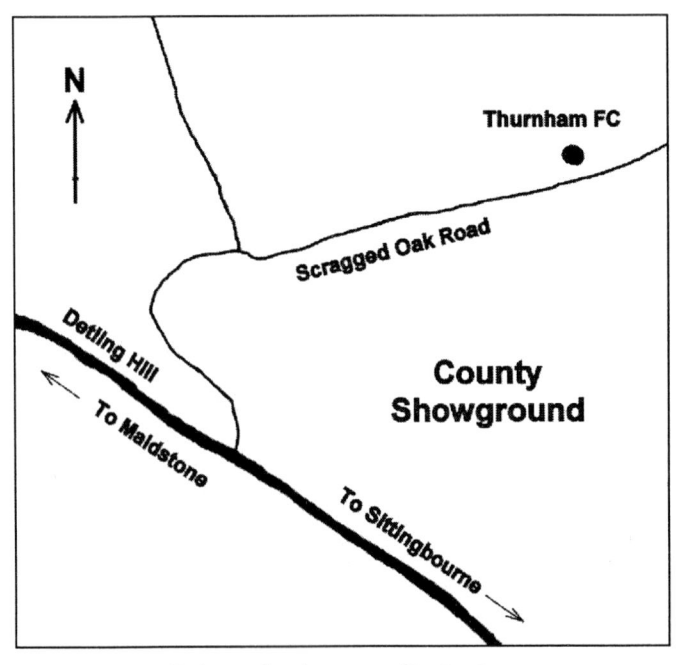

Both reproduced courtesy of Ian Lambert

Subsequently, they have used council pitches in Maidstone, and accept that, today, there is no link with the village apart from the name.

The first season was spent in Division Six of the Maidstone and District League, when they finished runners up to Wateringbury, having lost only two games but with seven ending in draws. Promotion was gained to Division Five where the next three seasons were spent. The first season, 1974/1975 was to provide the only cup final appearance when the club lost to Castle Sports in the League Group C Cup at the Athletic Ground on 16 April 1975.

In 1974/1975, a Reserve team was formed and entered Division Six. They remained in the lowest division for ten seasons, until they were disbanded at the end of the season 1983/1984. In 1977/1978, Division Six was withdrawn and both teams moved up a Division with the First XI having a successful first season in Division Four, finishing third on 37 points, behind RMS and United Banks, both on 38 points.

As a result of a reorganisation, the first XI found itself in Division Three for the season 1978/1979. It was probably the most successful season in the club's history. This transcript of report about the last of the season's matches appeared in the Kent Messenger, 4 May:

> The Division 3 title has still to be decided. Thurnham displaced Detling at the top of Division 3 on Tuesday on goal difference when they beat them 4-2. Goals from Keith Whitnell (2), John Brown and Barry Stevens.
>
> The outcome of the Division will be decided tomorrow when Detling visit relegated Hunton and Thurnham entertain Barming.
>
> | | P | W | D | F | A | Pts |
> |---|---|---|---|---|---|---|
> | Thurnham United | 25 | 18 | 4 | 88 | 37 | 40 |
> | Detling | 25 | 18 | 4 | 78 | 32 | 40 |

Reproduced courtesy of Kent Messenger newspaper group

This was the only time during the season that Thurnham had held top spot. Detling were the arch-rivals, being neighbouring villages, and their home pitches were in close proximity.

With a number of permutations possible, Thurnham beat Barming 2-0 and Detling beat bottom of the table Hunton 6-1, which was an insufficient margin to deprive Thurnham of the title.

During the season, Thurnham were involved in a number of high-scoring victories. These included 6-0 versus Barming; 6-1 versus RMS Reserves; 6-2 and 5-1 versus Frittenden; and 5-2 versus East Malling Reserves.

At the end of March, they were four points behind the leaders, with four games in hand. With four games remaining, they were three points behind Detling on the same number of games.

April saw the start of evening matches because of a backlog due to bad weather. A good late spell was the key to the eventual league title, with a win against Alabaster Passmore Reserves, who were top, and a draw against VCF who were in second position.

Players who featured regularly in the promotion campaign included Rod Bailey, John Brown, Mick Delaney, Dave Jenkins, Roger O'Brien, John Palmer, Mick Pay, Dave Smith, Barry Stevens, Phil Sutton, Keith Whitnell and Mick Williams.

About this time, Thurnham forged a link with an Irish village team from Waterford and several exchange visits were made.

Thurnham United Football Club

Thurnham were to remain in Division Two for three seasons, before being relegated at the end of the 1981 season, with this record:

P	W	D	L	F	A	Pts
22	1	6	15	38	80	8

The photograph below shows Roger Heyhoe, the secretary of Thurnham United Football Club in the late 1980s and early 1990s. Roger was also the Auditor of the League Management Committee.

Reproduced courtesy of Maidstone & District Football League

The following eight seasons were spent in Division Three. Only once did they finish in the top half of the table. They were third from bottom twice, next to bottom once and they finished last in the season 1989/1990, during which goals were at a premium. Scorers in the following defeats included:

- 4-1 versus Yalding (Dave Mills)
- 6-2 versus Leeds (Alan Hawkins, Steve Murrell)
- 7-4 versus Leybourne Grange (Steve Murrell 2, Allan Hawkins, David Mills)
- 5-1 versus MPE (Noel Hanley)
- 4-1 versus Leeds (Richard Pearce)

Leybourne Grange subsequently withdrew from League, removing one of Thurnham's better results from the records.

Unfortunately, Richard Pearce scored two own goals in the 7-0 loss against Minstrels.

There were occasions when it was difficult to maintain eleven players on the pitch. In another game against Leybourne Grange, Thurnham were 2-0 down and playing with ten men when skipper Dave Mills sustained a leg injury. He went in goal and keeper Nigel Cox was pressed into action as a striker. Within a minute of taking up his position, he had scored.

One of the better results was a 1-0 defeat against Yalding who, the Kent Messenger newspaper reported, expected to win by an avalanche against cellar dwellers Thurnham! Yalding had nearly all the possession, but could not improve upon a tenth-minute goal. Early in the second half, a Thurnham player was sent off for fighting, and near the end Richard Felton went off with cramp, leaving Thurnham with just nine men. Perhaps this match was the embodiment of a comment made by Malcolm Allison in 1989:

> …A lot of hard work went into this defeat…

Several of the team were playing with injuries in the 12-0 defeat against Staplehurst who won 10-0 in the return game. YMCA Sports won 9-1.

Thurnham United Football Club

This table shows Thurnham's position at the end of the season:

Division Three　　　1989/1990

	P	W	D	L	F	A	Pts
Cross Keys	18	14	3	1	66	10	31
Staplehurst	18	13	2	3	67	22	28
Yalding	18	11	3	4	47	26	25
YMCA Sports	18	8	4	6	50	33	20
MPE Reserves	18	9	2	7	42	30	20
APM 3rd	18	9	2	7	40	32	20
Minstrels	18	5	6	7	31	33	16
Chart Sutton	18	5	3	10	22	41	13
Leeds	18	3	1	14	24	64	7
Thurnham United	18	0	0	18	8	96	0

The next season, life in Division Four was only slightly better; defeats were generally by smaller margins than before, although the 'old enemy', Detling, inflicted the double over Thurnham. The solitary win was recorded against Lenham Reserves (2-1) and the only draw was against Staplehurst Reserves (1-1).

The season might be summed up following the 1-0 reversal against Woodfield, when it was reported that:

> ...a goal scored from a twenty yard free kick was the only highlight of a drab contest...

Reproduced courtesy of Kent Messenger newspaper group

At the end of the season, Thurnham finished bottom and were relegated once more, to Division Five (the lowest division).

Division Four　　　1990/1991

	P	W	D	L	F	A	Pts
Snodland Reserves	20	16	1	3	57	66	33
Woodfield	20	13	3	4	63	25	29
United Banks Reserves	20	12	3	5	61	30	27
Eccles Reserves	20	10	5	5	48	29	25
Detling	20	11	3	6	40	24	25
GSE Sports	20	10	3	7	41	37	23
Barming Reserves	20	10	0	10	47	49	20
Leeds	20	5	4	11	29	59	14
Lenham Reserves	20	4	3	13	30	49	11
Staplehurst Reserves	20	4	2	14	16	48	10
Thurnham United	20	1	1	18	15	81	3

This period was, undoubtedly, the low point in Thurnham's history and over the two seasons, only one league game was won with one draw. Undeterred, the team continued, and perhaps bore in mind Howard Wilkinson's memorable quote from 1983:

> ...I am a firm believer that if you score one goal, the other team have to score two to win...

The team's fortunes were somewhat improved the following season and there was an immediate return to Division Four after finishing runners-up in Division Five.

Over the next sixteen seasons, the number of teams in the Maidstone League fluctuated with the result that the number of Leagues varied. Thurnham have avoided relegation during this period on several occasions as they have been in the basement division which has often been Division Four. In the 2007/2008 season they were in Division Three, the lowest division.

Thurnham has often been in the news for the wrong reasons and it is therefore pleasing to end with a transcript of some positive headlines which appeared in the Kent Messenger, 2 November 2007:

Fant-astic Thurnham fightback

The outstanding game of the day took place in Division 3, where Thurnham United overturned a 3-0 half time deficit to stun Fant Falcons 4-3.

When Thurnham's Phil Thorogood forced a great save out of the Fant keeper early on he inadvertently stung the Falcons into action and playing down the Giddyhorn Lane slope they quickly went ahead, when Jamie Allen slotted past Dale Stringer.

Within five minutes, Fant struck again through Paul Goldfinch and when Jason Critchell tapped home the third from close range following a free-kick Fant must have thought the points were in the bag. Dale Stringer made another superb stop to keep it down to three at the break and a Churchillian half time team talk produced an instant reaction from the visitors.

Thorogood's cross looked harmless enough, but it was sliced into the Fant goal by Sean Pelling and when Thurnham then won a free-kick about 40 yards from the goal, Brian Peach produced a stunning shot to make it 3-2.

With Fant reeling Stuart Peach volleyed the equaliser through a crowded penalty area and an increasingly frantic home side finally buckled with a quarter of an hour to play as a partially cleared cross found Peach, who headed the winner.

Reproduced courtesy of Kent Messenger newspaper group

Ian Lambert

MPE Football Club

MPE football club was formed in 1970. Mick Rayner, a founder member, recalled that in the early days, there was dual use of the name Mote Park Estate and Madginford Park Estate, so to avoid any confusion, the football club decided to be known just as MPE. The club joined Division Six of the Maidstone and District League for the season 1971/1972.[1] The club badge is shown here on the left.

This photograph of Mick Rayner was taken in May 2008. His association and involved commitment with the club spans thirty seven years: he is now club president.

Both reproduced courtesy of Mick Rayner

In their first competitive season, the club won the league and were runners up in the Group C Cup, losing 4-1 to Star XI at the Athletic Ground, Maidstone. MPE's only goal was scored by Bill Poulton.[2]

From this excellent beginning, MPE developed into one of the most respected clubs in the area, playing in the Premier Divisions of both the Saturday and Sunday leagues. At its peak, MPE ran four senior teams. This article is mainly about these teams, but the contributions by officials, and parents, to youth football, with teams playing under the umbrella of the club at all age groups should not be forgotten. MPE won Division Five in 1972/1973 without losing a match and achieving an average of nearly six goals a game.[3] This photograph of the winning team appeared in The Gazette, 8 May 1973:

Reproduced courtesy of Kent Messenger newspaper group

<u>Back row (left to right)</u>: John Lucas, Dave Delahay, Charlie Ashley, Ray Hitch, Terry Rodwell, Mick Horrell, Gavin Spears, Bill Poulton, Bill Lock
<u>Front Row (left to right)</u>: Tony Hunt, Kenny Ling, Geoff Parker, Bernie Flanagan, Dave Read, Andy Anderson.

This undated photograph shows thirteen players from MPE before leaving on a trip to Beauvais, the French town twinned with Maidstone. The club participated in the eleventh international tournament. They took with them the Kent Messenger Travel Cup which was presented by Alderman Peter Robinson before their departure.[4]

Reproduced courtesy of Kent Messenger newspaper group and Maidstone & District Football League

Progress continued in 1973/1974 when the First XI achieved the double in winning both Division Four and the Group C Challenge Cup with a 7-0 win over Castle Sports following a replay. The team included: Difford, Nicholls, Sunnucks, O'Donovan, Smith, Hogg, Neaves, Whitelaw, Mulley, Tremayne, Black, Mayes, Baker and Chappell.[5]

An indication of the strength of the club was the formation of a Reserve team for 1973/1974. They played in Division Six.[6]

Five seasons later, in 1978/1979, the First XI were in the Premier Division and the Reserves were in Division Three where they were to remain for the next seven seasons.[7]

In 1977, MPE entered a float in the Bearsted and Thurnham Carnival and Fayre and this photograph was taken as the carnival procession moved through Madginford down to Bearsted Green:

Reproduced courtesy of Mick Rayner

MPE Football Club

1979 marked the departure of manager Bill Lock (pictured below) who was a newsagent and about to move to a new job in New Malden. He was presented with a silver salver to mark his eight winning years with the club.[8]

Reproduced courtesy of Kent Messenger newspaper group

MPE only remained in the Premier Division for two years, having finished their second season at the bottom of the table: [9]

1979/1980 Premier Division

	P	W	D	L	F	A	Pts
Bearsted	20	13	4	3	58	25	30
Maidstone Rangers	20	11	4	5	54	30	26
Alabaster Passmore	20	10	3	7	46	42	23
Eccles	20	11	1	8	35	32	23
Snodland	20	10	2	8	50	36	22
MALGO	20	10	1	9	41	36	21
Castle Sports	20	5	9	6	33	39	19
United Banks	20	7	5	6	35	42	19
Coombe Estate	20	8	2	10	36	39	18
Headcorn	20	6	2	12	39	54	14
MPE	20	2	1	17	21	73	5

Their return to Division One lasted only one season. As the table shows they finished second and were promoted to the Premier Division for 1982/1983: [10]

1981/1982 Division One

	P	W	D	L	F	A	Pts
Medway Brewery	22	16	3	3	72	32	35
MPE	22	16	2	4	84	39	34
Bearsted Res.	22	14	1	7	60	39	29
Staplehurst	22	13	2	7	48	40	28
Larkfield & New Hythe	22	13	0	9	57	40	26
United Banks	22	12	1	9	56	54	25
Aylesford	22	11	0	11	54	52	22
Maidstone Rangers Res.	22	9	3	10	47	44	21
Hollingbourne	22	9	0	13	56	63	18
Chart Sutton	22	5	3	14	34	64	13
Ditton Village	22	3	2	17	23	67	8
West Farleigh	22	2	1	19	26	80	5

In 1984/1985 the First XI drew 2-2 with old rivals Bearsted Reserves with David Pennel and Steve Amos having fine games. The goals were scored by Andy Bryan and Steve Turner. During the season, MPE Reserves beat Staplehurst Reserves 4-2 with goals by John White (2), Steve Brown and Ray Smith.[11]

MPE Football Club

For 1985/1986 an MPE team joined the Sunday League in Division Five., and were soon to achieve promotion.[12] MPE Reserves (still playing on Saturdays) were also winners of Division Three.

Division Three 1985/1986 [13]

	P	W	D	L	F	A	Pts
MPE Res.	22	18	4	0	99	28	40
Sutton Valence	22	17	4	1	111	14	38
Addington	22	16	2	4	83	36	34
Marden	22	16	1	5	85	27	33
Leeds United	22	10	5	7	54	34	25
Leybourne Grange	22	11	3	8	67	51	25
Minstrels	22	8	2	12	44	57	18
Thurnham United	22	7	2	13	43	83	16
Staplehurst Res.	22	6	2	14	39	75	14
The Rose Res.	22	5	1	16	28	88	11
Detling	22	3	3	16	25	83	9
Melrose	22	0	1	21	21	126	1

The MPE First XI were to remain in the Premier Division for six years. During this time, their best results were third and seventh places. In two seasons they escaped relegation by one place. They were relegated in 1987/1988 before bouncing back to the Premier League by winning Division One in 1988/1989:

Division One 1988/1989 [14]

	P	W	D	L	F	A	Pts
MPE	20	16	2	2	72	31	34
Barming	20	14	1	5	62	36	29
Trebor	20	13	1	6	60	41	27
Oakwood Res.	20	11	3	6	44	31	25
Wheatsheaf	20	9	4	7	60	44	22
Ulcombe	20	10	2	8	57	45	22
Sutton Valence	20	7	3	10	59	69	17
Coombe Estate	20	7	3	10	37	61	17
United Banks	20	4	4	12	38	58	12
Ditton Valence	20	3	2	15	35	68	8
Alabaster Reserves	20	2	3	15	23	67	7

There were mixed results for the other teams that season. The Reserves were relegated from Division Two. The Sunday First XI continued to impress, with Richard Knight scoring five goals in a 6-3 win versus Circaprint.

In 1989/1990 the newly formed Sunday Reserves won Division Five at the first attempt.[15]

Division Five 1989/1990

	P	W	D	L	F	A	Pts
MPE	21	17	3	1	102	12	37
Hoppers	22	17	2	3	91	27	36
Marlboro	21	15	1	5	94	37	31
LEM Res.	21	15	1	5	91	40	31
Allington Res.	19	14	0	5	99	27	28
Hollingbourne Res.	21	6	6	9	23	37	18
Yeoman	21	7	2	12	46	60	16
Trosley Res.	21	7	2	12	57	80	16
United Supporters	22	5	5	12	40	57	15
Larkfield Gr	21	3	4	14	28	86	10
Ketlon	20	3	2	15	36	117	8
YMCA Res.	22	2	2	18	25	141	6

1991/1992 was a season of overall progress for the club: the rapid progress by the Sunday First XI saw them playing in the Premier Division; the Saturday Reserves were back in Division Two and the Sunday Reserves in Division Four.

MPE Football Club

It proved to be a fine season for the Saturday First XI. At the beginning of April, a 3-2 win against Snodland, with goals by Marc Shaw (2) and Andy Baker took MPE to the top of the table. They were to end as winners of the Premier League. At the end of April, MPE played Blue Eagles in the Group A final at Eccles. The game was described at the most thrilling final in the League's history. It ended 5-5 after extra time, with goals by Steve Moorekite (2), Andy Baker, Roy Smith and Marc Shaw. MPE won the replay 1-0 to complete the double.[16]

The Saturday First XI remained in the Premier Division for the next nine seasons, until 2000/2001. During this time, they were league runners-up and losing finalists to Shepway Eagles in the Group A Cup in 1994/1995, and league runners-up the following year. They were champions in 1997/1998, when the title was clinched with an emphatic away victory against Larkfield and New Hythe Reserves, as shown in the following transcript of the report which appeared in the Downs Mail.

Their final record was P18 W15 D2 L1 F60 A18 Pts47.

MPE celebrate as the Maidstone Champions

It was a great night of celebration at the Coopers Cask, Bower Street, Maidstone, after MPE first eleven heard they had won the Premier Division of Maidstone's Saturday League. The team had just completed their season with a convincing 5-0 away victory over Larkfield and New Hythe Reserves with a hat trick from 16 year old Micky Colwell and goals from Simon Stockley and Steve Moorekite.

They had to crack in the goals because the championship looked like being decided in goal difference and their rivals Cherry Tree had reduced MPE's goal advantage to only four by winning 8-0 the previous week. But as MPE were winning, Cherry Tree faced a tough match with Eccles. When the news came through that Cherry Tree had lost unexpectedly 3-0, the tension was over and MPE were champions. It was a wonderful experience for the captain for the first time, Ian Stockley, son of the wife of the club secretary, Yvonne Taylor. MPE have regularly been in the hunt in recent seasons and last won the title about four years ago.

The winning team included: Gavin Palmer, Michael Rogerson, Roy Smith, Kevin Newland, Adam Tester, Simon Stockley, Marc Shaw, Derren Colwell, Tim Casey, Micky Colwell, Russell Debnam, Paul Edwards, Paul Weston, and Ian Stockley

Reproduced courtesy of Downs Mail

The Saturday Reserves were runners-up during 1996/1997. MPE had finished their fixtures and were top of their league, but Hunton won their outstanding game, to take the title by the narrowest of margins. The top of the table is shown below:

Division Two 1996/1997 [17]

	P	W	D	L	F	A	Pts
Hunton	18	13	2	3	48	17	41
MPE Res.	18	13	2	3	53	23	41
Ditton Res.	18	13	1	4	51	24	40

They advanced to Division One where they finished runners up two seasons later, with a playing record of P20 W14 D1 L5 F52 A28 Pts43.[18]

However, their arrival in the Premier Division in 1999/2000 was a disaster! They finished bottom without a single point and an average of nearly eight goals against them per game. The record was: P16 W0 D0 L16 F20 A132 Pts0. They were disbanded.[19]

The Sunday First XI had mixed fortunes. They were relegated from the Premier Division in both 1993/1994 and 1998/1999. In 1999/2000, a third place in Division One was sufficient to see them return to the Premier Division. An added bonus was reaching the final of the President's Cup where they lost 3-2 to the Freemasons Arms team who achieved what described as a 'thrilling victory'.[20]

The Sunday Reserve XI won Division Four in 1993/1994, having scored 112 goals in twenty one games with one game remaining. The team did not operate in 1996/1997 but they returned to Division Five in 1997/1998, which they won the following year. In 1999/2000 they were runners up to Walnut Wanderers in Division Four and in 2000/2001 they achieved the same result in Division Three.[21]

The success of MPE was carried through to the junior section of the club as the Under Nines team won the Elizabeth Harvie Memorial Trophy against Roseacre Raiders in 1999. This photograph shows the winning team:

Reproduced courtesy of Downs Mail

<u>Back Row (left to right)</u>: Graham Friend, Daniel Worthy, Michael Butcher, Scott Carmichael, Luke Nutt, Craig Letham
<u>Front Row (left to right)</u>: Matthew Fellows, Alisdair Reid, Robert Coleman, Toby Smith, Thomas Smith.

The club decided that they needed to redefine their direction, and withdrew their senior teams for two seasons, before starting again with one team in each of the lowest Divisions of the Saturday and Sunday leagues in 2003/2004.

In the first season following their return, the Sunday XI won Division Four and with two games remaining, they needed one point to secure the title. The top two positions in the final table were:[22]

	P	W	D	L	F	A	Pts
MPE	22	19	1	2	96	31	58
Boxley	22	17	4	1	100	31	55

The next season, 2004/2005, was to be even better, with promotion from Division Three. The final positions were:[23]

	P	W	D	L	F	A	Pts
MPE	18	13	2	3	80	30	41
Snodland Nomads	18	12	1	5	55	42	37

In the 5-2 win against Langley and Chart, the goal scorers were A Burke (2), M Jasper (2) and D Judges. In addition, the double was achieved with a 4-1 victory against P&H Medway to win the Group B Benevolent Cup. MPE's James Collins scored after the first ten seconds of play. He added a second goal ten minutes later and then a further two in the second half. The competition sponsor and local resident, Andy Ford, presented the trophy and medals. This included a well-deserved Man of the Match award to James Collins![24]

Two seasons later, in 2006/2007, the Sunday XI finished as runners up in Division Two to Boxley, followed by third place in Division One in 2007/2008. In this latter season, Paul Nicholls and Ali Simpson were among the leading League goal scorers.

This action photograph was taken during a game of MPE versus Icom was taken during 2006/2007 at a match played at Cobdown:

Reproduced courtesy of John Wardley and Kent Messenger newspaper group

The progress of the Saturday XI was not so dramatic. They began in Division Three and won this league in 2005/2006 as the top of the table shows: [25]

	P	W	D	L	F	A	Pts
MPE	16	13	0	3	58	23	39
Saxon Chief	16	11	1	4	56	37	34

After a season in Division Two, they were allocated a place in Division One for 2007/2008.

For many years, exchange visits have taken place between MPE and Arlington FC from Vermont, USA. In April 2008 the two teams met again at Cobdown and this pennant (left) was given to the team members as a small souvenir:

Reproduced courtesy of MPE

MPE Football Club

Teams from MPE continue to be a substantial presence within local football. This photograph shows the squad for MPE Sunday in the season 2007/2008, followed by two action shots during that season.

Reproduced courtesy of MPE

<u>Back Row (left to right)</u>: David Judges (Player/Manager), Dan Woods, Dan McCann, Sam Hampton (Captain), James Judges, Luke Watkins, Mark Judges, Ali Simpson (Vice Captain), Adam Demery, Ryan Vince
<u>Front Row (left to right)</u>: David Cox, Gary Bibey, Kevin Bibey, Matt Judges, Paul Nichols, Jack Higgins, Alex Burke.

Both reproduced courtesy of John Wardley and Kent Messenger newspaper group

Ian Lambert

Bearsted Golf Club: People and Personalities

Reproduced courtesy of Malcolm Kersey

A Golf Course has existed on the site currently occupied by Bearsted Golf Club since 1895, albeit smaller in area at the start. There are two interesting facts which emerge from this opening statement. First, it was the Maidstone Golf Club who were the initial occupants, and that the course is within the parish of Thurnham.

Towards the end of 1913, a majority of members opted to relocate Maidstone Golf Club to Oakwood Park. Their new course was officially opened 2 July 1914. The remaining members resolved to create Bearsted Golf Club which has gone from strength to strength to the present day.

These pages attempt to bring to life some of the personalities who have contributed to the club. Clive Horton's book, One Hundred Years of Golf at Bearsted 1895-1995, is recommended reading for those who would like a more detailed account of the club and its activities.[1] Clive was captain of the club in 1974 and President, 1995-1998. His wife was Ladies Captain in 1987. This photograph of Clive appeared in his book:

Reproduced courtesy of Bearsted Golf Club

Bearsted Golf Club: People and Personalities

It was Sir George Hampson, of Thurnham Court, who initially made fifty two acres of grass and woodland, part of which faced Ware Street and Thurnham Lane, available for the first course in 1895. It had been owned by the Hampson family since 1858.[2] Sir George was a keen golfer and was a most generous benefactor to the club. He was the first president, and club captain on six occasions. Hubert Bensted, an architect, who lived in Thurnham Lane, offered to design and layout a nine hole course. Hubert also undertook the duties of Honorary Secretary; a post which he retained for several years. The first Professional at the club was George Walls.[3]

Following the lease of further land, a new eighteen hole course was constructed. It was formally opened by the President, Sir George Hampson on 23 June 1923. This photograph was taken at the opening and includes:

Standing: P A Smith, R Toy, S Lee, J H Loyd, J Watcham, H Martin, Mrs Foord, Sir George Hampson, Ted Foord, J Gibbons, W G Sharp, Ted Coltman, R C Lloyd, Fred Post
Seated: J W Bridge, Miss Hampson, Harry Vardon, Miss J N Hampson, Mark Seymour, W Stirling.

To mark the occasion, an exhibition match was played between Harry Vardon (winner of six Open Championships) and Mark Seymour, the Professional at Cobham. 215 people paid for admission and the whole day was regarded as a great success. A notebook of events compiled by the then Honorary Secretary, Mr J W Bridge, reveals that he and the Captain, W Stirling, had met Harry Vardon from the 12.05 train at Maidstone East. They adjourned to the Secretary's house in nearby Brewer Street for lunch, where a half-bottle of whisky was consumed. They then drove to the club where Vardon drank three more doubles before he was ready to play. On every tee, Harry asked two questions: the yardage and the wind direction. He won the match![4]

This photograph of Harry Vardon and Mark Seymour was taken by the thirteenth tee, now known as the eleventh tee:

Both reproduced courtesy of Bearsted Golf Club

Sir George Hampson died in October 1936. The Kent Messenger newspaper report about the funeral said that he was buried in the family vault at St Mary's and the approach to the church was lined with beautiful floral tributes. A number of villagers and estate workers were among a large congregation that paid their respects to his memory. George's son, Sir Dennys Hampson, was elected President of the club the following year, but sadly died in March 1939, at the age of forty one.

The first Ladies Committee meeting was held 5 April 1898. Mrs Boyce, Mrs Hill, Mrs Prosser and Mrs Tasker were present. Among other matters, they decided to write to the Honorary Secretary to request a reduction in fees for lady visitors from five shillings to 2s 6d. [5]

In 1914, Mr and Mrs Watcham became Greenkeeper and Stewardess respectively. Alfred Watcham had originally been rejected for armed service as he was found to be medically unfit, but either a miracle cure or lack of manpower determined that he was deemed due to depart for military service in October 1916. He also took some of the duties of a Professional and Caddie Master. Following his departure to the army, the staff comprised Mrs Watcham and a lad. She was paid 7s 6d a week and allowed to live at the clubhouse. Mr White assisted and as a consequence was allowed to play at any time without fees. He also repaired clubs on the premises. Mr and Mrs Watcham both retired in 1931. [6]

Below are shown Mr and Mrs A Foord who were joint club captains in 1926. Over the years, there have been instances of husbands and wives being captains of the respective sections, but relatively few in the same year.

Both reproduced courtesy of Kent Messenger newspaper group

Mr and Mrs R Batchellor were the next joint club captains in 1933. They were followed by Mr and Mrs H Kettle during the Second World War, Mr and Mrs S Webb in 1980, Mr and Mrs P Hood in 2001 and Mr and Mrs Greagsby in 2006. This recent photograph shows Mr and Mrs Hood:

Reproduced courtesy of Mr and Mrs P Hood

Mr and Mrs Corbin were also club captains. William Corbin, usually known after his middle name of James, or Jim, held the post in 1980 and his wife was Captain of the Ladies section in 1992. Jim had a distinguished wartime career in the Royal Air Force. As a Flying Officer, he was awarded the DFC in 1943; whilst in North Africa he completed 500 operational flying hours. Jim was a teacher and completed his career at the Maidstone Technical School where he had once been a pupil. This photograph of Jim was taken whilst serving in the Royal Air Force: [7]

Reproduced courtesy of Bearsted Golf Club

This cartoon appeared in the Kent Messenger in September 1931, and shows some of the contemporary stalwarts of Bearsted Golf Club:

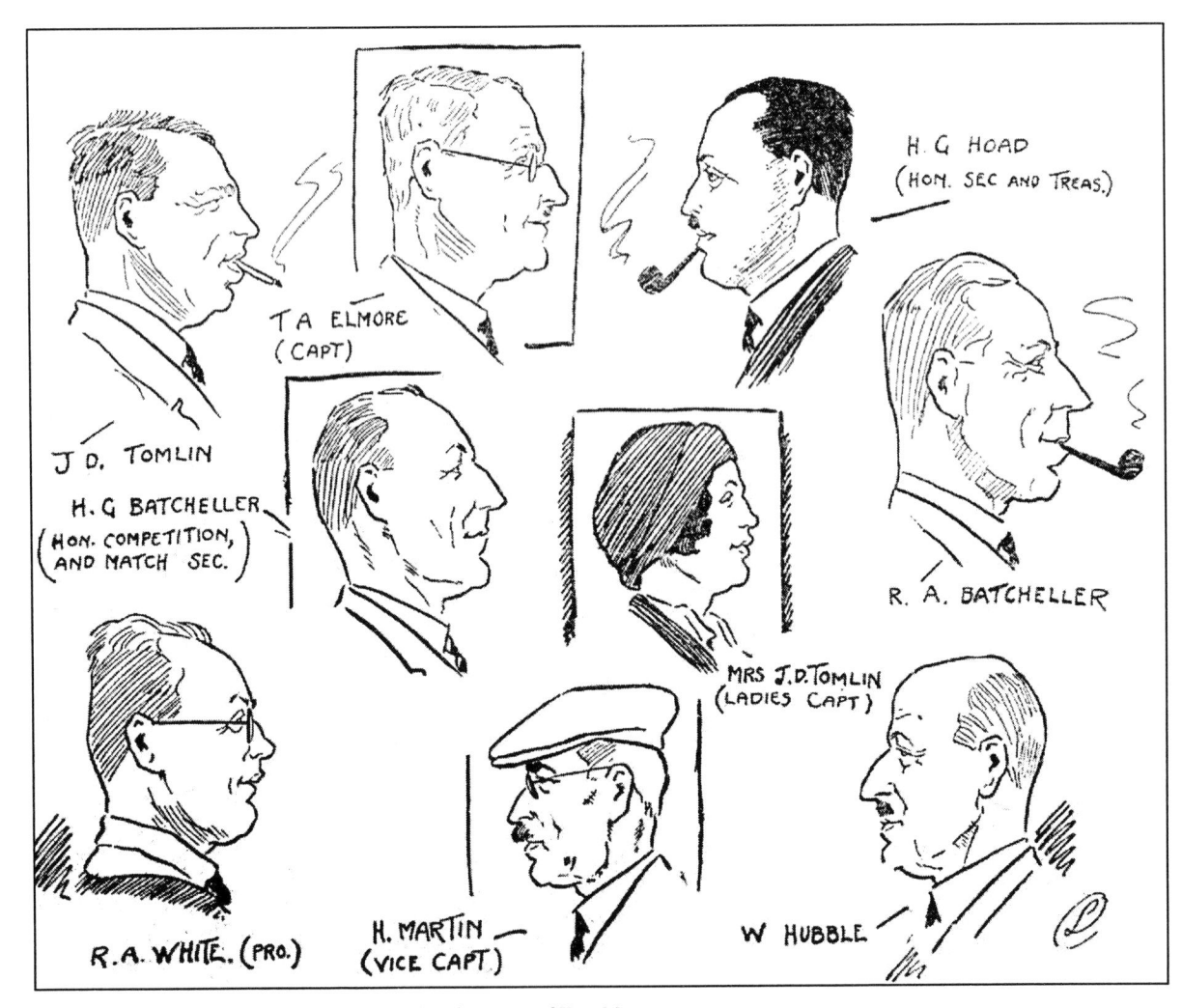

Reproduced courtesy of Kent Messenger newspaper group

Bearsted Golf Club: People and Personalities

The 1950s saw two cricketing legends who had represented Kent and England, and were resident in Bearsted, showing their prowess at golf. Godfrey Evans won the Courage Salver in 1950 and 1951 in partnership with Andrew Day. Leslie Ames was runner-up in the Kent Messenger Cup in 1954, which was an open competition. This photograph, taken in the late 1940s, shows Godfrey and Leslie amongst a group of fellow Kent cricketers who played golf: [8]

Reproduced courtesy of the Kent Messenger newspaper group

Back row (left to right): Eddie Crush, John Pocock, Arthur Phebey, Godfrey Evans
Front Row (left to right): Peter Hearn, Fred Ridgway, Leslie Ames.

1957 also saw the first appearance of another celebrity, although this was not on the golf course. Victor Silvester and his Ballroom Orchestra provided the music at the club annual dinner dance which was held at the Tudor House in April. The famous band leader and his strict tempo music ensured the occasion was enormously successful. The event marked the first of fifteen consecutive appearances at the annual dinner by Victor and his Orchestra.

Members and former members of the club continued to enjoy some spectacular successes too. In September 1962, a former member, Trevor Osborn won the Western Australian Open Golf Championship. Trevor had played at Bearsted from the age of 7 and in 1951 won the Junior Cup aged 14, the same year as his father H C (Bert) Osborn won the Senior Cup. Bert was made an honorary member of the club in 1993. Trevor turned professional after leaving the Maidstone Technical School.[9] This photograph below shows Trevor with the trophy of the Western Australia Championship in 1962. Sadly, after returning to this country, he died in 1974 at the age of 37:

Reproduced courtesy of Bearsted Golf Club

Bearsted Golf Club: People and Personalities

There have been many examples of fathers and their children being members of the club. Before the war, George Hughes and his son, Jack, were very successful in competitions. The photograph below shows Mandy Langford, the daughter of Lewis Langford. In 1974, Mandy won the English Girls Championship, represented Kent and won a place in the England Under-19 Team. Her career progressed and she turned professional winning Womens Professional Golf Association events and holding key appointments in women's golf.

Reproduced courtesy of Bearsted Golf Club

The following pictures show fathers who are playing today, together with their sons. The first photograph shows John and Simon France. In 2007, John was elected an honorary member for his services to the club, having joined in 1964. In a period spanning forty four years, he has been on the club committee for well over twenty years. He is also an active member of the veterans section, having been secretary for over ten years and veterans captain in 2002. He has won the Courage Salver foursome competition on three occasions, two of which were with Simon.

Simon joined the club in 1977. He has enjoyed considerable success representing the club as a member of winning teams for over twenty years and his individual achievements include the Scratch Cup, the Fremlin Cup, the Sir Dennys Hampton and the Sharp Cup and the Bearsted Open. He continues to represent the club 'A team' in the Kent League.

Reproduced courtesy of John and Simon France

Bearsted Golf Club: People and Personalities

Don Bramall and his son, Philip, joined Bearsted Golf Club in the early 1970s. Philip won his first tournament - the Captain's Day Trophy when he was fourteen. He went on to win many more tournaments including the 'Scratch Cup' (Club Champion) on seven occasions. These pictures below show Don (right) and Philip, and Philip with his son, Ben, sitting in the Scratch Cup.

Both reproduced courtesy of Don Bramall

Don is an active member of the Veterans section and in the past has won, amongst other competitions, the 'Packer Spoon' with Vic Harnford.

There have been other family relationships involved in Bearsted Golf Club over the years, including the four Milstead brothers who were popular and very committed members for around twenty years after the Second World War.

The Ladies section has always been a thriving and active part of the club, at both competitive and social levels. The picture below shows the Ladies Spring Meeting held in 1963:

Reproduced courtesy of Bearsted Golf Club

<u>Back row (left to right)</u>: Winnie Sharp, Peggy Parker, Nancy Holdstock, Maureen Edwards, Lorna Nickles, Vera Hollis
<u>Middle row (left to right)</u>: Dorothy Cramp, Nora Taylor, Mollie Sharp, Terry Cairns, Gwen Appel, Ruth MacDonald, Winnie Richardson
<u>Front row (left to right)</u>: Eileen Wells, Ina McLaren, Joan Benson, Jean Cox, Gladys Clifford (Captain), Dorothy Buckley, Doris Allen, Kit Hay.

Bearsted Golf Club: People and Personalities

In 1964, the club won the Medway Trophy which was played at Bearsted. The picture below shows the winning team with the President, W H Gatward, holding the trophy. Also shown are Ray Sharp who was the club captain in 1964, (his wife Mollie was Ladies Captain in 1971), Frank Duhig who won the club Scratch Cup in eleven consecutive seasons and Brian Beavis, who is currently the longest serving member, having joined in 1956:

Reproduced courtesy of Bearsted Golf Club

<u>Left to right</u>: J R Butterworth, D Hammond, W R Sharp, F Duhig, E F Harvey and B L Beavis

In September 1965, a family tradition ended at the club when the professional, Peter White, retired. His father, Reginald, had been the professional at Bearsted for twenty three years before him. Peter was the last of the 'old style' professionals, with wide-ranging responsibilities, including that of barman! In this photograph, Peter is shown with his wife, Florence which appeared in the Kent Messenger, 28 May 1965:

Reproduced courtesy of Kent Messenger newspaper group

Peter was succeeded in the post of the club professional by Don Masey. This photograph shows Don in conference about the course during Captain's Day, 1970:

Left to right: W F Pentecost (Captain), R F Cummins, Don Masey (Professional).

Over the years there have been many matches and exhibition games organised for charity. In May 1965 an exhibition match was held to benefit the Forces Aid Society. It raised £560. Tom Page and club professional Ken Bousfield took part. This photograph was taken during the event:

Both reproduced courtesy of Bearsted Golf Club

Left to right: Tom Page, Dai Rees and Peter Alliss.

In June 1969, an exhibition match was held in aid of the National Society for Cancer Relief. Max Faulkner, Bernard Gallagher, Brian Barnes and Nicky Job all participated.

In 1972, John Ryan became Kent Amateur Champion. John was a member of the golf club but was also a professional footballer; his clubs included Fulham, Luton Town and Manchester City. This undated photograph shows John in action on the golf course:

Reproduced courtesy of Bearsted Golf Club

This transcript of an interview with John appeared in a programme for a football match during 1974: [10]

How is your golf these days?
Well, it's not as good as it could be. I don't get a lot of time to play during the season. My handicap now is four, although I have not been playing in any Competitions lately. I have had it down to three, but it is something you have got to work on consistently if you are going to keep the figures low. I have just joined the Northamptonshire County Golf Club and incidentally, linked up again with Bill Dodgin who, as you know, is the Northampton Town manager.

What has been your biggest prizes as a golfer?
Quite definitely the Kent Championship. This is for all Amateurs who are members of Kentish clubs and played over three days. I won that one in July 1972. Within the space of two or three weeks I also won the Club Championship - that is the Maidstone Club - and the Canterbury Open, and a few quid in prize money as well which can't be bad. I have been playing golf for seven years now.

What other sports do you play?
I used to play cricket. I had trials for Kent Schools and when I lived in Kent before I moved to Luton and got married I played for the local village side. That was before the golf bug took over and that seems to be all-consuming these days. I also like water-skiing. We used to go most weekends at one stage. It wasn't exactly Mediterranean conditions. It was off the coast by Gillingham. In fact you could see the Gillingham ground from there.

Reproduced courtesy of Luton Town Football Club

There have been other professional footballers associated with the club, notably John Ballagher, a current member who played for Gillingham in the 1963-1964 season when they were promoted as Division Four Champions. Former member Andy Ford also played for Gillingham costing them £30,000. In his career, he made sixty two senior appearances and scored three goals. His previous clubs were Bournemouth, Southend and Swindon. His sons Matt and Jon were also members, winning many trophies and both represented the County. Matt is currently a professional golfer.

Bearsted Golf Club: People and Personalities

Another former professional footballer, Sir Trevor Brooking, was the special guest at the official opening of the newly extended golf course in 1980. Thirty professionals including Max Faulkner and former junior member, Paul Hoad, and ninety amateurs, took part in a Professional/Amateur match. This photograph shows part of the action during the match:

Reproduced courtesy of Bearsted Golf Club

<u>Left to right</u>: a caddie, Trevor Brooking, Ray Sharp and Max Faulkner.

The new course was designed by Club Professional Bob Henderson. He joined the club in 1971 from Knole Park Golf Club, Sevenoaks, where he assisted the legendary Sam King. He eventually left in 1984 to return to his native Scotland and ran a small hotel. This photograph of Bob appeared in the Kent Messenger newspaper, 30 March 1979:

Reproduced courtesy of Kent Messenger newspaper group

Ken Lambeth was another former footballer who was employed by the club as Head Greenkeeper. This photograph, showing him hard at work during his greenkeeping duties, appeared in the Gazette, 1 September 1970. He had been a centre forward with Maidstone United Football Club in their amateur days and enjoyed both golf and cricket. He later emigrated to Australia.

Greenkeeping at Bearsted seems to have attracted some special people with excellent golfing skills overall: Graham Godmon used these to great effect at both junior and senior level. In 1985, he reached the semi-finals of the English Amateur Championship at Woodhall Spa, in Lincolnshire. The eventual winner from the other semi-final was the former Ryder Cup player, David Gilford. This photograph shows Graham receiving the Kent Messenger Open Challenge Trophy in 1977, at the age of eighteen, with a single figure handicap:

Both reproduced courtesy of Kent Messenger newspaper group

Left to right: Michael Finley; Jeremy Baldwin; Graham Godmon; Fred Nock (Club Captain), Mr A S Hewling-Luson (Secretary); and Geoff Wood (Vice Captain).

It is important to have stability behind the scenes and in 1979, Linda Siems was appointed as Administrative Secretary. It was twenty eight years later that she retired from the post! Her award of Life Membership was a just reward for the high esteem in which she was held. In this photograph, Linda is standing in front of one of the golf club honours boards:

Reproduced courtesy of John France

In 1993, the club enjoyed great success as the B team created two records when they won their division of the Kent League for the fourth year in succession and for a record number of times.

Reproduced courtesy of Bearsted Golf Club

Back Row (left to right): Gordon Milne, Eddie Calvert, Alan Buxton, Paul Speed, David Bignell, David Bowman, Roy Milne, Peter Samways
Front Row (left to right): Adrian Foster, David French (Past Captain), Ken Rosier (Team Captain), Tony O'Caroll (Club Captain), Doug Slaughter.

Bearsted Golf Club: People and Personalities

Kath Seager (1910-1991), was a good neighbour, and supporter of the club. In 1990, the club purchased thirty three acres (previously leased) of her landholdings in Chapel Lane. Miss Seager pledged that the money would be donated to the club upon her death. This most generous bequest was used for the construction of the new clubhouse. This photograph of Kath, is not dated but it is believed to have been taken around 1960.

Reproduced courtesy of Bearsted Golf Club

Danielle Masters has associations with a few local clubs, including Bearsted. The Curtis Cup team sweater that she wore when representing her country as an amateur in 2004, is on display in the clubhouse.

These photographs of Danielle were taken during the Curtis Cup:

Both reproduced courtesy of Danielle Masters

Danielle started playing golf as a youngster with her family, enjoyed success as an amateur and qualified for the Ladies European Tour in 2006, finishing third in that year in the Ladies English Open at Chart Hills. She could not repeat that success in 2007, finishing just sixteenth, although she was second in the Ladies Scottish Open. She continues to enjoy the mixed fortunes of golf, but few would argue with her status amongst the top lady professionals.

Over many years, Bearsted Golf Club has been particularly fortunate, surviving uncertain times when many members relocated to Oakwood Park in 1913, the storms of two World Wars and being able to purchase their premises when the opportunity arose. That the club continues to flourish into this current century, is in no small part due to the enthusiastic members and players of a sport that is now world wide.

Ian Lambert

Bearsted Golf Club: Around and About the Course

Although many people will be aware of Bearsted Golf Club, there are many aspects of the course which, by and large, remain invisible to the general public. Through these pages can be found an impression of these treasures, and a glimpse gained into some of the best-kept local landscape secrets which may still lie hidden from view!

The current clubhouse, the third building erected by the club was opened in 2000:

This replaced the clubhouse that was finished in 1972. A single storey building, it was opened by the club captain John Semmons, assisted by the President, Eric Sibley. This photograph shows the Secretary, Jack Matthews, standing to one side of the new building:

Both reproduced courtesy of Bearsted Golf Club

Bearsted Golf Club: Around and About the Course

The first clubhouse was opened in 1899. No contemporary photograph of the building has survived, but this photograph of play in progress in front of the clubhouse was taken around 1930:

Reproduced courtesy of Bearsted Golf Club

This summary shows the development of the clubhouse and other buildings:

1899	Clubhouse costing £500 was completed and officially opened in March
1921	Flush toilet installed in clubhouse
1922	Gas supply laid on to clubhouse
1927	Telephone installed
1954	Electricity supply laid on to clubhouse
1964	Major extension to clubhouse which included locker rooms and bar at cost of £7,010
1972	New clubhouse built on new site within grounds
1982	Fire destroys professional shop
1984	New professional shop built
1989	Major development of clubhouse lounge, dining room and kitchen
2000	New clubhouse opened
2008	Existing Groundsman accommodation demolished New enlarged building erected at same location

This photograph of Bearsted railway station, which is undated, clearly shows the location of the first clubhouse on the highest point of the landscape, left hand side:

Reproduced courtesy of Jean Jones

The proximity of the railway station was found to be a convenient means of transport to the club for many members. A pedestrian link still exists between the platform and the golf course.

In 1903, some cottages named 'Golf View' were built between the railway station and the Methodist church in Ware Street. The photograph below shows part of these properties. How many people have passed by these cottages without realising the significance of the name?

Reproduced courtesy of Ian Lambert

Bearsted Golf Club: Around and About the Course

This is a summary of the development of the course:

1895	First nine hole course laid out
1923	Official opening of extended eighteen hole course
1924-1962	Various parcels of land purchased with some changes to course
1974	Reservoir and pump house built
1976	Land from Chapel Farm, Ware Street, purchased, total area of club and course now 124 acres
1977	Course re-designed by Bob Henderson and developed by Golf Landscapes Ltd
1985	Land purchased up to Hockers Lane to allow the Twelfth Hole to be extended
1990	Further land at Chapel Farm purchased which had been previously leased. Small area compulsorily acquired for M20 widening
1993	Purchase of land to increase water storage capacity
1990s	Greens reconstructed to improve drainage

This photograph shows the most recent work at the club; the Greenkeeper's accommodation in the process of demolition, during 2008:

Reproduced courtesy of Ian Lambert

In December 1932, a series of articles on golf courses in Kent appeared in the Kent Messenger. The article about Bearsted included the following comments: [1]

> ...It is a bijou course, set in pastoral charm....a golf club where the nature of the locality is in harmony with Kent's reputation as the Garden of England....it is all so truly rural; even romantic. Alighting from a train onto the Bearsted platform after a few minutes journey from Maidstone East station, one passes through a wicket gate and 'Open Sesame'; one is on the golf links. Its allurement has already been discovered, for each year, nearly two thousand players sign the Visitor's Book...

Reproduced courtesy of Kent Messenger newspaper group

Bearsted Golf Club: Around and About the Course

The Second World War comprehensively affected normal life, and the club was no exception. During play, on 8 September 1940, members saw some of the horrors of war as an RAF pilot unsuccessfully baled out of a Hurricane aircraft, P3201. Sub Lieutenant J C Carpenter, of 46 Squadron, had been attacking a Luftwaffe formation when he was shot down. His body was found by wardens in Thurnham Lane, in the area between the railway and the current motorway bridge. He was twenty one years old and based at Stapleford Tawney, Essex.[2]

Ironically, a week later, on 15 September, a Messerschmitt aircraft crashed and burned at 12.45pm at Aldington Court Farm, Thurnham after combat with fighters. Oberleutnant Rudolf Schmidt baled out but he was either too low for the parachute to deploy or the parachute failed. He was found on the fairway of the Thirteenth Hole on Bearsted golf course and subsequently buried in St Mary's churchyard.[3]

During the war, sections of the course were requisitioned by the armed forces and used as a camp. To assist with local defences, two concrete emplacements of anti-aircraft guns and thirty railway sleepers were placed in an upright position on the course to prevent enemy aircraft landing.

Some local men that were not able to serve in the armed forces volunteered to join the Bearsted branch of the Observer Corps, later called the Royal Observer Corps. Their first lookout post was sited on the golf course before being relocated to land in the vicinity of Roseacre Farm which was owned by Mr Bradley.

This undated photograph shows the members by the first lookout post: [4]

Reproduced courtesy of Bryan McCarthy

After the war with the resumption of normal life, the golf club became a popular venue as the sport gained a wider following. In 1953, a publication, Golf in Kent, by Robert H Browning, briefly described the course as an outstanding example "designed for the pleasure of the handicap golfer".

Ken Trafford produced the course layout diagram for the club which appears on the next page, and several of his paintings are hanging in the clubhouse. Ken has been a member of the golf club for over forty years and as well as being a talented artist, has appeared in many musical productions; the most recent with the Maidstone Operatic Society.

Bearsted Golf Club: Around and About the Course

This is Ken Trafford's diagram of the current layout of the course:

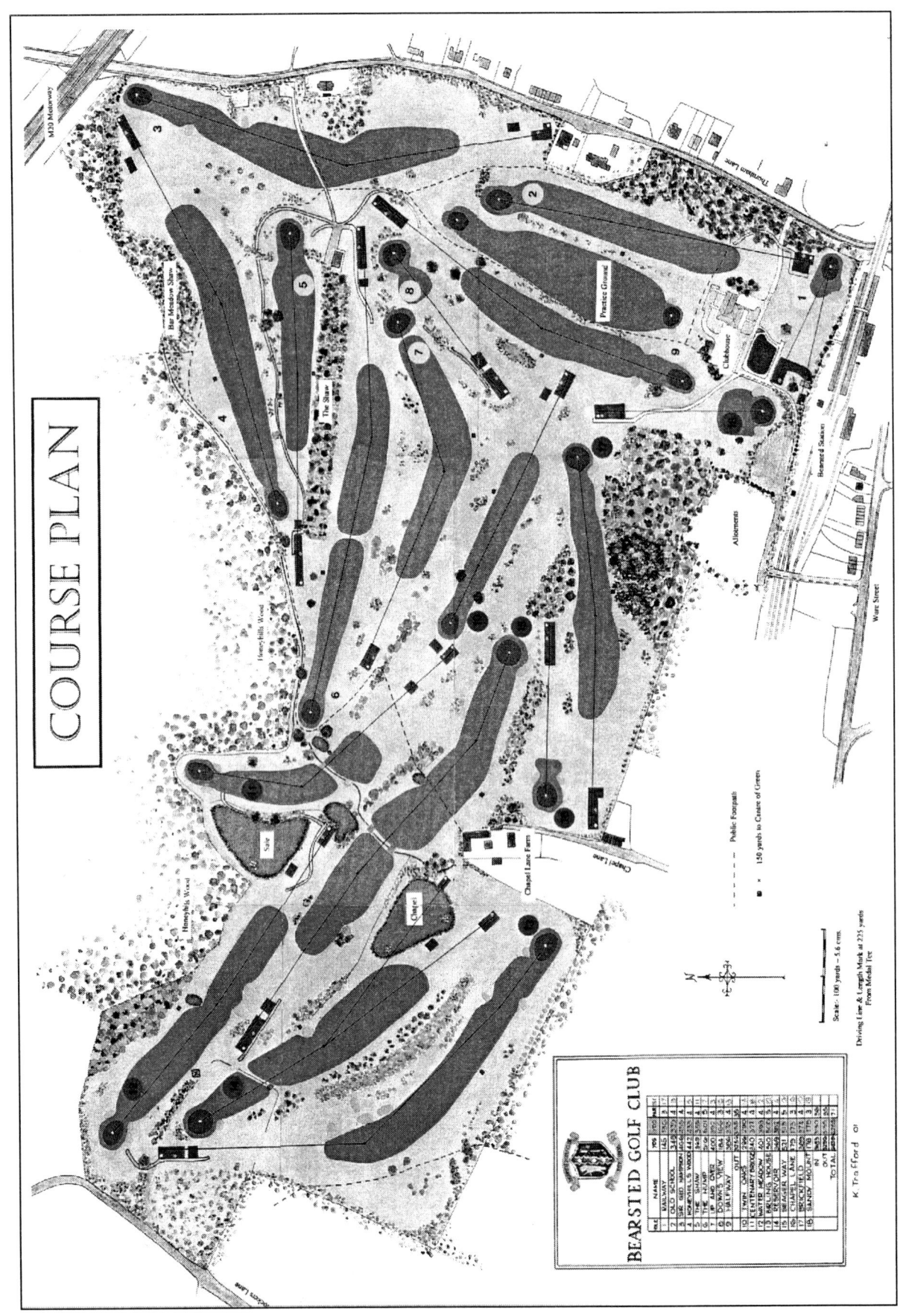

Reproduced courtesy of Ken Trafford

Bearsted Golf Club: Around and About the Course

This set of photographs comprises a short visual tour with some unusual views of the area to be seen during a round at the golf course. The first shows members putting on the First Green which is clearly visible when crossing the footbridge at Bearsted railway station. The platform and station sign can be seen in the background.

Reproduced courtesy of Ian Lambert

This view of the rear of the former Thurnham School building in Thurnham Lane was taken from behind the Second Green:

Reproduced courtesy of Malcolm Kersey

Behind the Third Green, a Eurostar train is shown passing at high speed; the track runs parallel with the M20 motorway. Note that part of the landscape around Thurnham castle is in the background.

Reproduced courtesy of Malcolm Kersey

This view of the Eleventh Green from the Twelfth Tee is very attractive. The lake is a haven for wildlife.

Reproduced courtesy of Ian Lambert

This photograph shows part of the North Downs and landscape which can be seen by looking back at the Thirteenth Tee. Note that Jade's Crossing at the bottom of Detling Hill is also visible in the background:

This unusual view of some of the houses in Chapel Lane, off Ware Street, is taken with the Thirteenth Green in the foreground and note that Sandy Mount is also in the distance:

Both reproduced courtesy of Malcolm Kersey

Bearsted Golf Club: Around and About the Course

It is generally acknowledged that the club has come a long way since it first opened in 1896. The name has changed and the membership has seen great fluctuations, the club now owns the course instead of leasing the land. Recent developments such as the new clubhouse and improved course facilities show that the club is well equipped to continue through the twenty first century. What a difference from these two ladies, shown during play at the original Sixth Green – an undated photograph, but a perfect example of all our yesterdays!

Reproduced courtesy of Bearsted Golf Club

Ian Lambert

The Tudor Park Hotel and Country Club

The Tudor Park hotel has 120 bedrooms and includes restaurants, bars and conference/meeting rooms with parking for 250 cars. However, it is probably better known locally for the popular leisure facilities it offers. These include a championship 18 hole golf course, an indoor heating swimming pool, sauna, steam room, spa bath, cardiovascular theatre, tennis course, a resistance gym and aerobics studio in addition to a health and beauty spa and solarium. It is an impressive list!

A view of the exterior (top) and the swimming pool (bottom):

Both reproduced courtesy of Marriott International

The Tudor Park Hotel and Country Club

The Tudor Park literally arose from the ashes of the former Tudor House, which had comprised a restaurant, ballroom and banqueting hall. It had initially opened for business in 1927 as a roadhouse which provided meals. A fire in July 1983 destroyed the premises with the exception of the mock Tudor façade.[1] This is a photograph of the original building:

Reproduced courtesy of Chris and Sue Hunt

Following negotiations during 1983 and 1984, the site of the Tudor House was purchased by a Bristol based company, Country Club Hotels, jointly owned by Whitbread and the J T Group, a building firm. Included in the purchase was a further 120 acres of Milgate Park.

In July 1985, a planning application was made to build a new hotel, golf course and other leisure facilities. Work began in July 1986 with a traditional sod-cutting ceremony and the new complex was topped out on 30 September 1986 by Norman McIndoe, the managing director of County Club Hotels. By 1988, the new hotel and its associated development was finished. It had taken nearly five years work to bring the scheme to fruition at a cost of £8.5 million.

Prior to the official opening, the Leisure Club already had 1300 of its intended 1500 members signed up. This is one of the early receipts issued for membership:

Reproduced courtesy of Marriott International

The Tudor Park Hotel and Country Club

The official opening took place on 29 April 1988, when the Whitbread Chairman, Sam Whitbread, launched the new complex by firing a cannon from the patio and unveiling a plaque. Sports Minister, Colin Moynihan was a special guest. Amongst the guests were representatives from the Borough of Maidstone and the parish councils of Bearsted and Thurnham. The first general manager was Tony Snowden.

This photograph accompanied the report of the opening from the Kent Messenger, 6 May 1988:

Reproduced courtesy of Kent Messenger newspaper group

In 1995, Whitbread acquired franchise rights for the Marriott name in Great Britain. On 26 April 1996 the hotel was renamed to become the Marriott Tudor Park and Country Club.

Today, the leisure facilities are available to hotel guests and a variety of options and tariffs enable the general public, of all ages, to become members. Many friendship groups have been formed between participants and there is no better example than the Nifty Fifties, who have enjoyed such classes as aerobics and chi-ball since the early 1990s. This photograph shows them gathered on the patio:

Reproduced courtesy of Mary Lambert

The hotel frequently accommodates guests with sporting connections. For example, there are overnight stays for teams playing against Gillingham Football Club.

The golf course was launched on 8 April 1988. It was designed by Donald Steel, one of the country's leading golf architects. Almost immediately, it was over-subscribed with 550 members and a further 30 waiting to join. The course was built on what is believed to be the former Milgate deer park, and recently hosted the Professional Golf Association Euro Pro Tour.

The Tudor Park Hotel and Country Club

Below are further details of the course from the score card:

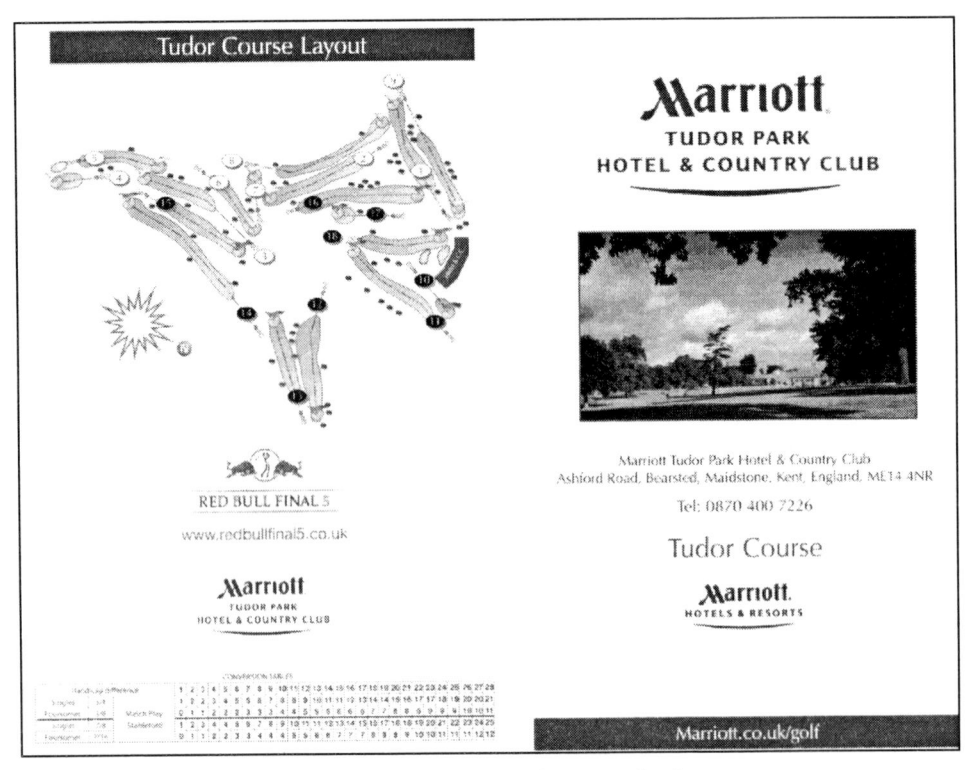

Reproduced courtesy of Marriott International

This photograph shows the course looking up to the Ashford Road. Note the car travelling along the road in the background:

Reproduced courtesy of Malcolm Kersey

The majority of leisure activities available to local residents are provided by clubs run on a voluntary basis. The Marriott Tudor Park is an exception, but nevertheless, it makes a valuable contribution to the welfare of its members and visitors with a range of activities which can be enjoyed by all age groups. The original hotel holds a special place in the memories of older inhabitants but there is no doubt that the same will be true to more recent residents who have attended social and leisure events at the modern replacement.

Ian Lambert

Bearsted and Thurnham Bowling Club

Anyone who ventures up Church Landway on a warm evening in the summer is met with a sight that seems essentially, and eternally, English: the members of the Bowling Club and their immaculate green and clubhouse. This photograph was taken during their twenty-fifth anniversary year in 2008:

Reproduced courtesy of Bearsted and Thurnham Bowling Club

It was not until 1983, five years after Bearsted parish council had purchased a private road leading to Mote Hall and farm, that the bowls club was formed. It was the dream of Margaret Tate and James Ravenscroft.[1]

Two years prior to this, Bearsted and Thurnham Residents Association had called a public meeting to discuss the possible use of the land. Bearsted and Thurnham Lawn Tennis Club was already occupying part of it and the Scout Association was also interested in securing a plot for a headquarters. Dr Frank Alston, Chairman of the parish council, confirmed that the council would be willing to support the formation of bowls club, renting the land at a nominal sum of £1 per annum. From the outset, the Tennis Club was most supportive of the new club, lending the use of their pavilion and other facilities over many years.[2]

A Steering Committee was formed with James Ravenscroft as Chairman, Mrs Braga as Secretary and Mrs Bowman as Treasurer. The priority for membership would be those living within the parish and would be open to both men and women, which at the time was unusual for a bowls club. The founder members were to pay £50 for two years in advance. Ordinary life members were charged £20 entrance fee plus a £20 subscription. Life membership was available for men aged over 65 and women over 60 for £100. Associate members would be charged £5. [3]

On 5 February 1982, the lease for land was granted. The site was cleared and levelled and a water supply was laid on from the tennis club. Construction of the bowling greens was undertaken by Crossway Construction Limited. The final surface of Cumberland turf was laid over a thick layer of sand. The costs for the green and the setting up of the club came to around £25,000. The club's fledgling existence was highlighted to the rest of the community by the running of a side show at Bearsted Fayre. A fund-raising committee was formed with Margaret Lyne as Chairman.[4]

The first Annual General Meeting was held at the tennis club pavilion in November 1982. A new management committee was formed: [5]

President	Mr J Ravenscroft
Vice Presidents	Dr Alston (Chairman of Bearsted Parish Council) Mrs V Braga, Mr G Bassett, Mr E Swift
Chairman	Mr E T Rayner
Secretary	Mrs V Braga
Treasurer	Mr D Hider
Mens Captain	Mr S Braga
Mens Vice Captain	Mr E Swift
Ladies Captain	Mrs V Braga
Ladies Vice-Captain	Mrs V Banner
Trustees	Mr J Ravenscroft, Mrs V Braga, Mrs Bowman
Committee	Mr G Bassett, Mr J E Fermor, Mr B Head, Mrs K Radford, Mrs P Stevens, Mr Lyne
Auditor	Mr Truscott

It was agreed that the club colours would be green, black and white. A design for a tie was approved using an idea by Jack Potter but slightly modified to reflect a proposal by Eddie Fermor that the foundation date of 1983 should also be included. The design was subsequently used on a club flag and badge. For matches the following uniform would be worn: [6]

> White tops with grey trousers or skirts for weekday matches, but bowling whites at weekends...Blazers could be blue or black but no uniform was required for 'roll ups'. Bowling shoes to be worn at all times...

Both reproduced courtesy of Bearsted and Thurnham Bowling Club

During the early winter, heavy rain flooded the green and showed that there was need for additional drainage. Whilst this problem was addressed, footings were also sunk for a retaining wall, steps were inserted and some alcoves were built to accommodate seats. Grass seeding of the banks was abandoned due to the weather. To ensure that the green was not overplayed, there was a restricted fixture list.[7]

In the opening ceremony, held on 11 June 1983, the President, James Ravenscroft, mentioned that it was the first bowling green in Bearsted. However, he believed that games of bowls had once been played some considerable time ago at Thornham Friars. Dr Alston then unfurled the club flag and bowled the first woods of the afternoon.[8] The photographs on the next page were taken during the official opening. Note the tent in use as a temporary pavilion!

At the opening, the following trophies were donated: [9]

Trophy	Donor
Presidents Cup for the Mens Championship	President James Ravenscroft
Mixed Pairs Trophy	Mr & Mrs Braga
Mens Handicap Trophy	Mr & Mrs P Laws
Ladies Handicap Salver	Mr & Mrs E T Rayner
Ladies Pairs Cup	National Westminster Bank
Mens Pairs	Mr Bishop of Page & Wells
Ladies Single Rose Bowl	Mr King from Whitbread Fremlin Ltd

All reproduced courtesy of Bearsted and Thurnham Bowling Club

The season comprised twenty seven fixtures: twelve home and fifteen away matches, all arranged by Alf Cork. Included in these matches were several against Milton Regis, which is one of the oldest clubs in the country, and two ladies games, at Westborough and Loose. The trophies were presented the following year after a Fun Day with the Tennis Club on 10 June. The winners were: [10]

Presidents Cup, Mens Champion	E Swift
Mens Singles Handicap	S Braga
Mens Pairs	G Bassett and B Head
Mixed Pairs	Mrs C Hart and A Cork
Mixed Triples	Mrs V Craven, Ms S Murphy and W Brown
Ladies Pairs	V Braga and P Stevens

1984 saw a great deal of consolidation as the club became established. It was realised that for members to be able to enter the County and National competitions, the club needed to affiliate to the English Bowling Association, English Women's Bowling Association, Kent County Bowling Association and the Kent Women's Bowling Association. However, it was recognised that the club was too new to be accepted for these associations, so it was decided to affiliate to the County Bowls Association. The club also resolved to enter the Maidstone Triples League, and was accepted for the 1985 season.[11]

During 1985, Jack Prior played at the club for a short time, although he had originally joined the club in 1982. He was blind, but bowled with immense skill using a cord stretched along the middle of the rink. His wife stood at the other end to inform him of the length of the jack and the results of his bowls.

Jack later moved to the Brighton area to improve his chances of competing in the St Dunstan's Match Cup which was held there for blind bowlers from all over England. He hoped to realise his ambition of gaining a place in the national team. When he left, he gave £75 for a trophy, but the Committee reserved it for the provision of a trophies honours board.[12]

This undated photograph shows Jack (on the right hand side) standing by Ernie Swift. Ernie was club President 2000-2003.

Both reproduced courtesy of Bearsted and Thurnham Bowling Club

Although the club had only been running for a few years, it was quickly realised that a pavilion was a necessity. During the summer, a tent could be used but everyone recognised that this could only be temporary arrangement. A budget was drawn up:

```
BEARSTED AND THURNHAM BOWLING CLUB

ESTIMATED COST OF PAVILION                             November 1985


Planning Applications and Fees as paid                        178
Foundations      as quoted                                  5,290
Foul Drainage
             Pipes at cost                    469
             Cost of laying pipes as quoted 2,480           2,949
Flooring
             Timbers       estimated          300
             Floors         -do-              600
             Joist Hangers at cost            118           1,018
Brickwall        as quoted    (rear wall)                   1,510
Walls
             Timber        estimated          350
             Outside boarding   "           1,000
             Plaster Boards at cost           145
             Insulation    estimated          500           1,995
Doors and Windows
             Glass                            150
             Doors and Windows                650
             Furniture                        100             900
Roofing
             Trusses       given
             Wood          estimated          850
             Felt          at cost            110
             Ceiling       estimated          150
             Guttering     at cost            125           1,235
Partitions                 estimated
Kitchen Furniture          given
Floor covering             say                                590
Tables and chairs                                             350
Electricity Supply         as quoted                        1,259
Electrical Fittings        say                                500
Plumbing and water supply                                     200
Sundries                                                      391

                                                        £ 18,585
```

Reproduced courtesy of Bearsted and Thurnham Bowling Club

A great deal of effort and ingenuity by all the members of the club went into the project. The pavilion was mainly constructed with the materials obtained from a large sectional wooden building. This had been offered to the club from Notcutts garden centre, if the club members could dismantle and remove it.

The construction of the building was marked by very challenging weather conditions: in January 1987, six inches, nine inches and three inches of snow fell on three consecutive days! This was followed in early February by bitter north-easterly winds which blew whilst Peter Lyne and Ewin Rayner attached the uPVC cladding to the outside of the building. Sam Mackeddie tackled the electrics. Joe Essex asked his son to plumb and tile the pavilion. Glazing was undertaken by Jack Langridge. A donation of cabinets from Elsie and Michael Brooker were fitted in the kitchen. With considerable skill, Bernard and Vera Banner rescued sixty metal chairs from the Women's Institute hall which were re-painted and re-seated.[14]

Bearsted and Thurnham Bowling Club

These three photographs show some of the stages of construction:

All reproduced courtesy of Bearsted and Thurnham Bowling Club

The pavilion was ready for use on the first day of the 1987 season, although the official opening took place before the first match, on 2 May.[15] In this photograph, the President, James Ravenscroft, is about to enter the pavilion after cutting the red ribbon:

It is a mark of the sturdiness and quality of the construction that during the Great Storm on 15 October, when winds over 100mph were recorded in Kent, countless trees came down and buildings were damaged, the pavilion stood firm and unscathed.[16]

At the 1990 Annual General Meeting, it was specifically noted that the quality of facilities attracted the Kent Womens Bowls Association to seek permission to play the Divisional final of their tournaments.[17]

The tenth anniversary of the club in 1993 saw it in good shape. The grounds had been further landscaped and enhanced despite the problems caused by some long, hot and very dry, summers. The original pavilion had been extended and a verandah built. The anniversary was marked by a set of matches on 13 June. A photograph of the Founder and the first president, James Ravenscroft, was hung in the pavilion. James had retired in 1989 when George Bassett took over as president.[18]

During the anniversary year, the A side in Division One of the Triples League had reached the semi-finals before losing in the Knock Out Cup. Sandro Braga and Brian Davison had also reached the quarter finals of the County Pairs. An application had been made for entry to the Maidstone and District Women's League and the club was now on the waiting list.[19]

In 1994 Alf Cork, a life member, received a tankard in recognition for all his sterling work and commitment to the club. It bore the following inscription:

> Alf
> Thanks for all your help over the years
> Bearsted and Thurnham Bowling Club

Both reproduced courtesy of Bearsted and Thurnham Bowling Club

In 1995 the club saw further success, being placed as runners up in the area finals of the County Ladies Pairs. This was especially pleasing because it was the first season of the club belonging to the Maidstone and District Ladies League. In the Maidstone Triples League, the Mens A Team did the double, finishing as Champions and winning the Knock Out Cup. The ladies achievement was consolidated the following year by winning their league, whilst the Mens A team won the Triples League for the second year running. The C team also reached the Knock Out Cup Final as runners up.[20]

This photograph shows the ladies league winners:

Reproduced courtesy of Bearsted and Thurnham Bowling Club

<u>Back Row (left to right)</u>: Ruth Frisby, Gretta Danson, Phil Stevens, Janet Stubbs, Gwen Hayman
<u>Middle Row (left to right)</u>: Else Brooker, Doris Potter, Olive Monk, Audrey Eastwood
<u>Front Row (left to right)</u>: Vi Craven, Margaret Lyne, Vera Banner, Betty Reith, Sylvia Howard.

The next few years saw the club continue in their success with further League wins for the Ladies and A teams. In 1998, the club lost the valuable service of Vera Banner as Social Secretary after seventeen years in the post and the following year, the first President, James Ravenscroft, sadly died.

The arrival of the new millennium marked some changes within the sport and much success by the teams from the club. The national organisations and associations leading bowls in the United Kingdom reviewed aspects of the sport; including the introduction of coloured clothes for matches. In 2006 teams from the club began to play in pale blue polo shirts trimmed with emerald green around the sleeves and collar, with an updated club badge.[21]

The club also decided to investigate the possibility of a further extension to the pavilion. The Mens Changing Room was altered, as was the kitchen and bar area. The work was completed in time for the County semi finals to be played at Bearsted the following year. Further work on the pavilion was undertaken during the winter of 2004 to 2005. The pavilion was enlarged and large windows were fitted. As the pavilion is higher than the green, a much improved view was gained. New lighting, heating and furnishings have also recently now been fitted providing room and comfort for members and visitors.[22]

In 2002 the A team reached the top of their division within the Triples League and the B team had also gained promotion. The club agreed to play in the Wealden League. The following year saw Graham and Jenny Walkling as husband and wife captains. In 2004, both B and D teams earned promotion to the Triples League and Sandro Braga, Robin Lunn, Maurice Goldacre, Peter Acott all gained their County Badges.[23]

On 17 November 2005, a tree was planted in the Bearsted Woodland Trust site by the club. The inscription from the accompanying plaque is shown below:

> This Maple was donated by Bearsted and Thurnham Bowling Club,
> planted by Joe Riggs, a member,
> and dedicated to Past, Present and Future Members 2005

This photograph shows the team from Bearsted competing in the Maidstone Triple A League during September 2007:

Reproduced courtesy of Kent Messenger newspaper group

<u>Left to right</u>: Robin Lunn, Andrew Barnes, Andrew Tree, Maurice Goldacre, Sandro Braga, Brian Davison.

The club is now in a strong position, having built upon the hard work and achievements of their founding members. As their website says, the club continues to go from strength to strength, underpinned by sound financial management and a strong self help ethos. Support for club friendly fixtures is high, 76 matches were planned for the 2007 season.[24]

The clubhouse is a key to the success of the club. The next two photographs illustrate its many uses:

Reproduced courtesy of Trevor Coleman

The club now enters a total of nine teams in four different competitive leagues. Club competitions form an important part of the season's bowling programme. During May and September, six evenings are allocated for one-off team competitions which maximise the capacity of the Green. The competition programme is run principally over five days during the season, culminating in a semi final week-end and a Finals Day.

Specific evenings are also run to play rounds of team competitions.[25] Altogether, the club runs seven adult singles competitions: Veterans, Two Wood, Mens Singles, Mens Singles Handicap, Ladies Singles, Ladies Singles Handicap and the 100 Up. There are a further seven team competitions. Junior players may enter adult competitions but there are also two designated junior competitions: Singles and 100 Up.[26]

This photograph shows the game of bowls at its best!

Both reproduced courtesy of Trevor Coleman

The club celebrated its Silver Jubilee in 2008. Club members may continue to engage in friendly debate over the outcome of matches and the skills of players, but the dream of Margaret Tate and James Ravenscroft has surely been fulfilled.

Ian Lambert

Tennis in Bearsted and Thurnham

A tennis club was formed in 1923 as a section of the Bearsted and Thurnham Sports Club. At first, matches were played on the Green, so posts and nets had to be taken down every evening. It is believed that Mr R Palmer was Captain and Honorary Secretary. These were the club rules: [1]

> **Bearsted & Thurnham Sports Club.**
>
> **TENNIS CLUB RULES.**
>
> 1. The Subscription shall be 5/-, to be paid in advance.
> 2. The Courts shall be open to members at all hours during the week, except Sundays.
> 3. All members must wear Tennis shoes when playing.
> 4. Each member must bring his or own racket and tennis balls.
> 5. Members last to leave the Courts shall be responsible for taking down the nets and posts and putting them in the place selected to store them.
> 6. In the event of friends being introduced, they shall be charged 6d. per day or 2/6 per week.
> 7. Persons wishing to join the Club to apply to the Secretary, who shall submit their names to the Committee for approval.
> 8. No member shall play two sets in succession when other members are waiting to play. All sets to be "short."

In 1924 Mr J L Ollett became Honorary Secretary and wrote to Henry Lushington to ask if the club could be allowed to have a piece of ground in Thurnham Lane to use for two courts, at a nominal rent. The club remained at this location until the early 1940s. This is a copy of the response from Henry Lushington, together with a transcription (which is on the next page):

Both reproduced courtesy of Bearsted and Thurnham Lawn Tennis Club

Tennis in Bearsted and Thurnham

> Dear Mr Ollett
>
> I have much pleasure in sending £1 for the Tennis Prize.
>
> I shall be very glad to let you have a piece of ground for three or four tennis courts, and will charge you no rent provided you can do the fencing. I think it would be best if you select some spot, and I shall be glad to try and make arrangements. The difficulty is to keep the colts and stock away.
>
> Yours very truly
>
> Henry V Lushington
>
> 3.11.24

As seen in a previous chapter in this book, Bearsted and Thurnham Sports Club combined cricket, football and tennis. Evidently, each sport had a degree of autonomy as there were separate advertisements in local publications. The club disbanded in 1937, as by that time, each of the sports had decided to manage their own affairs.[2]

This photograph gives an impression of some of the properties in Thurnham Lane during the 1920s:

Reproduced courtesy of Jean Jones

In 1929, there was a reference in the Bearsted parish magazine to the tennis club and the two courts situated near Thurnham School.[3] Below is a transcript of an advertisement which also appeared:

> **E W M TAYLOR**
> Slazenger's Tennis Balls
>
> ENSIGN and KODAK films
> Developing and Printing
> BEARSTED

Reproduced courtesy of Holy Cross church

In May 1930 there were two courts available for play and the following report appeared in the parish magazine: [4]

> Arrangements have been made whereby beginners will have the courts on Monday evening, and are promised the help of one or more of the committee for coaching; they will also be able to play at any other time; with the exception of Wednesdays or Friday evenings, which are club nights. The subscription is 7/6.

Regular advertisements continued in the Bearsted parish magazine highlighting the facilities of the club over many years.

During the Annual General Meeting of the Sports Club in November 1930, Mr Whitehead was elected President to replace Major Craig who had left the village. It was noted that everyone connected with the sporting life of the village was deeply indebted to Major Craig [5]

The following year, tennis formed part of Bearsted Fayre. An American Tournament (mixed doubles) was held. The entrance fee was two shillings per player and spectators were charged a penny for a seat.[6]

In 1932, at the Annual General Meeting, Mr A Barker was re-elected as Chairman, Mr Charles Harnett, Captain and Mr Ollett was Secretary. Committee members were Misses K Perrin and L G Dibble, Messrs P Wenham and R Gooch. It is not known when the H V Lushington Cups were first presented as trophies for single matches but in 1932 they were won by Miss J Lloyd and Mr R Gooch. The following year, in the finals for the trophies, Miss B Perrin beat her sister, known as 'K', 6-4, 6-5 and Mr Barker defeated Gerald Goodman 6-4, 6-1.[7]

In 1935 the competition for the Lushington Cups was interrupted by bad weather which prevented the games being completed on grass. Fortunately, Mr and Mrs S H Loweth offered the use of their hard court at their home, Westways, as an alternative venue.[8]

During 1936 Mr J C Lloyd was appointed Captain and Miss M O Jones was Vice-Captain. A groundsman was sought. Both Mr Lloyd and Miss Jones were re-appointed the following season but the matches were only completed with great difficulty due to bad weather. The courts were rendered unfit for play for the majority of June and members were advised of the condition of the courts through a notice displayed in the window of Mr Moss's shop at Chestnut Place.[9]

In 1938, the annual subscription was increased to ten shillings, but this included tennis balls. There was also a rather ironic report in the parish magazine about a match held at The Mount: [10]

> 'Lost all the events', sounds bad, but when we say '166 games to 109', it does not sound so much like a colossal defeat.
>
> Mr Charles Whitehead always gets a team which is 'just too good for us' but we do thank Mr and Mrs Whitehead for the annual opportunity for playing on their splendid courts.

Both reproduced courtesy of Holy Cross church

It seems that there are few photographs of the tennis club before World War Two. This one was taken in 1938, although no further details are known:

Reproduced courtesy of Bearsted and Thurnham Lawn Tennis Club

During the Second World War, very little tennis was played on weekdays as most of the club members were undertaking Air Raid Precaution work in and around Bearsted and Thurnham. However, the games played on Saturday afternoons provided some relaxation from work and anxieties about the hostilities. A junior section continued though, and thirteen members regularly attended on Monday evenings. In 1940, an away game against Lenham Juniors was lost. The team included Muriel Brown, Milly Baker, Violet Merrill and Vera Croucher.[11]

The 1940 season was brought to a premature end because of an increasing number of daylight air raids: in August there was particularly heavy raid on nearby Detling airfield. The Annual meeting was held at the Rifle Club. Despite the wartime conditions, the club decided to continue in both 1941 and 1942. As there were difficulties in collecting subscriptions, a reduced subscription of five shillings was agreed, but members now had to supply their own tennis balls. Members were also expected to help mow and mark the court.[12]

It is likely that as the war continued, the club then fell into abeyance. There are no references to tennis in local publications until 1946, when the parish magazine reported a meeting was to be held at the Tennis Courts, Thurnham Lane, on 15 June. The meeting was to consider the possibility of reforming the club. Tennis enthusiasts were urged to attend the meeting to show the Committee that the club would be well supported.[13]

Evidently, there was a good attendance at the following meeting on 8 July 1946 at which it was formally agreed that the tennis club should be reformed. Mrs Ling was elected Honorary Secretary. Mrs Lushington expressed a wish that the club should continue to use her premises in Thurnham Lane but as the courts were in poor condition and the fencing needed repair, perhaps it would be better to use them the next year. Fortunately, Mr and Mrs Whitehead were able to offer the immediate use of their facilities at The Mount for what remained of the season. A subscription of seven shillings and sixpence was suggested in order to raise funds to prepare the courts in Thurnham Lane for the next season.[14]

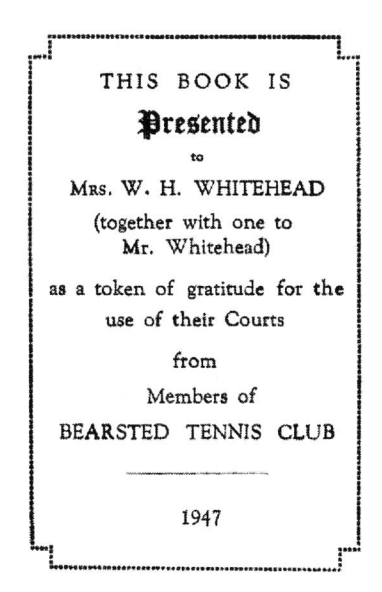

```
┌─────────────────────────────┐
│      THIS BOOK IS           │
│      𝔓𝔯𝔢𝔰𝔢𝔫𝔱𝔢𝔡              │
│          to                 │
│   Mrs. W. H. WHITEHEAD      │
│    (together with one to    │
│       Mr. Whitehead)        │
│                             │
│  as a token of gratitude for the │
│      use of their Courts    │
│                             │
│           from              │
│         Members of          │
│    BEARSTED TENNIS CLUB     │
│                             │
│           1947              │
└─────────────────────────────┘
```

Reproduced courtesy of Bearsted and Thurnham Lawn Tennis Club

At the Annual General Meeting on 15 April 1947 it was noted that Mr and Mrs Whitehead had again kindly offered the use of their courts at The Mount, but there would be no play on Sundays. On 2 December, during a social evening held at the Memorial Hall, Mr and Mrs Whitehead presented the Lushington Cups to Mr C Hawkins and Miss M G Brown. Two books were also presented to Mr and Mrs Whitehead by the club as a small token of their gratitude for the use of their courts. A bookplate from one of them is shown on the left.

However, during that meeting, the President referred to the matter of the courts used by the club. Those loaned by Mrs Lushington had been taken over by the Kent War Agricultural Committee and their continuing work., and so were no longer available for use. Mr and Mrs Whitehead had loaned some courts on a temporary basis. The club was now without courts, so it was time for the members to address this problem.[15]

Fund-raising began immediately: dances were held at the Women's Institute hall and Whist Drives took place. At the Annual General Meeting in 1948, it was reported that grounds for courts had been found at a site between St Faith's Home and Roseacre Lane. It was owned by Mr Loweth and leased by Mr Thomas. However, a great deal of money was required to prepare the site; Mr Brakefield quoted £32 for the ground works. This sketch map is not to scale, but it gives an indication of the location of the new courts:

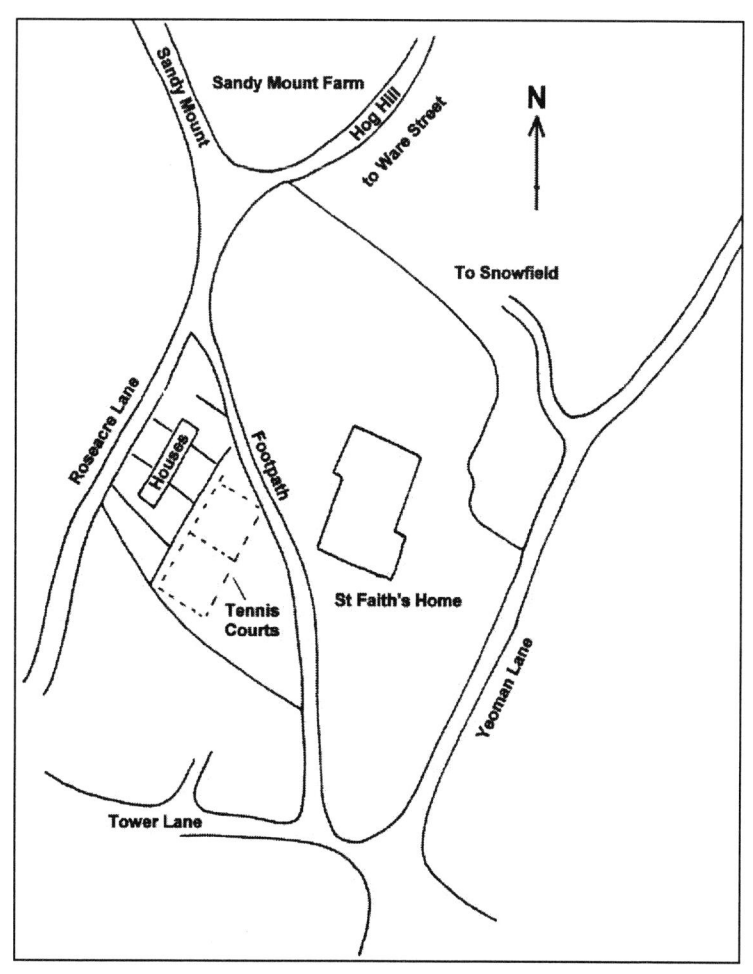

Diagram by Kathryn Kersey based on Ordnance Survey

Whilst funds were being raised, and the courts prepared, Lieutenant Colonel Thomas offered the use of his court to the club members. Frederick Grout renovated two mowers which were most welcome, but there were delays in obtaining wire netting for the surrounds.[16] Mrs Ling was forced to resign as Honorary Secretary of the club due to ill health, and Mr J Lyle and Mr G Pearce then shared the post. In June 1948, Samuel Harnett became Ground Secretary and Mr G Pearce was appointed Honorary Secretary. During 1949, it was noted that a great deal of money had been spent on the preparation for the new courts, so members volunteered to undertake the groundsman's duties. A small loan was secured to purchase a motor mower to assist members to maintain the courts.[17]

In 1950 the Lushington Cups for single matches were again presented to the winners: Miss Mary Meech and Mr R Usmer. A further trophy was presented for mixed doubles matches by the Vice Presidents, Mr Loweth and Lieutenant Colonel Thomas. By 1951, club membership had risen to forty four. The subscription was also slightly increased to thirty five shillings. Junior Members aged 16 to 18 paid twenty five shillings.[18] During 1952 the club joined the Maidstone Tennis League and were played in the first of three divisions together with teams from APM, Queens, Medway A and Tovil A.[19] In June 1953, the club officials were determined to build upon the league membership and in June the parish magazine carried a report in which it referred to the importance of encouraging younger people to the club and welcoming them. Junior members would now be accepted aged 14 to 18 at reduced fees.[20]

Despite this optimism, the club quickly encountered a major problem the following year. This is a transcript of the report which appeared in the March edition of the parish magazine: [21]

> The Annual meeting of the Tennis Club was held at the Women's Institute Hall on 15 February. Nine members were present and they decided that, as the ground on which the courts are situated has been sold, and that there is little likelihood of obtaining new courts, to disband the club.
>
> This ends another chapter in the annals of the Bearsted Tennis Club which made a beginning in 1922 on the Green. In 1924, the late Mr Henry Lushington provided, free of costs, sufficient ground in Thurnham Lane for two courts. There, for many happy years, the club remained until about 1940 when the too-frequent appearance of 'Messerschmitts' caused the club to close. The courts in Roseacre Lane have been in use for about five years.
>
> The existing Committee is to be responsible for disposal of equipment and any money to be deposited in a Post Office account, for, who can tell, there may be another chapter.

Reproduced courtesy of Holy Cross and St Mary's churches

There was indeed to be another chapter to tennis in the villages but no-one foresaw that it would take over twenty years to resurrect the idea of a club! Alan Ferrell was central to this and these are his reminiscences:

The formation of a new tennis club in Bearsted was considered by almost sixty residents at a meeting in October 1978, as a result of interest shown by a survey conducted earlier by the Bearsted and Thurnham Residents' Association. This had been instigated after enquiries made by one or two fathers of young families. The meeting learnt that Bearsted Parish Council was prepared to make available a site next to the allotments adjacent to Church Landway. A Steering Committee of nine residents was formed to explore methods of financing the project and progress the matter further.

Grants were not forthcoming from the numerous organisations approached, the only offer being a loan of £1,000 from the Kent Playing Fields Association. In an endeavour to raise the necessary capital, applications were invited from residents to become Founder Members who would be prepared to advance a payment of £100 to cover an entrance fee and annual subscriptions for three years. Understandably, this was not too successful.

A second meeting was held in January 1979 for the Committee to report back and propose additional annual family, senior and junior membership. In the light of the enthusiasm and support shown, Bearsted Parish Council offered to donate a sum of £5,000 providing an equivalent amount was first raised by the residents.

Tennis in Bearsted and Thurnham

The Steering Committee subsequently decided that the generous offer of land and cash gift enabled the proposals to become reality, and so, the Bearsted and Thurnham Lawn Tennis Club was formed. A Management Committee of seven was duly elected and fresh applications were invited from virtually every household in the two parishes.

£10,000 was eventually raised, mainly by advanced membership fees and some generous gifts and loans, to supplement the sum of £5,000 from the parish council, which allowed the project to proceed.

Planning permission was obtained and a local woodsman commenced work on the site, which was a derelict orchard. He felled and removed the apple trees free of charge, but with the provision that he could take away the wood! Crownways Construction Limited then completed clearance and constructed three Tarmacadam courts with surrounding netting, levelling an additional area for a possible further two courts. These photographs show some of the site clearance; note the houses in Manor Rise in the background:

Both reproduced courtesy of Joy Ferrell

Tennis in Bearsted and Thurnham

Finally, the whole site between the courts and the perimeter fencing was weeded, raked, seeded and rolled by the club's new members, just in time for the official opening of the courts on 1 September 1979, when a cheque for £5,000 was received from the parish council. Play commenced the following day.

This photograph was taken during the official opening. Dr Frank Alston is standing by the gate (left hand side) and is handing the parish council cheque to Alan Ferrell (right hand side):

Reproduced courtesy of Joy Ferrell

This is a transcript of a report about the official opening: [22]

Bearsted & Thurnham Lawn Tennis Club

'Today is a day to remember and the morrow is time to enjoy' - said Dr Frank Alston, Chairman of Bearsted Parish Council, when he formally declared open the courts of the Bearsted and Thurnham Lawn Tennis Club. Dr Alston also handed a cheque for £5,000 to Alan Ferrell the Club's Chairman to honour the Council's promise to give the amount when the Club had raised a similar sum. Mr Ferrell expressed thanks to the parish council and all who had worked hard to bring about the inauguration of the club.

Both Dr Alston and Mr Ferrell paid tribute to the late Mr Richard Lambert, the parish council's former chairman, who had realised the need for more sporting facilities in Bearsted, and with his Council, had played a large part in the success of the project.

Dr Alston added that the council believed in furthering sport in the parish and hinted that some of the four acres of the council land which remains might house in future a bowling club.

Within a year, three hard courts have been installed and it is hoped that during the next year, two grass courts will be added. At present membership is confined to parishioners of Bearsted and Thurnham.

Reproduced courtesy of Holy Cross and St Mary's churches

Behind the scene activities were also taking place, during, and after, the construction period. Guarantors were secured for all financial borrowing and the appointment of trustees, presidents and officers. The constitution and rules and various sub-committees to set the standards of play, dress code, fund-raising, maintenance, etc., were all created. Not least of all, a twenty five year lease with provision for an extension for a further twenty five years was agreed between Bearsted Parish Council and the trustees of the Bearsted and Thurnham Lawn Tennis Club, to safeguard the interests of the council and secure the long-term future of the club.

The original concept of the Steering Committee was a tennis facility of five courts and a pavilion, upon which the overall area of the site was based. However, the club's immediate well-being and future growth depended upon the continuing support of the founder members and the ability to attract new members and raise funds. The club's future beyond the formative, euphoric period remained as an unknown entity.

In the closing months of 1979, two pre-fabricated office buildings, measuring 60 feet by 24 feet each were offered for sale by tender by the Kent County Council. They were too good an opportunity to miss, and the club was successful in its bid to acquire one for use as a clubhouse at a cost of £514 (allegedly only £14 more than the unsuccessful bid).

A condition of sale was the removal of the buildings from the site at Albert Street not far from the KCC's Springfield complex in Maidstone by 7 January 1980. With the aid of the County Council's Manpower Services Commission youth training team, arranged by one of the club's members free of charge, supporters set to work. The building and its contents were dismantled and transported over the Christmas and New Year holiday period to the site at Church Landway.

There was no money available in the foreseeable future for re-erection, so the materials were stored on site, but off the ground, on a series of timber A-frames and protected by tarpaulins.

However, thanks to a member's generous offer of a long-term interest-free loan of £5,000, it was possible to give early consideration to providing a clubhouse. The club also became eligible to be considered for financial support by the Sports Council and subsequently received a £4,000 grant. Work therefore began in April 1980, again, with the help of the KCC's youth training team. The following fourteen months were a hive of activity as gradually re-erection of the building took place. Specialist contractors were necessary to carry out certain items of work, such as the electrical installation, felting the roof and laying a sewer from the site all the way along Church Landway to connect to the mains in Ashford Road. However, most other works were carried out unselfishly by members in their spare time and the club owes much to them. After a great deal of hard work and financial wheeling and dealing, the grand opening of the clubhouse took place on 6 June 1981.

The next photographs show some of the work undertaken to build the clubhouse:

Reproduced courtesy of Joy Ferrell

This photograph was taken during the official opening on 6 June 1981: the club's first President, Peter Monckton, is cutting the ribbon across the door. Note the guard of honour formed by tennis racquets held up by players behind Alan Ferrell.

Both reproduced courtesy of Joy Ferrell

In 1999, the club reached its twentieth anniversary and these photographs were taken during the celebrations held on 18 July:

Both reproduced courtesy of Bearsted and Thurnham Lawn Tennis Club

From humble beginnings the club has now matured with age and experience over the years, paying off its debts and becoming financially stable. Two further hard courts with flood-lighting for all five courts have been constructed. Ever-growing numbers of members and their guests now enjoy a fully equipped clubhouse.

Extra links with the community have been developed; the finals of the annual Kent Messenger winter tennis tournament have been held at the club for twenty four years. The Bearsted and Thurnham bowls club used the clubhouse as temporary facilities before they were able to build their own pavilion in 1987. The clubhouse continues to be used by other local organizations; the Bearsted Ladies Lunch, run for Bearsted Area Churches Together, use the clubhouse as a venue, and Bearsted Woodland Trust have also held recent Annual General Meetings there.

Currently, the club has 600 members with nearly half of them being juniors, who enjoy the services of five resident coaches. Over two dozen teams participate in local and county leagues.

Bearsted and Thurnham Lawn Tennis Club was created to provide an active interest in the leisure-time activity of playing tennis, whilst having due regard to its relationship with its neighbours, other village organizations and residents. The club believes this objective has been met and, as it looks forward to celebrating its thirtieth anniversary in 2009, is the envy of many clubs in Kent, with a stable and secure future – what a far cry from those early days in 1979!

This is the club's badge:

Reproduced courtesy of Bearsted and Thurnham Lawn Tennis Club

Alan Ferrell and Ian Lambert

From Boer to Bull's Eye: Bearsted Rifle Club

Bearsted Rifle Club has been described as not only one of the oldest in England, but one of Bearsted and Thurnham's best kept secrets! It was started by John Hampson, the younger brother of Sir George Hampson of Thurnham Court. It is believed that whilst John was serving in the Boer War, he was alarmed to see that the Boers were much better at shooting than the British. He became determined to improve matters. He decided to see if there was any local interest, and, after carefully explaining matters to members of the community, it was decided to begin a club in Bearsted.[1]

The first General Meeting was held at Thurnham School in Thurnham Lane, 11 December 1901, with members coming from Bearsted, Thurnham and Detling. This meeting was to inaugurate and appoint officers. At that time, the club was called the Bearsted and District Rifle Club. This meeting was presided over by Mr Badcock of Detling, who was appointed Chairman for the evening, with Mr Hampson as Secretary and Treasurer. Other members of the committee included Messrs John Brown, James Ellis jun., Charles Brisley and William Hunt.[2]

Between 1904 and 1908, Dr Richard Thompson Caesar was Chairman and President of the Rifle Club. James Ellis succeeded John Hampson as Secretary and Treasurer before William Hunt took on the post, serving in this role at the Rifle Club for twenty years. He later became Chairman and his hard work promoting the club meant that it was able to continue to run through the First World War, unlike many other village organisations.[3]

These two photographs show John Hampson (left) and William Hunt (right):

Both reproduced courtesy of Chris and Sue Hunt

Some early meetings were held in a large room at the far end of the White Horse public house. Several village societies and clubs held meetings there. It did not take long to ascertain that the room would accommodate a twenty five yard range of shooting from one end to the other. Sandbags were piled against the wall at the end of the hall to form a butt, whilst the firing point was the opposite wall, at the road end of the building.

However, the main venues for the club were outside: a chalk-pit in Thurnham Lane, and, it is thought, the former brickyard and tile works in Ware Street. A site in Water Lane, where there were sand-pits was also used occasionally. The first shoot took place on a Saturday, at another location which was opposite the Black Horse. The weather was not good, being December, but Mr John Brown managed to make a bull. Mr James Ellis was top scorer with fifteen points on this occasion. Firing days were fixed for Wednesdays and Saturdays for the men, and Thursdays for the ladies.[4]

These two photographs are undated but show part of a shooting match between the Inns of Court Volunteers and the Bearsted and Thurnham Rifle Club held at the chalk pit. The first photograph includes Thomas Hunt, John Hampson and Thomas Golding:

The back row of this photograph includes B Carr, who is fourth from left in the back row. Note the chalk cliff face in the background and the bank of chalk used as a seat:

Both reproduced courtesy of Bearsted and Thurnham Rifle Club

A concert in 1903 was held to raise funds for a permanent undercover site, as this poster indicates: [6]

The Village Hall, BEARSTED.

A Grand Smoking CONCERT

WILL BE HELD IN THE ABOVE HALL ON

WEDNESDAY, NOV. 18th, 1903,

In aid of the Bearsted and Thornham Rifle Club.

SPECIAL ENGAGEMENT OF

FREDERICK CHESTER,

Of LONDON VENTRILOQUIST & COMIC ENTERTAINER.

HORACE DANN, THE OLD FAVOURITE

WITH ENTIRELY NEW SONGS.

WILL KELLY, Laughing Comedian.

Mr. FRED BAXTER,

THE BROMLEY AMATEUR, HUMOROUS VOCALIST,

And several other well-known Artist have kindly consented to appear.

Reserved Seats, 2/-. Second Seats, 1/-.
A LIMITED NUMBER 6d.
Doors open at 7 o'clock   Commence 7.30.

5079).   "KENT MESSENGER" TYP., MAIDSTONE

Reproduced courtesy of Bearsted and District Local History Society

At the end of April 1932, the club sought permission from Mr John Hampson to use a chalk pit off Thurnham Lane, near Langham Wood, on land farmed by Mr C Brown. Mr Hampson thought that application should be made direct to the farmer, with a caution that it might be necessary to apply to his brother, Sir George Hampson, who was the landowner. It would also be necessary to have its suitability assessed by a qualified officer of the Society of Miniature Rifle Clubs. Sir George was quite happy for the chalk pit to be used. A letter from the Secretary of the Society of Miniature Rifle Clubs suggests that the site had been used earlier in the life of the club, but that its use had lapsed. A captain from the Queen's Own Royal West Kent Regiment, based in Maidstone Barracks, came in June to make the inspection. He recommended that some fencing would be necessary, or alternatively, did they 'propose to post a man near the wood while firing is in progress?' Following a further exchange of letters, the Safety Certificate was issued at the end of August.[7]

Despite the lack of indoor facilities for the club, the members enjoyed success as this slightly edited report from the Kent Messenger, which appeared 23 November 1935, shows:

> **Rifle Shooting**
>
> Bearsted A and Yalding A are still first and second respectively in the Maidstone League championship. K C O are third, but Maidstone A have come up to fourth with their B team now running fifth.
>
> In the individual championship, Mr A Maxted, captain of Bearsted A, still leads the field with an average score of 99.5, with Mr Tom Hartley a close second only one point behind.
>
> There have been three maximum possible scores this week in the League – Mrs Hallam, (Yalding A), R Middleton (Maidstone A) and S A Jenner (East Malling). It is understood that this is Mr Jenner's first maximum possible score in the match shooting for the past two years and he is to be congratulated.
>
> Next week sees the commencement of the President's Cup matches, when Bearsted A and Yalding A meet for the second time this season.
>
> It will be remembered that the conditions under which this cup is shot for are entirely new to the League. Half the team shoot at home, while the other half shoot away. If possible the two matches are to be shot on the same night and in any case, the same week. All shooting is to be done on metric cards.

Reproduced courtesy of Kent Messenger newspaper group

Around 1936, the club opened negotiations with Fremlin's Brewery to erect a permanent range at the back of the White Horse. An alternative site outside at Stockbury, on land belonging to Mr Ken Beaver, had also been under consideration, but the parish council thought the access road was too narrow. In spite of this, members thought that this would have been a very acceptable site too.

In September 1937, agreement was reached with the brewery about the range and an annual rent of £10. The opening ceremony was performed by Major Leney, the chairman of Fremlin's a year later.[8]

The first shot at the new range was fired by the President, Major Harry Ernest Chapman, who was then Chief Constable of Kent. It is not known what prompted Major Chapman to join the Bearsted Club, when there was at least one other rifle club in Maidstone.[9] The photograph on the left shows Major Chapman in 1935.

Reproduced courtesy of Chris and Sue Hunt

The parish magazine carried the following report:[10]

> **Bearsted's New Rifle Range**
>
> Major H E Chapman fired the first shots on the new 25 yard range of the Bearsted and Thurnham Rifle Club, Friday 26 November. It has been built in the garden adjoining the White Horse Inn by the brewers, Messrs Fremlins Ltd, from plans prepared by the Society of Miniature Rifle Clubs and is considered one of the best ranges in the Maidstone and District League.
>
> If you are interested in rifle shooting, you are invited to come along on Wednesday or Saturday evenings, from 7pm to 9.30pm. The annual subscription is 3s 6d, lads under 18, 1 shilling. The club has three teams in the Maidstone and District League and is affiliated to the Society of Miniature Rifle Clubs and is in the West Kent League.
>
> Officers elected were:
> | | |
> |---|---|
> | President | Major H E Chapman, OBE |
> | Chairman | Mr George Russell |
> | Hon Secretary | Mr J L Ollett |
> | Competition Secretary | Mr M W Corps |
> | Hon Treasurer | Mr William Hunt |
>
> Committee: Lt Comdr. A J Trewett, Messrs W E Wickens, F Harnett, C Carr, A J Pearson, J Sharpe, A Maxted, A V Pearson and W Foster.

Reproduced courtesy of Holy Cross church

Mr Ollett first came to the club to take details of the AGM in his capacity as a reporter for the Kent Messenger. During the course of the evening he became highly interested and left as an officer of the club! He remained as a non-shooting member, eventually becoming President.

The club remains affiliated to the Society of Miniature Rifle Clubs. It is believed that the word 'miniature' was used to distinguish the guns they used from the Army's .303 rifles. Long-standing club member Vic Matthews recalled going with other members of the team from Maidstone Grammar School to shoot at the Barracks in Sandling Road. The sign on the door included the word 'minature'. The boys would laugh heartily at the spelling mistake, but nobody ever altered it, and so the sign remained the same for many years.

When the range was first opened, the club had three teams in the Maidstone and District League. Mrs Scott of The Friars wished to form a Ladies team and other interested ladies were invited to a meeting about it. Despite this, it is not clear if a separate ladies team was started.[11]

Around this time, Arthur Maxted bought a little clock from Marks and Spencer for the club room. It cost about five shillings and lasted for years. It had to be wound every time that someone came in because it was only a day clock. Then one night the spring broke, so another member offered a replacement. When installed, it was seen to be about the same age as the club itself and it is still there. It was made about 1901 in Connecticut, and has a strike, although that is never used in case it interferes with the shooting.

The club room had no heating, apart from a German paraffin heater which members sometimes used to roast chestnuts in the winter. Eventually the heater disintegrated, and there was no money to replace it. The club existed on the £10 grant received each year from the Bearsted Fayre, which was then held on the August Bank Holiday, the first Monday in August. The grant helped to run the club, but did not extend to paying for anything new. One member offered to put up ten shillings if other members would contribute five shillings and so a pale green Aladdin heater was purchased. A member who was also a fire officer had a special tray made, so that if the heater leaked, the spillage would be contained. A shed was built to accommodate it, and gas laid on, but that was all. Many years later, an electric heater was installed.[12]

This photograph of the interior of the range was taken in the 1930s. It is believed to include Thomas Gilbert but nothing further is known about the occasion. Note the target papers displayed on the wall in the background.

Reproduced courtesy of Debbie and Richard Gilbert

In June 1939, a note in the parish magazine advised villagers that the Rifle Range would be open during the summer months on the first Wednesday of each month from 8pm to 9.30pm. By September, when the AGM was held, Major Chapman expressed the wish that the club would carry on through the war, as had the Society of Miniature Rifle Clubs. He pointed out that this was work of national importance, and would, at the same time, provide recreation during the winter months. He added that, as an experiment, the club room would be open from 6.30pm to 9pm on Saturdays, commencing 30 September, and thought that it might be necessary to arrange an earlier time for juniors, who would be taught to shoot. Ladies were invited to join. Almost every club in the Maidstone and District League had lady members, many of whom could beat the men.[13]

Trophies have always been awarded by the club, and are often fairly small items such as silver spoons. Vic Matthews, currently the oldest member, one time Postmaster and shopkeeper at the Roseacre Stores and Post Office, joined the club in 1936. He won a trophy the first year that he was a member; it was a silver spoon which was awarded because he had made a score of 99. Silver Spoons were always awarded for Best Score. Unfortunately, the spoons were not dated, and the designs changed from year to year, so however many were won, they did not match! Bill Woolven had a spoon belonging to his grandfather, who was a member of the Police Force in Stoke Newington. Bill first saw a .22 round at his grandmother's house. Among other trophies listed at the 1938 AGM were the Commander Stafford Cup; the Bell Medal, which was a national award; and the George Barnard Cup. There was also the Maidstone Shield, which was a District trophy and Bearsted won it several times.[14]

In March 1940, John Hampson died and the Kent Messenger newspaper carried a short obituary in which he was credited with founding the rifle club. It also added that during the Great War, he had served as a member of the Kent Cyclist Battalion, and later as a lieutenant in the Royal Defence Corps. During the Second World War, until his death, his home was used as an air raid warden's post, and he was 'an energetic warden, devoting much time to his duty.' In his will, he asked that his gardener and housekeeper should both receive gifts, and that every indoor and outdoor servant in his service at the time of his death should receive a sum equal to three months' wages. He also left an annuity to his house keeper, in recognition of many years of ungrudging service. John was a generous and community minded man who was much missed.[15]

After the outbreak of the Second World War, many of the members of the club were called up to the Armed Forces. However, the range remained open and became an important part of the local defences that were in place should an invasion become imminent. Almost immediately, the club provided a centre for the Local Defence Volunteers, later called the Home Guard, who had not been issued with rifles. Since many of the Home Guard were local farmers and farm workers, the club provided the valuable opportunity to practise shooting. Older residents of the villages can recall their families also regularly, but very quietly, practising at the range. As everyone knew, the close proximity of Detling airfield, a railway line, Maidstone barracks and even the naval base at Chatham, all meant that if there was a German invasion, there was a distinct possibility that the villages would be involved in some sort of action. People felt that they needed to be prepared. Fees for visitors were also introduced, at the rate of 6d per evening.[16]

During the war, Robert Skinner, the headmaster of Bearsted School, was also Chief Observer of the Bearsted branch of the Observer Corps. He was also determined to be thoroughly prepared for enemy action and as part of his duties both at the school and Observer Corps, introduced a good many of his pupils to shooting. In November 1941, it was noted that every Tuesday, there was shooting at the Rifle Range for the children from Bearsted School. At that time, the minimum age for using the range was twelve. Later, it was raised to sixteen when some of the young lads misbehaved and acted foolishly.[17]

Many of the boys from Bearsted School that went on to Maidstone Grammar School then joined the Combined Cadet Force. They were able to develop their shooting skills first acquired at Bearsted by using the range at the grammar school. James Clinch, a former member of the Cadet Force from Maidstone, recalled that matches were sometimes held between them and Bearsted Rifle Range. There was one occasion during such a match when the Cadet Force realised that they were severely hampered; they had not been permitted to bring their own firearms. As a result, the Cadets shooting performance was significantly reduced as they were not used to shooting with anything other than a Lee Enfield rifle!

Bill Woolven, a member of the club for many years, was in the Air Training Corps at the beginning of the war. Those desiring to join the RAF had to learn to shoot, and Bearsted was the only available club, nearby, or the only one that would co-operate. So Bill started shooting, liked it and found that he was good at it, so he joined the club. The club trained many members of the Air Training Corps and some cadets. The cadets provided their own Nosworth rifles, which were considered to be fairly poor target weapons. This was because although they were like a service rifle, their barrels were not sufficiently accurate. The Nosworths were handed back after the war.

Other members of the club can still recall some aspects of the range during the war: Vic Matthews, recalled that the windows of the club room were painted black to comply with the black-out regulations, and there was a double entrance, for the same reason. There was a screen around the door with cloth over it. Members came in through the first door and closed it, and then came through the cloth screen. Vic later became a bomber pilot in the war. He eventually became president of the club, but no longer lives in the village. Dennis Gibbons related how obtaining ammunition was not a problem during the war. He said that there was no choice, it was what the Army issued: .22 ammunition. Vic Matthews added that as long as it went bang, that was all one could expect of it!

Dennis Gibbons joined in 1942, becoming secretary in 1968. He already owned an air rifle when he came to Bearsted. It was his father who suggested that Dennis joined the rifle club. Vic Matthews, like Bill Woolven, had been a member of the 'A' team at Maidstone Grammar School, where he was a member of the Air Training Corps. He recalled that at school the boys were allowed to go to the range outside of school hours whenever they liked, and they could shoot as much as they liked. He and a group of friends went to the Grammar School range, took out 500 rounds and could shoot all evening without it costing a penny.

At that time, Maidstone Rifle Club also used the range. One evening when the boys went in, the Maidstone Club had left their cupboard open. The boys found some rather strange rifles with odd sights and a funny action. The boys were accustomed to using bored-out Army rifles, so they tried the others, and liked them. Soon after, Vic went down to the Bearsted range. Arthur Maxted was the duty member. He put out ten rounds, and watched carefully as Vic shot. When Vic had finished, Arthur asked him for payment: Vic only had pocket money, and it had never occurred to him that he might be charged for ammunition!

Members used to arrive at the club on foot, though some had bicycles or motorbikes which they could leave under a shelter. They carried their rifles slung across their backs. Bill Woolven recalled cycling through six inches of snow to attend a match. Dennis Gibbons and his wife came from Rochester on a motor bike one bright moonlit night. When they reached the Bell bridge they found that the road had flooded and then frozen – but they managed to get across without mishap. Dennis reported the matter to the police, who treated the ice so that by the time Dennis was ready to return home, the ice had melted. Now, of course, members arrive by car but are discouraged from parking outside the range.

Dennis Gibbons remembered that after the war ended, when Bert Pearson was station-master, ammunition was purchased from the Miniature Rifle and Smallbore Association. It was sent down by train to the railway station, where Mr Pearson would load it on to a trolley, wheel it down to the range, and put it on the doorstep. No-one ever touched it but this may have been because an order was usually five thousand rounds, weighing about a ton and a half!

However, the legislation surrounding the ownership of firearms became far more strict. Firearms certificates were introduced in 1946. The guidelines from the Home Office stated that they were only issued if a person had a legitimate sporting or work-related reason for owning a gun. If a member moved away from the area, and there was no club within easy reach, the certificate had to be given up and the gun sold: civilians had to belong to a club. Firearms certificates cost 2/6 and remained at this price for many years. Every year the local policeman came round to tell owners that it was time to renew their certificate and to request the half-crown. The certificate then arrived through the post a couple of days later. Now a firearms certificate costs about £40, and the police have to come to inspect where the gun is kept, and to make sure that it is secure.

John Hardy joined the rifle club at the age of eleven. The boys section met on a Saturday night, and under the guidance of Arthur Maxted, known to all as Mac, learnt to shoot, and to respect rifles. Mac had been a superb shot in the Home Guard and encouraged many of the young lads of the village to learn how to shoot. He was an engineer who worked at Bockingford, near Tovil, in the paper mill.

This photograph shows Mac in 1935.

He rode an ancient Royal Enfield motorcycle which he had owned from new, probably purchasing it in 1937. It was certainly a 500cc model. He kept the bike spotless, and used to say that the secret was to give it 'plenty of hoil'. When riding his motorbike he always wore an old oil-stained mackintosh and a flat cap and goggles. This was before crash helmets became compulsory. When he voluntarily gave up riding, he gave the bike to Mick Jones, who then lived in Thurnham Lane. Mac lived with his brother at Crismill, and enjoyed taking black-and-white photographs which he developed and printed himself. Mac was also keen on railways, and often took a group of children on the Romney, Hythe and Dymchurch Railway to Dungeness.

Reproduced courtesy of Kent Messenger newspaper group

John started shooting as a team member when he was about fourteen or fifteen then subsequently became captain of the 'C' and 'D' teams. He was also reasonably proficient at pistol shooting. He has many happy memories of 'shoulder to shoulder' matches in the Maidstone league and of matches held at the open range in Thurnham. These matches acquired the name because they involved one member of each team shooting from the firing point lying almost shoulder to shoulder. Matches were arranged against teams from Maidstone, Wateringbury with Teston and Yalding. The locations for 'away' events included several Territorial Army halls, small village ranges near public houses and one in the vicinity of a graveyard. Postal matches using rifles and pistols were also popular. This involved sheets of ten targets being sent to a central inspector after ratification by a second member of the club. The inspector would compare the targets, mark them and then declare a winner.

This undated photograph was taken of John whilst he was lining up a target at the range. Note the prone position adopted:

Reproduced courtesy of John Hardy

During the 1960s, there were evenings when the rifle club would compete in a match against an Army team, usually from 36 Engineer Regiment. The club had their rifles, and the Army team used Army issue guns, but they were no match for the rifle club. On one occasion, there was plenty of time left after the competition, and the soldiers suggested another shoot. To make it a bit more fun, Bearsted suggested that they shot left-handed, all except one, who was left-handed anyway, so he shot right-handed. At the end of the match at the Barracks, the door opened, and in came the cooks with curry for everyone. As it was a very cold evening, this was very welcome. However, it presented a problem when the 36 Engineers were invited to Bearsted for a return match, as there were no facilities for cooking. Terry Jones brought his caravan down and parked it outside, and it was arranged to have fish and chips for everyone. At the appropriate time the fish and chips were collected, and served from the caravan, together with beer and other drinks.

In 1967 the range was re-evaluated by the Ministry of Defence so that air pistols could be used. Dennis Gibbons later recalled an incident concerning a young member which occurred shortly after the re-evaluation of the range. He was about sixteen and an experienced shot, so he knew, as Dennis put it 'far more than was good for him' about fire-arms. He used to buy a box of fifty rounds and store it in the club cupboard. One night after he had been shooting, he missed the bus back to Maidstone, so he went to the railway station, only to discover that he had missed the train too. Desperate to return home, he decided to steal a car. In the course of breaking in to the vehicle, the son of the car's owner appeared on the scene. The young lad produced a pistol, so the owner's son very wisely left him and went to the telephone box by the shops at Chestnut Place to contact the police. Meantime, the young man decided that it would be better to walk home, and walked down to the Ashford Road. Once there, he thumbed a lift - from a police car which was out looking for him! It did not take long to clear up the matter of the firearm: he had a starting pistol which he had bored out to take a .22 round, and had taken some ammunition home with him that night. Perhaps he had done the same thing before. When the police picked him up he asked, 'Will this have a bad effect on me joining the Air Force?'[18]

In June 1978 Whitbread Fremlin's carried out major alterations to the White Horse, and this led them to alter access to the club. They also realised that there was no written agreement for the use of the range and saw it as an appropriate time to review the rent, and to draw up a proper tenancy agreement. There was a certain amount of dissension about this, as Whitbread maintained that the club had no security of tenure, while the club's solicitors believed that the club was protected by the Landlord and Tenant Act. The matter was settled with the brewery seeking a rental of £250 per annum, with the club to pay the insurance premiums, and to be responsible for internal repairs. However, in July 1979, the brewery intimated that they thought the club should pay a premium to the brewery insurers, and that both sides should include the phrase "fair wear and tear" into the repair agreements.[19]

In 1987 there was a new draft lease drawn up for three years at a rental of £225 per annum. The club offered to buy the site, but this offer was declined by Whitbread. Later correspondence suggests that they set up a sub-committee to investigate possible alternative sites which included an area behind the downside platform at Bearsted railway station, and in the approach road to the railway station at Hollingbourne. The club, under the chairmanship of Stanley Buss, approached the parish council for help in finding an alternative site, with a minimum area of 120 feet by 40 feet, but they were unable to assist. However, they did advise that if a suitable site was found, the scheme would be given positive consideration. The idea was subsequently abandoned.[20]

In 1989, the club established a link with Monschau, a club in Germany. Visits were exchanged between the two clubs, with anything between sixteen and twenty one members in attendance at the early fixtures. The visits continue to this day, with the home team almost always enjoying dominance in the matches.

The club celebrated its centenary in 2001 with two events: 23 September there was a Dewar competition in the morning, and a clay pigeon shoot in the afternoon at the Sittingbourne range. This was followed by a buffet meal at the Royal Oak on 28 September for club members. In the past hundred years, the highest number of club members at any one time was seventy one. Today there are around forty people that attend the club. Just as membership has varied, the number of rifle clubs has fluctuated and today the number has substantially decreased. In the Maidstone Division there remain just two: Bearsted and Wateringbury with Teston. In the Kent League there are nine and this includes Ashford, Black Lion (incorporating Snodland), Swalecliffe and Canterbury. Some clubs are affiliated to companies.

Reproduced courtesy of Bearsted Rifle Club

Bearsted has the most County teams, and were recently the County champions. They have four individual County champions, and one member has also shot for England. A small number of lady members have recently formed a team. Sadly, there are no longer shoulder to shoulder competitions due to reduced number of members in local clubs. Instead, there is a similar system to postal contest: members shoot a total of ten targets, which are then ratified and then sent to the Division marker, who decides the winner.

In 2003-4, the club purchased the freehold of the range, which has put them on a much more secure footing. To mark his four decades of service as Secretary, it was agreed to dedicate the range to Dennis Gibbons, pictured here on the left. Dennis sadly died in 2006 and he continues to be missed by the club. It is fitting that one of the oldest rifle ranges in the country now bears the name of such a dedicated member.

Rosemary Pearce

Rights of Way and Footpath Walking around Bearsted and Thurnham

In addition to the metalled roads of Britain, there is a vast network of green lanes, bridleways, and footpaths. From the earliest times these have provided links between communities and between people's homes and their churches, inns, workplaces (farms or manor houses) and, more recently, schools. Hence these paths often provide quicker, more direct routes than the roads. Kent is particularly well-endowed with such rights of way not only because it has always been the gateway to England from Continental Europe, but also because our ancient ancestors practised transhumance; moving their animals from agriculturally rich North Kent to graze in the Low Weald. A glance at a map of Kent will reveal the predominance of these NNE/SSW routes.

Local authorities were obliged by a Parliamentary Act of 1949 to prepare a definitive map and written statements concerning all green lanes, bridleways and footpaths within their areas. The issue of draft, and then provisional, maps allowed challenges to their correctness to be made through the courts. Thence, it was decided that definitive maps with an appropriate code for each path were to be compiled by county councils by mid-1982.

In Bearsted and Thurnham, some exploration of local paths was made by the several branches of the Women's Institute during the 1960s. However, systematic walking and assessment of routes on the draft definitive maps began with the formation of a Footpaths Group as part of the Bearsted and Thurnham Residents' Association founded in September 1972. The group's original aims were to walk all the paths within a circle of three-mile radius centred on Bearsted Green, familiarise local people with them and report faults and obstructions to the Kent County Council.

The group proceeded with this work, using draft definitive maps supplied by the county council under the leadership of Bob Tate with the able assistance of Elizabeth Harvie as secretary. A pattern of walking developed: longer walks of 6-8 miles, on the third Saturday afternoon of each month, excepting December when the walk was on Boxing Day and, from Spring to Autumn, shorter (Friday evening) walks were organised by Oliver Spendley. In these early days large numbers of people took part in the walks, many using them to exercise their dogs. Eventually, dogs had to be excluded because of risk of damage by the animals and, more so, by owners trying to recover lost pets. As a consequence numbers of walkers declined significantly.

This photograph accompanied a report in The Gazette newspaper, 19 August 1975 which featured the footpaths group in Ware Street. Shown as leading the group are Clifford Pearce (left) and Bob Gee.

Several members of the Association took on the task of suggesting, reconnoitring, and leading some of the walks, including the author. He thought that his map reading skills might be of value after attending a walk when the joint leaders lost their way, and completed a full circle in Hucking before finding a road and hurrying homeward.

Reproduced courtesy of Kent Messenger newspaper group

Today, when rights of way are clearly shown on the 1:25,000 scale Ordnance Survey maps, and their intersections with roads are usually marked by sign-stone and/or post, as this photograph on the right shows, it may be difficult to imagine the problems of finding and navigating paths in the 1970s. On one of their first exploratory walks, members of the Footpath Group failed to locate the access from Thurnham Lane to paths across the golf course!

Sometimes, walkers were accosted by irate farmers or landowners, one such typically claiming that his crop was being destroyed, and, on being shown the line on the draft definitive map, claiming (erroneously) that he had had the path officially diverted.

On one memorable early walk, a house owner, upset by the seemingly endless stream of people and dogs passing close to his windows, produced a ciné camera and started filming us, and issued a threat of legal action despite being shown the path on the map. That path remains unaltered to this day, although others in the same parish (Leeds) and similarly situated paths in Thurnham and Hollingbourne have since been officially diverted.

Reproduced courtesy of Michael Perring

The crossing of streams and rivers posed greater difficulties and in due course, Kent County Council provided bridges. Examples of these are situated at Ripple and across the Lilk stream and the River Len, near Otham Lane, and Milgate Park. Another was the bridge over the Lilk stream, on land below Gore Cottage, which was provided at the request of the Footpath Group. The level of the silted-up stream had risen above the original stone bridge. The group provided labour to improve the way across the boggy path and on the steep slope west of the bridge.

The land is now part of Bearsted Woodland Trust and the bridge has recently been replaced at a cost of £13,500 which was met by an appeal and a Kent Countryside Access Service donation. It was built very quickly by the 70 Gurkha Field Support Squadron (part of 36 Engineer Regiment) supervised by Dave Johnson from the trust. It was officially opened on 26 September 2007 by the Mayor of Maidstone (Bearsted resident, Richard Ash) and Major MacCullum. The trust has also installed alternative paths providing gentler gradients for the less able.

This photograph shows the bridge shortly after it was opened.

Reproduced courtesy of Malcolm Kersey

Rights of Way and Footpath Walking around Bearsted and Thurnham

Problems with rights of way were gradually overcome during the period when the Footpaths Group was represented on the Kent Rights of Way Council. However, the most rapid progress was made in the period when the Kent County Council devolved its authority to local councils. Rights of Way officers worked closely with local groups of walkers and riders, seeking their help with way-marking, path clearance and stile building projects. The Bearsted and Thurnham Footpaths Group was involved in these activities in parishes within its walking area. It was in this period that a long-standing problem with one path in Thurnham was resolved. The Footpaths Group had found it obstructed by derelict glasshouses on a smallholding between Milgate Park and Caring Lane. It had obviously not been used for many years, but provided an important link to paths in Leeds parish. Despite many representations, the matter was not resolved until a Maidstone Rights of Way Officer was able to divert it to the present route.

The Wildlife and Countryside Act of 1981 and subsequent amendments, and particularly the Countryside and Rights of Way Act of 2000, have given local authorities more responsibility for the maintenance of paths. There are now greater powers to enforce rights of way. Hence access to the marvellous countryside in and around the villages has improved in recent years. However, problems remain such as; flooding, deep mud, cattle, overgrown vegetation, inadequate waymarking, difficult and also broken stiles, like that on a path south of Harrietsham (below left). Occasionally wilful obstruction is encountered, as on the same path (below right):

The most common problem is that of unrestored paths following disturbance by ploughing. Although many farmers do compact paths during cultivation and burn ways through crops with weed killers as is shown for a path in Harrietsham (below left), others do neither. Sometimes, the width of the path is inadequate so that crops such as oil seed rape collapse across it, as on this path in Hollingbourne (below right), and make walking extremely arduous:

All reproduced courtesy of Michael Perring

Rights of Way and Footpath Walking around Bearsted and Thurnham

With government concern for the health of British citizens, walking has been advocated as a a means of reducing cardio-vascular problems, obesity, etc., and people are now often to be seen walking the roads, but less frequently, using footpaths. This is a pity, because navigating country paths requires not only greater co-ordination of eyes and legs, but also exercises the brain and most muscles in the body when walking in woodland, and climbing stiles, ascending or descending steep gradients, as shown below in these photographs.

Maybe the Footpath Group's survival is the best advertisement for the health benefits of country walking! Its parent body was absorbed into the more active Bearsted and Thurnham Amenity Society, recently relaunched as the Bearsted and Thurnham Society.

But it is the mind that really benefits from the delights rarely seen or felt when using the roads: the sights and sounds of the countryside, its vegetation, birds, butterflies and animals, extensive views as from this path above Lenham (shown below), and the ever-changing colours and cloud and crop patterns.

All reproduced courtesy of Michael Perring

The eagle-eyed walker may discover fossils left from when the landscape was formed below a warm sea, millions of years ago, or objects lost or discarded by our not so ancient ancestors. Some remains of their work are rather more obvious, but some can only be seen from footpaths: the White Horse Stone and Kits Coty are two examples. This photograph shows the author standing by Kits Coty:

Reproduced courtesy of Norman King

Over the years, the walking area to the west and south of Bearsted has become urbanised and the Footpath Group has sought quieter routes beyond the original three-mile circle. Recently, the walks have been routed and timed to accommodate particular views, flora, fauna and attractive buildings. Frequent use of the same paths has been avoided as much as possible.

Proposed building developments in Thurnham, Hollingbourne, Leeds and Langley threaten much of the Group's original walking area, the feeder routes to the Area of Outstanding Natural Beauty to the north and the enjoyment of the idyllic views from the crest of the North Downs. However, the Group currently continues to appreciate the sights and sounds of the lovely countryside around Bearsted and Thurnham and enjoys introducing it to newcomers.

Michael Perring

Roll Up! Roll Up! The Circus comes to Bearsted and Thurnham

Horseman and soldier Philip Astley created the circus in its present form but the origins of the entertainment go back a lot further. Parts can be traced to chariot racing and the athletic contests of ancient Rome. Strolling minstrels, court jesters, jugglers, mountebanks and rope walkers are thought to date from medieval times, whilst the equestrian displays are thought to date from displays mounted on village greens in the eighteenth century.[1]

Astley was particularly gifted in trick horse riding and so headed to London to display his equestrian talents. He opened a riding school near Westminster Bridge in 1768 where he taught riding in the morning and performed 'amazing feats of horsemanship' in the afternoon. The school had a circular arena because he and his riders realised that the centrifugal force gained by galloping around in a ring made it easier to keep their balance in performances, which could then be in full view of the audience. Astley's ring was made of rope and stakes, which he then called his circle or 'circus', a word which is based on the Greek for circle or ring, *kirkos*. Originally this meant a circular area enclosed by rows of seats for audiences watching such events as athletic games or chariot races.[2]

Within two years, Astley was able to purchase land near Westminster Bridge, and to create covered seating for his audience. In 1780 he built a wooden circus building but this was not without its risks as it burned down three times! Astley took the circus to Paris, founding it in Europe, and from there, other entrepreneurs took it to Russia and America.[3]

Later, the circus was to be presented in gigantic tents. Astley discovered that the optimum size for the ring was forty two feet in diameter. These tents are still called Big Tops after the biggest post used to erect them. There are still permanent buildings in Europe, but only two static circuses in England, in Great Yarmouth and in Blackpool.[4]

John Lawson's circus first came to Bearsted in 1988, and has visited every year since, entertaining many small children and families alike. This is a typical poster for the circus:

Reproduced courtesy of John Lawson Circus

At first, the Big Top was pitched on the green where the children's playground is now sited. Then it moved down to its present site, between the pond and the White Horse. When asked "Why Bearsted?" John's response was "Why not?" The village meets the criterion of a small(ish) community, and when the circus first arrived on the green, there was a good range of shops to supply commodities and to display advertisements.

John Lawson's Circus De Reszke was founded in 1974.[5] The founder, known as Captain John, was ringmaster as shown below in this undated photograph:

For five years, John Lawson's Circus appeared all over the country at open air events before purchasing a small second-hand 'flower show' marquee and a Bedford lorry. This photograph shows the Big Top which many local residents remember:

Both reproduced courtesy of John Lawson Circus

From then on, he began touring the country with what was possibly the smallest circus in Britain. The first venue was the playing field at Hadlow, near Tonbridge in September 1980. The show was very well received, and it went from strength to strength. Captain John passed away in November 1985, and leadership passed to his widow Vonni De Reszke and their children Daniela and Niven. They maintained the original intent of the show, to bring traditional live entertainment to small communities across the country, where such entertainment is rare.

Early in the twenty-first century, audiences were falling because there were so many other leisure attractions and because there were fewer shops in Bearsted and Thurnham, there were fewer opportunities to advertise. It was realised that the circus had to attract increasingly sophisticated audiences, and so new toilet facilities and luxury bucket seating for 500 people were provided and improved heating and lighting introduced.

The Big Top now takes five hours to erect, and two and a half hours to pull down. Family 'house' acts are now augmented by artistes from outside England, many from Eastern Europe; Hungary, Bulgaria and Romania. These people stay from March to October, and then return home for the winter, while the circus takes up a permanent home in Tonbridge. The photographs below show some of the current artistes working with the circus:

Both reproduced courtesy of John Lawson Circus

In 2004 negotiations brought about a new use for the Big Top when a Palm Sunday procession and service was initiated. The procession, led by a donkey, involved all the local churches. It came down from the railway station, went around the Green, and was followed by a service in the Big Top. It proved very popular and has been repeated in each subsequent year when the visit of the circus coincides with Palm Sunday.

The following photographs were taken during the procession in April 2007:

Reproduced courtesy of Douglas Chenery

Reproduced courtesy of Douglas Chenery

This is a slightly edited transcript of a report which appeared in the parish magazine, May 2004:

Palm Sunday in Bearsted

We met in the station car park, a gathering of people from the Churches in Bearsted, and the surrounding villages. We walked behind the donkey to the green, singing joyfully although those at the end of the column were always slightly behind the choirs at the front! As the head of the Procession reached the entrance to the Big Top, the tail was just passing The Oak. Such was the support for the occasion. Once in the Big Top, the marshals did an excellent job of settling us in, not an easy job in the comparative gloom. The clergy from the various churches welcomed us and young Alex Brabyn ran excitedly in, and with such confidence told us to prepare as Jesus was on his way, riding on a donkey, the crowd following singing praises and shouting Hosanna.

We all joyfully joined in singing the Palm Sunday hymns and enjoyed the theme supporting the performance of our own Bearsted Clown, Well Done Ed! Bishop Gavin talked on the meaning of Easter, and following the performance of Ed, spoke of 'the three S's; 'Silliness', which is felt about Jesus riding into Jerusalem where he knew the crowds wanted to see him killed; 'Sadness' felt by Jesus as He foresaw the events ahead resulting in the crucifixion, and 'Special;' as Jesus was and ever will be'. The message would appear to be that we are sometimes silly, sometimes sad, but always so very 'special' to God.

Reproduced courtesy of Holy Cross and St Mary's churches

Roll Up! Roll Up! The Circus comes to Bearsted and Thurnham

When the circus first came to Bearsted it included ponies, llamas and a performing pig. At the time Mote Park had a ban on entertainment involving live animals. They were tethered on the Green, and after the visit, several large, neatly cropped circles were to be seen. Then in 2001 there was an outbreak of foot and mouth disease, and so the movement of animals was banned. Those belonging to the circus were found new homes or not replaced as they died. The programme was revised so that it featured only human acts.

In 2007, John Lawson's Circus was voted the Best Small Circus in Great Britain. These are some of the staff who received the award:

Reproduced courtesy of John Lawson Circus

John Lawson's circus certainly adds a splash of colour to the Green in the springtime. Although it looks rather cluttered during a visit, overall there is very little environmental impact to the area. Shortly after the circus departs, there are only a few traces of sawdust and a ring of flattened grass to indicate that the Big Top has ever been there.

Rosemary Pearce

Drama in Bearsted and Thurnham

During the twentieth century, there were two main organisations active in producing plays and entertainments within the two villages: the Women's Institute and the Bearsted Amateur Dramatic Society. The latter was eventually borne out of the determination of the Rev Frederick Blamire Brown, vicar of Bearsted (1914 to 1928), to do something to encourage the younger people. Initially, after the First World War, 'Activities' were laid on at the vicarage; John and Margaret Blamire Brown could remember people eagerly arriving at the house for meetings organised by their father.

One of the first accounts concerning a formal entertainment appeared in the May edition of the parish magazine, 1923. This is a transcript of the report:[1]

> There was a most charming rendering of a fairy play, The Sleeping Beauty, at the Women's Institute on 3 and 4 April, in which some twenty of our young people took part. The stage management and dresses, for which Miss M Higgins was responsible, were unusually good, and the enunciation, dancing and action, of all the performers were above the average.
>
> Misses W Taylor, E Swift, C Holmes, B Hickmott, M Hickmott, F Hickmott, E Hazelden and A McConnell were the fairies. The Court party consisted of Misses L Blandford, E Wellard, F Hickmott, M Hickmott, M Higgins, R Hazelden, D Jeffrey and M Gorham. Other parts were taken by E McConnell, A Camfield, Wellard and Mr O Higgins.
>
> Very cordial congratulations to the whole team for the excellent performance and it was good to see a full house for each performance.

Reproduced courtesy of Holy Cross church

It is believed that this photograph is one of the scenes from The Sleeping Beauty. Regrettably, the identities of the players are not known.

Reproduced courtesy of Roseacre School

In 1924, the West Kent Federation of the Women's Institute held a pageant at Lullingstone Castle by the invitation of Lady Emily Hart Dyke. Members of the drama group from Bearsted Women's Institute performed in the section called, The Coming of Christianity in AD 597. The cast included Mildred Higgins, Muriel Moss, Mrs King, Alice Mendel, Mrs Groombridge and Eileen Blandford.

Drama in Bearsted and Thurnham

This is a section of the programme and a photograph of one of the scenes:

NORTH DOWNS DISTRICT.

District Secretary: Miss Farmer, Leeds & Broomfield W.I.

Stage Manager: Mrs. Mercer, Otham W.I.

Wardrobe Mistress: Mrs Richmond, Bearsted & Thurnham W.I.

Music Representative: Mrs. Kitchen, Boughton Malherbe W.I.

The Coming of Christianity, A.D. 597.

Characters.	Institute.
Bishop Luithard	Mrs. de V. Watson, Harrietsham W.I.
King Æthelbert	Mrs. Webb, Lenham W.I.
Queen Bertha	Mrs. Moss, Bearsted and Thurnham W.I.
Augustine	Miss Mendel, Bearsted and Thurnham W.I.
Messenger	Miss Champers, Otham W.I.
Æthelburga	Miss Eileen Blandford, Bearsted and Thurnham W.I.
Augustine's Chaplain	Miss M. Higgins, Bearsted and Thurnham W.I.

Courtiers, people, monks, soldiers, etc.: Members of Bearsted, Boughton Malherbe, Harrietsham, Langley, Leeds, Lenham and Otham Women's Institutes.

Reproduced courtesy of Jessie Page

Reproduced courtesy of Jenni Hudson

Drama in Bearsted and Thurnham

Bearsted Amateur Dramatic Society was founded in 1924 by Mr and Mrs Sierakowski borne out of the work at the vicarage. Under the direction of Miss Higgins, it produced Scenes from Early Church History, Robin Hood, The Charm School, Tilly of Bloomsbury, and several other short plays. The productions were of a high standard and usually performed in the Women's Institute hall.[2]

In December 1930 the Dramatic Society gave the first of a series of play readings every Monday. There was an admission charge of 6d.[3] Further plays and other productions took place during the 1930s, all faithfully recorded in the parish magazine. They were very popular and well attended. Many different local organisations benefited from the proceeds of admission to the productions including St Faith's Home.

This is a scene from an early production by the society: Damsel in Distress, a three-act farce by Ian Hay and P G Wodehouse, which was staged in 1931. The cast included members of the Foster family and Thomas Gilbert.

Reproduced courtesy of Sheila Foster

During 1933, a production of The Middle Watch – a Romance of the Navy, was mounted.[4] The cast included Stanley and Mildred Sierakowski, William Foster, Sarah Fuller, Rowland Gregory, Mildred Smith, Alice Camfield, Brian Brook, Martin Corps and Thomas Gilbert. This is a photograph from one of the scenes:

Reproduced courtesy of Jean Corps

This was followed in 1934 by Thark, a farce in three acts by Ben Travers The review in the parish magazine commented: [5]

> Thark was a good choice from the point of view of the audience – a point which must always be taken into consideration – was amply experienced by the whole hearted enjoyment and rapturous applause that greeted the performance on the first night...
>
> ...Stanley Sierakowski's performance as the irresponsible Romy was most delightful and showed an appreciation of its absurdities, whilst winning sympathy from the audience in his many predicaments.

Reproduced courtesy of Holy Cross church

In 1935, the Kentish Express newspaper highlighted the work of the society in a special report which gave a good overall impression. This is a slightly edited transcript:

> ...the society is limited in its constitution to fifty members. These are at all times forthcoming and there has always been a waiting list. This goes to show that the human element on the stage is very much alive in Bearsted. A series of one-act plays and sketches are presented during the year at the invitation of local organisations, and the society gives an annual entertainment at the County Sanatorium, Lenham.
>
> All the arrangements and work in connection with the scenery, effects and lighting are made by members of the society. The officers are - President; Mrs A J Brook, Director and Producer; Mr Sierakowski, Stage Manager; Mr J C Ollett, Stage Carpenter; Mr L Buller, Committee; Mesdames Abery, Brook, Groombridge, Sierakowski, Messrs Corps, Ollett and Sierakowski.
>
> Approached by a representative of the Kentish Express for his views on the amateur movement in drama today, Mr Sierakowski said that it was a sincere and hard working group which was in fact truly representative of English drama. 'Dramatic instinct should be encouraged in young people,' he said, 'as it is a thing of beauty. It is a creative and expressive art to be held and developed. For students of drama everything should hold beauty'.
>
> Mr Sierakowski would like to see a revival of the plays of the type of The Scarlet Pimpernel. 'You may say', he said, 'where are our Terrys, Trees and Irvings? But I say, give us the script and we will find the substance, apropos of our two modern masterpieces Noel Coward's Cavalcade and Sheriff's Journey's End. In the latter, Stanhope, Raleigh and Uncle will live long in our memories.'
>
> Above: Mr Stanley Sierakowski

Reproduced courtesy of Kent Messenger newspaper group

Just before the outbreak of the Second World War, the officers of the Dramatic Society comprised: [6]

President:	Mrs H J Brook
Director:	Mr E S Sierakowski
Hon Secretary and Treasurer:	Mrs M Sierakowski
Committee:	Mrs Abery, Mrs Groombridge and Mr Ollett

Reproduced courtesy of Holy Cross church

Drama in Bearsted and Thurnham

During the war, the society decided to do everything possible to continue readings and, perhaps, mount productions, but there were problems with interruptions to rehearsals by air raids. Assembling sufficient people for productions was not straightforward; many were undertaking important shift work with the Observer Corps, Home Guard or fire-watching. The Women's Institute hall was in almost constant use as canteen, so it was not always available as a venue. Despite these difficulties, some plays were produced including works by Ian Hay and J B Priestley which were a brief respite to wartime anxieties.[7] The Women's Institute drama group was also active during the war and in 1942 produced an excellent rendition of Jane Eyre.[8]

After the war, the Bearsted Amateur Dramatic Society was re-launched and in 1945 three plays were performed: Little Ladyship, a comedy by Ian Hay, A Man's House, by John Drinkwater and Living Room, by Esther McRacken.[9] This is a typical scene from Little Ladyship:

Reproduced courtesy of Thomas Gilbert

In 1946, a production of Noel Coward's Blithe Spirit was performed by the society. Bearsted resident and mayor of Maidstone, Samuel Lyle, was keen to support the production and brought the council to a performance. The congratulatory letter he wrote to Stanley Sierakowski is reproduced on the next page.

Between 1946 and 1948 there were further productions by the Dramatic Society which was joined by some members of the Women's Institute who were interested in drama.

Towards the end of 1948 there was a production of The Bully, a comedy. This was staged by the Women's Institute but the play was preceded by a song recital by Miss Arabella Tulloch. During November the Dramatic Society staged a three-act comedy, Fly Away Peter, by the Ashford playwright A P Dearsley. A review appeared in the Kent Messenger and revealed that the society had received a telegram of good wishes from the author. The newspaper thought the society was probably the first amateur company to present this topical comedy of a suburban family. The parish magazine advised readers wishing to purchase tickets that they could be obtained at the Box Office at Yeoman Nurseries.[10] It would be good to think that the purchase of tickets was regarded as a separate transaction from ordering potatoes!

The letter of thanks and congratulations from Samuel Lyle:

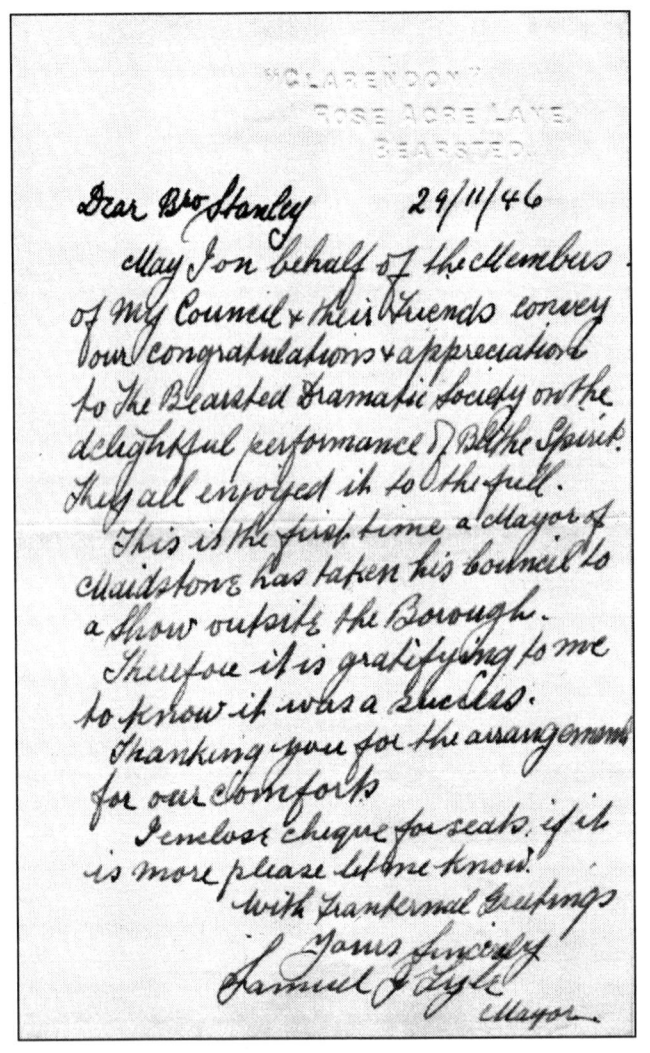

Reproduced courtesy of Bearsted and District Local History Society

1949 was a significant year for the dramatic society as it was asked by the organisers of the Royal Air Force Week to present a production of Flare Path by Terence Rattigan at the Corn Exchange. Further distinction was achieved when Dame Sybil Thorndyke agreed to become patron as a mark of confidence by a professional actor in the work of the society.[11] This is one of the scenes from the production:

Reproduced courtesy of Kent Messenger newspaper group

This slightly edited report, which accompanied the photograph, in the Kent Messenger commented:

> ## *Maidstone remembers epic battle of 'the few'*
>
> ### Anniversary Celebrations help funds of RAF organisations
>
> ...It is difficult to think of a more apt play for Battle of Britain Week than Terence Rattigan's Flare Path, and it is difficult to imagine a better amateur presentation of the play than that which is being given by the Bearsted Dramatic Society in the Corn Exchange...the atmosphere of stress underlying the bright insouciance of typical RAF crews is brilliantly captured in an excellent production.
>
> A strong and well-balanced cast skilfully directed by Stanley Sierakowski re-creates vividly the authentic spirit of the time when scores of inns near scores of bomber stations were the daily scenes of unspectacular courage in the face of heartbreak and under the ordeal of waiting for the return of men who all too often did not come back.
>
> Wilfred Green, as the bomber pilot who feared he was 'lacking in moral fibre' gives a superb interpretation of a young man with a bright exterior masking the hidden fear that his nerve was going whilst Gladys Boddy, his wife, torn between passionate love for one man and protective love for another, gives a performance of considerable power.
>
> Kay Collins, the ex-barmaid wife of a Polish count, is triumphantly successful in creating the cheerful vulgarity of a girl with a deep, warm generosity of heart. As the self-centred, vain, yet, pathetic figure of an ageing film actor out of tune with the spirit of the age, Wilfred Hopkins is excellent and Stanley Sierakowski would be difficult to better as the Polish count.
>
> Eric Weale, extracts all the dry humour latent in the character of Sgt. Miller, the rear gunner, while Pat Lattin has a good time with the rather grotesque piece of caricature which passes as Sgt. Miller's wife. Others in a good cast are Margery Hopkins, Norman Ross, Phillip Smith and John Miller.
>
> Last night, the Mayor, Sir Garrard Tyrwhitt-Drake, congratulated the cast upon their performance and expressed thanks to both the company and the audience for their support of the charities for which the week is being held.

Reproduced courtesy of Kent Messenger newspaper group

Members of the Society gained further technical insights into their work on 23 January 1950 when Mr Hughes, the County Drama Advisor spoke to them on Drama, Lighting and Speech. He was able to highlight an extensive need for drama in the rural areas of the county and appealed to the society, with twenty five years experience to take their expertise to other areas of Kent. He concluded with some pithy advice those who wished to make the stage a profession: 'Don't'.[12]

Performances of play readings, three act comedies and one-act plays by the Women's Institute and the dramatic society continued throughout the first half of the 1950s.

During May 1951, the Society presented Bona Venture by Charlotte Hastings.[13] The parish magazine advised that a taxi service could be arranged for people who lived in the Ashford Road and Royston Road and wished to attend performances. The fare would be approximately two shillings a head for the two journeys. Tickets for the show were priced at three shillings or one shilling and sixpence.[14]

Drama in Bearsted and Thurnham

In 1952 the Women's Institute hall was once again filled to capacity. Two short plays were presented by the Women's Institute drama group. The programme also included an hour's magic display given by Richard Lambert and Larry Ross. This advertisement shows one of the tricks which was successfully performed. The reviewer subsequently commented that the magic was very clever, but even Mr Lambert could not convince the audience that he could eat razor blades! [15]

DO NOT BE MISLED!

If you need the ORIGINAL SENSATIONAL Swallowing Razor Blades Trick GET IT FROM THE MAN THAT FIRST PERFORMED IT IN ENGLAND.

From the Man that Startled the Members of the Magic Circle, and International Magicians. Who also made a Film for the Ideal Sound Cinemagazine.
Photographs in the leading Daily Papers, etc.

THE EFFECT.

Reprinted from the Leading Music Hall Paper, "The Era.":—
What to do with your old razor blades? In a new Trick, performed for the first time in England, Mr. George Davenport showed us what he did with his. Placing Ten Blades one at a time on his tongue, he drank them down with a little water, a length of thread followed with more water, to re-appear a moment afterwards with the blades gleaming at intervals along the thread."

A Sensation on any Programme.

NOTE THESE APPLAUSE-WINNING POINTS!

Performer's mouth may be examined before and immediately after the trick, proving that there is no deception! Water is unmistakably drunk and the blades and thread to all appearances swallowed! Finger tips only used for production and you may pause at any moment to show blades coming direct from mouth. Trick may be performed anywhere. Clean, efficient, it is a beautifully made piece of apparatus as originally used by Mr. Davenport.

Imitated but far from equalled.

Get the original Swallowing Razor Blades and have your audiences gasping!

Price 10/6.

Copyright by L. Davenport & Co., London.

Reproduced courtesy of Ian Lambert

The dramatic society continued until 1956. As other popular entertainments, such as television, became more widely available, the membership and large audiences once attracted by productions could not be sustained. The Kent Messenger reported: [16]

> **Bearsted Dramatic Society finishes after 33 years**
>
> Thirty three years ago a number of young people connected with Bearsted Church became interested in amateur theatricals. Encouraged by their success with one-act plays they became ambitions and later the Bearsted Dramatic Society was formed. From then on, full-length productions were given in the W I hall to crowded houses, and during the winter months, members enjoyed weekly play-readings. Proceeds of the plays were for charitable organisations, and well over £700 was given away.
>
> There had been a waiting list for membership, but at a special meeting on Monday, a different story was told. The membership was only 17 and the chairman Mr M W Corps, said the young people could not be persuaded to take an interest and there was a lack of support in plays produced by the society. He thought perhaps television had something to do with it. They could not, he said, continue the society at a financial loss and as much as the committee regretted it, they would have to wind up the society.
>
> After a long discussion this was agreed to and also to offer the society's lighting and scenery to the Women's Institute. It was agreed to donate £35 which belonged to the society to the Mission to Seamen, a Mission in which Mrs Sierakowski, a founder-member of the society was greatly interested. Thanks were accorded to Mr Sierakowski, for many years, producer, to Miss Bennett, hon. secretary and Mrs Fletcher, treasurer.

Reproduced courtesy of Kent Messenger newspaper group

Although the Dramatic Society had ceased, the drama group of the Women's Institute continued to mount productions. In November 1957, they presented a three-act play called Before You Leap written by a Women's Institute member.[17]

In more recent years, the drama group has staged concerts and plays. Productions now include a pantomime which is produced every two years. The group continues to enjoy great success and performances remain immensely popular with audiences from Bearsted and Thurnham.

Ian Lambert

Scouting and Guiding in Bearsted and Thurnham

The Scout Association celebrated a national centenary in 2007 and GirlGuiding UK is set to mark a centenary in 2010. In 2012, Bearsted Scout Group will also be a hundred years old. What makes both of these movements so special and why do they continue to appeal to young people today?

Scouts and Cubs

The Scout Law, devised by Robert Baden-Powell, actively promoted an almost-revolutionary belief that friendly participation with other Scouts was undertaken regardless, of rank, colour, nationality, wealth or class. This appealed to prospective members from the outset.

An enrolment certificate survives for James Elliott, who was one of fourteen boys that joined on 24 July 1912. James was patrol leader 1912-1914 and went on to become the Scout Master in 1920. Other boys from Bearsted and Thurnham that were founder Scouts included Harry Smith, (who also later became Scout Master), James Flood, W White, and two boys known only by the names of Delves and Hooper.[1]

This photograph shows the front of James' certificate:

Reproduced courtesy of David and Theresa Elliott

The troop was one of the earliest in Kent and was named The Scarlet Pimpernels. The name was taken from Baroness Orczy's most famous fictional character. The Baroness, who lived at Snowfield, was one of the founding sponsors. Montague Barstow, her husband, painted the first troop flag which bears an appropriate scarlet pimpernel flower. To this day, Bearsted Scouts are known as The Scarlet Pimpernels. The colours of the scout group scarf, red and green, reflect the flower and an attractive, stylised pimpernel embroidered badge decorates the back.[2]

Scouting and Guiding in Bearsted and Thurnham

In October 1912, a rally of over three hundred local Scouts took place in Sandling Park and boys from the troop eagerly attended, keen to know more about scouting. George Draikes was the first Scout Master but he died, very unexpectedly, in February 1913, aged only 22. At his funeral, which took place at Holy Cross church, the cortege was met by the troop and was accompanied by other Scout Masters and Scouts from the district.[3] George was laid to rest in the churchyard and his gravestone proudly bears the Scout Association emblem.

Burton Tobitt was the next Scout Master and under his leadership, amongst many activities was an enjoyable outing to London in September 1913. They also attended another rally of Scouts at Sandling Park.[4] This photograph was taken during the camp and includes James Elliott, Harry Smith, W White, and J Cowell. Note also the pimpernel flag on the left hand side of the picture:

Reproduced courtesy of David and Theresa Elliott

The Scouts regularly held concerts and entertainments, although it is not clear whether they met at a special headquarters and where this might have been located. Details of the activities were regularly included in Bearsted parish magazine. This is a slightly edited transcript of a report from 1914: [5]

Scarlet Pimpernel Troop of Boy Scouts

At the Bearsted Institute on Wednesday, 27 May, a very excellent programme was provided by the Bearsted and Thurnham Scarlet Pimpernel Troop of Boy Scouts. After a pianoforte solo by Miss Minnie Baker, the curtain rose on a picturesque camp fire scene in which boys recited and sang Scout choruses and songs, which were loudly applauded by the large audience which completely filled the hall. Assistant Scout Master Cowell and Scout J Flood then gave a most satisfactory First Aid Display treating Scouts Elliot, Barling and Rumble for fractured arms, legs and jaw.

A sketch, *White Eagle's Revenge*, written by Scout G Fuller, proved a very thrilling episode and was brought to a conclusion by a realistic struggle between Cowboys and Indians in full war paint. The Assistant Scout Master's song, *PC 49*, was enthusiastically encored, as was also *Redwing*, sung amidst appropriate scenery by Scout C Hyde, attired as an Indian girl. A sketch entitled *Mr Ford Turns Up*, was particularly well done and Scouts G Fuller as a shrewish housewife, W Wilkinson as her long-suffering husband and N Harnett as a blustering seaman, succeeded in keeping their delighted audience in perpetual laughter. The troop sang some of Scott Gatty's ever popular Plantation songs and at the end of the programme, Brigadier General A J Whitacre Allen gave the Scouts a most inspiring address.

A most successful evening terminated with Scouts giving hearty cheers for General Allen and for Baroness Orczy who had kindly rehearsed them for the entertainment.

Reproduced courtesy of Holy Cross church

During the First World War the Scout Group was disbanded and it took some time to revive it after the Armistice. However, by 1927, the headquarters of the scout troop was at the home of Scout Master, R C Gregory; a house called Hill View, in Tower Lane. The Assistant Scout Master was Henry Elliott, a relative of founder-scout, James Elliott.[6]

During the 1930s, there were two Patrols and many weekend camps were held in the grounds of Mr Watson's house on the Ashford Road. In July 1935, Scouts Baker, Barton, Blundell and Old showed the values of the Scout Promise to the wider community: they witnessed a terrible accident involving two motorcars on the Ashford Road. At great danger to themselves, they extracted the occupant of the burning car through the sunroof. The man was badly burned, but survived.[7]

In 1938, meetings were held in a room above Westwood Garage in Thurnham Lane. The premises were owned by Mr Waight and were next door to the shops in Chestnut Place.[8] Bernard Croucher joined in 1938 and recalled that some of the activities were highly energetic:

> I remember helping to pull and push the two-wheeled trek cart loaded with camping gear from headquarters, between the butcher shop and Westwood Garage, to the Green. We also pulled the cart up Thurnham Lane, past Thurnham School and St Mary's church to a field near the Black Horse. We managed to find a flat part to pitch a bell tent. Our sleeping and lying positions inside it was 'all toes to the middle pole'. Scout Master Bert Smith had his own tent. A favourite game while camping involved a small party going to the highest point at Thurnham Castle and sending back a message by semaphore to camp...

Meetings of the scout troop were formally suspended during the Second World War, but the members were certainly encouraged, and expected, to be involved in such wartime activities as the local branch of the National Waste Paper Collection. Along with the Guides, they attended church services held on the Green. A number of Scouts and Guides also accompanied the Beating of The Bounds ceremonies in their uniforms as this undated photograph shows:

Reproduced courtesy of Jessie Page

The scout troop restarted in 1950: the Scout Master was Henry Elliott and he was assisted by Jim Peat who had been a Senior Scout with Maidstone Grammar School Troop. Bearsted now had a Wolf Cub pack too; Akela was Mrs Matthews and her assistant was Miss Joyce Hunt, later to be Mrs Dobson. Joyce Dobson became Akela in 1951 and remained with the Cubs until her retirement in 1989. She was an exceptional leader, always willing to help and embodied the main spirit of Scouting, always giving her best and serving others regardless of the reward. This is a record of some of the activities during a typical meeting: [9]

Cubs Meeting 11 April 1951	
6pm	Subs and inspection
6.10pm	Collection of Bob a Job Money
6.15pm	Nature Observation Game
6.30pm	Spaceship and Rocket Game
6.45pm	Instruction groups for the Highway Code, Knots, Cleanliness, Semaphore and First Aid
7.20pm	Grand Howl

Meetings were held in an ancient timber-framed Nissen hut dating from the First World War, which was located in Church Lane. The hut held the village fire pump, which had to be wheeled out of the way before meetings and then carefully wheeled back afterwards! In 1951, the Scouts were advised that the land had been sold for housing and were offered the hut, provided it could be located elsewhere. A site was offered on the Snowfield estate in Roseacre Lane by Captain John Litchfield.

A massive effort to raise funds to renovate the building, was led by a Parents Association chaired by Richard Lambert. After much dedicated hard work, it was officially opened 25 July 1953 on the new site. This photograph shows Captain Litchfield receiving the key from Wolf Cub Robert Whibbley during the opening ceremony: [10]

Both reproduced courtesy of Bearsted Scout Group

In 1954 the troop held their first camp after the Second World War, at Broadstone Warren in Sussex. All the equipment travelled in a Roseacre Laundry van as the owner, Mr Gregory, was the Group Chairman and a keen supporter. It was the start of many such camping trips.[11]

A troop of Senior Scouts was set up in 1956 and soon became of the largest in Maidstone District; Senior Scout Master was Ted Francis. Two boys from the First Bearsted Troop, Michael Stratton and John Parks, attended the Scout Jubilee World Jamboree in Sutton Colefield on 1957. They camped in the Lake District and were most surprised to see the Jamboree featured on a newsreel when they visited the cinema in Keswick! In 1958, the first Bearsted Scout to achieve the Queen's Scout award, the highest honour in Scouting, was Roger Hall.[12]

In 1962 Eric Haydock joined the Wolf Cub Pack. It was the start of a very distinguished career in scouting: he was later a Scout, Venture Scout and Assistant Group Scout Leader. His thorough participation the movement and entries into many local events such as Bearsted Fayre, the Gang Show (both in Maidstone and a local one held at the Memorial Hall), and even broadcasting on Radio Medway, led to the award of a Medal of Merit in recognition of outstanding services. Eric was sometimes assisted by his wife Sue in the broadcasts. His untimely death in 1994 was a great loss. This undated photograph was taken before the transmission of Guylines, a programme specifically for Scouts and Guides on Radio Medway. He is standing, third from the left in the back row: [12]

By 1964 it was realised that the number of boys attending Scouts and Cubs was too great to be safely accommodated in the Nissen hut. After some negotiation with Bearsted Parish Council, the Scouts moved to the Glebe and met there for many years.[13] A further move was achieved in 1988 when fresh premises were officially opened in Church Landway on 11 June, by Joyce Dobson, Cub Scout Leader. This picture was taken during the opening ceremony:

Both reproduced courtesy of Bearsted Scout Group

<u>Left to right</u>: Colin Musselwhite, Group Scout Leader; Joyce Dobson and Alan Morton, District Commissioner.

Throughout the 1960s, Bearsted and Thurnham developed; new housing estates were built and many more families moved into the area. In response to demand, two new cub packs were opened for boys who lived on the south side of the Ashford Road. They met at Madginford Junior School with Mark Akhurst and Audrey Fermor as Assistant Cub Scout Leaders. Eventually, all these packs transferred to the Scout Hut in Church Landway.[14]

During this decade, Scouting began to change. A new uniform was introduced and new regulations were drawn up; some of the rules for awarding badges became much more demanding and stringent. Michael Ede became the first Bearsted Venture Scout to achieve the Queen's Scout award in 1971 under the new rules. The work undertaken for the award included a 150 mile journey through the mountains of Morocco and twenty eight days attending an Outward Bound course in the Bavarian Alps.[15]

In the 1980s, the Scout Association introduced the idea of Beaver scout colonies for boys aged six to eight. Two colonies opened at Bearsted in 1986 under the leadership of Angela D'Souza and Pam Rawlings. A further colony opened at Downswood Community Centre on 25 April 1990. This colony then transferred to Bearsted Scout Hut in 1998 with Robert Reid as the Beaver Scout Leader.[16]

This photograph shows the badge that was designed and worn by the Scout Group in 1997 to commemorate its eighty fifth anniversary:

Reproduced courtesy of Malcolm Kersey

Guides and Brownies

At the scouting movement's first rally, held at the Crystal Palace in 1909, a small group of girls turned up. They represented hundreds of other girls and insisted that they wanted to be Scouts too. In an age when skirts were ankle length and young ladies never ran, the idea of girls being involved in camping, hiking and similar activities received a mixed response. Angry critics denounced 'girl scouting' as a 'mischievous new development', a 'foolish and pernicious movement' and an 'idiotic sport'.[17]

However, Robert Baden-Powell evidently was thinking about a scheme for girls and in 1910 he formed the Girl Guides. Agnes Baden-Powell, Robert's sister, was initially appointed to look after it but in 1918 Olave Baden-Powell, Robert's wife, took over and became Chief Guide. In 1914, the Rosebuds were formed for girls between 8 and 11 years of age. They were later known as Brownies.

It is not entirely clear when Brownies and Girl Guides began in Bearsted and Thurnham as the records to confirm a specific date do not appear to have survived. It is possible that the schemes actually began in the villages before the First World War but, like the Scouts, were suspended indefinitely during the hostilities and it took some time to be re-established. Norah Giles (née Pettipiere) could certainly remember attending Brownie meetings in the 1920s.

This is one of the earliest photographs of the Bearsted Brownies. It is believed to have been taken around 1925:

Back Row, left to right: Eileen Blandford, Margaret Oswald Jones, Dolly Foster, Jean Wilkinson, Kath Playfoot
Front Row, left to right: -----, Norah Pettipiere, Dorothy Frost.

In 1936, Pamela Thorpe started a Brownie Pack. Doris Britcher recalled that Pamela was a very popular leader and as Brown Owl, would invite the Brownies to tea at her house on the Ashford Road once a year during the summer. Doris progressed to the Girl Guides when she was ten years old. She enjoyed the activities and the joint meetings with Companies from Leeds, Harrietsham and Hollingbourne. There were two Captains that Doris particularly remembered: Miss Eileen Blandford, later to be Mrs Howard, and Joyce Hunt. Eileen lived in a cottage called The Retreat opposite the pond on the Green. She had no favourites in the company, but everyone was made to feel that their presence mattered.

Eileen and Joyce ran the Guides for many years before Joyce became involved with the Scout Group. This photograph shows one of Eileen's many warrants:

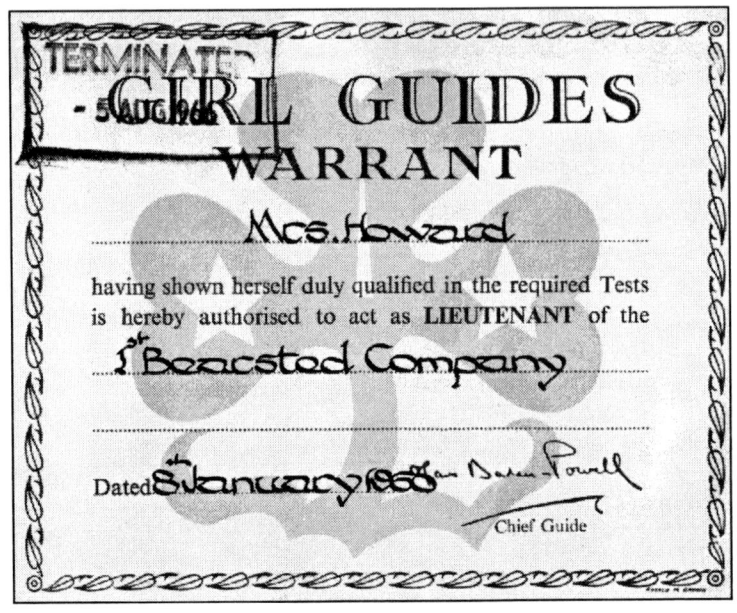

Both reproduced courtesy of Jenni Hudson

Scouting and Guiding in Bearsted and Thurnham

Many local people offered help in running activities for the Brownies and Guides. Doris particularly remembered that Mrs Grout, allowed her house, Rusaker, to be used to work for badges that had a practical element to them. In this way, many Guides earned their Homemaking badges.

The company ran many activities for the girls in the village. Meetings were usually held at the Memorial Hall. Camps took place locally in the large gardens of houses such as Snowfield and Commonwood but were also held in smallholdings such as Artily on the Spot Farm Estate. Local farmers were also happy to give permission for camps, as they knew that the land would be well-respected. Other camps slightly further afield were the Brabourne estate in Mersham and the grounds of Homewood School, Tenterden. In July 1939 there was a Guide camp at Maidenhead, Berkshire during which this photograph was taken:

This photograph of the 1st Bearsted Guide Company was taken around 1940:

Both reproduced courtesy of Jenni Hudson

<u>Back row from left</u>: Barbara Spendley, Betty Gibbons, Joyce Hunt, Pam Batkin, ----, Evelyn White, Betty Ware, ---, June Monckton, Marion Smith, Pam Sendles, Audrey Lee, Pat Batkin
<u>Front row from left</u>: Muriel Tutt. Ann Cheshire Martin, Ann Coveney, Marion Shales, Barbara Cox, Christine Lee.

Scouting and Guiding in Bearsted and Thurnham

The Brownies and Guides regularly held shows and other entertainments. This photograph of the Guide Company was taken after an entertainment held in the Women's Institute hall on 22 May 1943:

Back row includes: Captain Eileen Blandford, Audrey Lee, Christine Lee, Marion Smith, Betty Vane, Betty Baisley, Joyce Hunt, Evelyn White, Barbara Spendley, Pam Batkin, Betty Gibbons, Ann Cheshire Martin, Muriel Tutt, June Monckton, Pat Batkin, Lieutenant Joyce Eversden
Centre Row includes: Marian Shales, Peggy Ann Jessel, Pam Sendles, Barbara Cox, Audrey Humphrey, Ann Coveney
Front Row includes: Celia Pantin, Dorothy Green, Margery Green, Margery Avery, Eileen Chittenden.

Camping with outings continued to be popular after the war. In 1960, a camp was held at Mersham. There was an outing to Littlestone and this photograph was taken during the day:

Both reproduced courtesy of Jenni Hudson

Back Row includes: Mary Kirk, Angela Howard, Hilary Ravenscroft, Monica Harden, Janet Woodruff, Eileen Howard
Centre row includes: Elizabeth Wisby, Lorna Gardner, Penny Keast
Front row includes: Sally Avis, Hilary Hodges, Rosalind Cooper, Judith Hodges.

Another regular event which continues to this day is the church parade. This undated photograph shows the company leaving Holy Cross church after a service:

Reproduced courtesy of Jenni Hudson

The Brownies and Guides occasionally hold joint meetings with the Scout Group. In the 1950s they were sometimes known as Great Camp Fire evenings and were hugely enjoyed. This photograph was taken on 16 December 1950 and shows a joint Christmas party in the Scout Hut in Church Lane. Leaders included in the photograph are Mrs M E Matthews (Cub Mistress), Miss J Hunt (Assistant Cub Mistress), Mr H W Elliott (Group Scout Master), Mr James Peat (Assistant Scout Master), also present was Eileen Howard:

Reproduced courtesy of Doris Britcher

In 1984, the parish council offered the Girl Guides a lease for some ground in Church Landway alongside the Scout Hut. It was a wonderful opportunity for the Guides to have a base of their own in the parish and was warmly welcomed by leaders and parents alike. An immense amount of hard work and fundraising by everyone involved in the Guide movement in the local area took place. Construction of the permanent premises began in 1989, but the fitting out and equipping took nearly three more years. It was officially opened on 31 January 1993. This photograph was taken at the opening: Lorraine Wilkin, District Commissioner, is being handed the keys by George Wright, chairman of the Bearsted Guides and Brownies Supporters Association:

Reproduced courtesy of John Wardley and Kent Messenger newspaper group

The Movements Today

There continues to be an excellent spirit of mutual co-operation and help between the leaders of both the Scouts and GirlGuiding, assisted by the close proximity of the Scout and Guide huts in Church Landway.

For nearly twenty years both groups largely ran and benefited from the Fayre held on the Green, (although for a time it seems to have been known as a Fete). The event was then revived in another form for the Silver Jubilee in 1977. [18]

A Summer Fayre, specifically for the Guides and Brownies, is held in the grounds of Snowfield. The front of a programme for 2002 is shown here.

Girlguiding Bearsted District

Invite you to their

Summer Fayre

at

Snowfield, Yeoman Lane

on

Saturday 13th July 2002

at 1:30 - 3:45

Admission: Adults 50p Children 20p

Reproduced courtesy of Malcolm Kersey

Both groups continue to participate in Bearsted Fayre, and many local people are of the opinion that the event would not be the same without the Scouts ably running the burger and hot dog stall! One event held during the Fayre which has been the subject of keen rivalry between both groups is the tent pitching competition. Success is never guaranteed by any one team and in 1970, the Scouts specifically noted: [19]

> **Bearsted Fete**
>
> The weather was extremely good to us and the Fete was a great success. The results are now known and the total of £3,000 has been divided equally between the Scout and Guide Groups. We would like to thank the Fete Committee, both from ourselves and from our sister organisations, for running such a fine event. The Scout Band from Gravesend, we thought magnificent and proved their merit a week later by winning the Kent County Supreme Champions Trophy for Boys Bands. The Scout versus Guide Competition resulted in a win once again from the Guides who very ably showed their prowess in erecting a tent, lighting a fire and brewing a cup of tea all within 4 minutes!

Reproduced courtesy of Bearsted Scout Group

2007 was the Centenary of the Scout Association which was marked by many special events. 26-27 May a Centenary camp was held at the Scout hut in Church Landway. During August, there was a Jamboree in Essex which was attended by four Scouts as representatives from Bearsted. On 1 August, members of the movement all over the world took part in Scouting Sunrise during which they renewed their Promise. Some Scouts from Bearsted even chose to renew their promise as dawn broke at Thurnham Castle.

This photograph shows the Centenary badge which was worn during 2007:

Reproduced courtesy of Malcolm Kersey

Plans are well underway to mark the Centenary of GirlGuiding UK with a very full programme of events throughout Britain and the wider world in 2010.

Today all sections of the Scout Association and GirlGuiding UK continue to be popular with the younger representatives of the community. Perhaps the real secret of the appeal is that they have moved with the times. Both organisations have retained the values of dedicated service to all of the community but include contemporary schemes such as Jamboree on the Air and Jamboree on the Internet, and Guiding Overseas Linked with Development projects. Through these schemes both movements have a truly international modern appeal, particularly as travel and communication becomes faster, quicker and easier.[20]

Bearsted Scout Group today includes Beavers, Cubs, Scouts, Young Leaders and Explorers. All of these accept both boys and girls. They are based at the Scout Hut in Church Landway. The Bearsted branch of GirlGuiding UK includes Rainbows, Brownies and Girl Guides, Ranger Guides and Young Leaders. The majority of these sections meet at the Guide Hut also located in Church Landway but some Brownies and Rainbows still meet in the Memorial Hall and Madginford Hall.

Kathryn Kersey

Traditional pub games and other miscellaneous pastimes

A great variety of other traditional pursuits and miscellaneous pastimes have taken place in Bearsted and Thurnham. Some of them enjoyed a brief heyday but others have continued to be pursued to this day.

Pub Games

Public houses were once largely a male domain in which to enjoy a pint and a traditional game of darts, cards or pool. Games of quoits and darts were once regularly played in both villages. Quoits is a pub game played throughout Britain and as far away as South America. There are various forms and is thought to be related to an earlier game which involved throwing a horseshoe at a pin in the ground.[1]

A transcript of a report from the Kent Messenger, 19 May 1894:

> The Members of the Yeoman Quoits club held at the Kentish Yeoman, Bearsted, are open to receive challenges from other clubs within a distance of six miles from the clubhouse…

A year later, the Kent Messenger reported on 27 July 1895:

> On Monday evening, a friendly visit was made to the Bearsted Quoits Club by the players at East Farleigh who were chaperoned by Mr J W Tapsfield. A well-contested match was played which ended in favour of Bearsted. A smoking concert was afterwards held at the Club House, Mr J W Tapsfield presiding. The harmony was sustained, amongst others by the Chairman, Messrs R Fleet, Water, Crittenden and Dalton.

Both reproduced courtesy of Kent Messenger newspaper group

Quoits continued to be popular in the 1920s; the Bell Inn at Thurnham entered a team in the Maidstone and District Quoits League. Games of darts were also played at the Bell Inn and in 1937 this photograph of a team outside the establishment was taken:

Reproduced courtesy of Norah Giles

The tradition of the Bell Inn entering teams in local sports leagues continued for many years.[2]

During the Second World War, it did not take long for The White Horse to become part of the circuit of public houses visited by airmen from the Royal Air Force which were based at Detling aerodrome. This included sergeants from Thurnham Court, and their officers based at The Friars and Cobham Manor. A magazine, called the Detling Bulletin, was produced by some of the staff at the aerodrome between November 1939 and August 1940. It cost three pence and carried many local advertisements.[3]

This is a typical advertisement from the Detling Bulletin, showing what games were available:

> **WHITE HORSE INN**
> **BEARSTED.**
>
> *"The Kicker."*
>
> Always at Home to Greet You
> **UNCLE BEN & AUNTIE BEN.**
> (BROOK)
>
> Darts, Shove Half-penny,
> **GOOD BEER,**
> **GOOD COMPANY.**

Reproduced courtesy of Centre for Kentish Studies

In 1949, Mr Leslie Sargeant presented a cup for annual competition between members of the Men's Institute Darts Club[4] who played in the Bearsted and District League. The cup was won by Mr F Pollard.[5]

In 1951, an extraordinary display of dart throwing was witnessed at the Men's Institute. Jim Pike, a champion from the News of the World newspaper and Leo Newstead, Metropolitan champion spent an evening there as guests of the president, Mr L J Sergeant. They gave an exhibition of dart-playing skills which included splitting a hair held by two members of the club. During the display, Alan Croucher courageously volunteered to have a cigarette knocked from his mouth and then faced Jim Pike in order to have a dart thrown through his ruffled hair into the bull of the dart board!

During the same evening, the semi finals and finals of the Presidents Darts Cup were played. In the semi finals L Elswood knocked out J Davis and E White beat P Gould. L Elswood won the final by straight legs. The Red Cross hidden number competition was won by E Chawner who beat J Smith in the final.

Other games were also played at the Men's Institute. In 1953, the results of the Winter Games competitions were as follows:

The Whitehead Billiards Cup	J Springett
Snooker	L Elswood
Whist	E White & J Davis
Single Crib	W Thompson
Double Crib	W Tolhurst
Single Darts	E Harden
Double Darts	E White & J Davis
Single Shove Halfpenny	H Humphrey
Double Shove Halfpenny	W Foster & H Humphrey

Badminton

The first reference to a badminton club is found in Bearsted parish magazine for October 1931. It was reported that the club could only be run that winter if there was sufficient interest. By implication, the club had already been established but perhaps was suffering from a decline in membership.[16]

Regular, but not annual, notices appeared in the parish magazines until October 1940. In that month, parishioners were advised that badminton could not continue to be played owing to the usual venue being unavailable. Badminton was later played in the Women's Institute hall on Saturday evenings during the winter and the club was run by Mr Wenham of Fairlands, Tower Lane.[17] In 1946, a notice in the parish magazine indicated that the club intended to resume its activities and that it would meet on Thursday evenings at the Women's Institute hall. It would be necessary to limit the number of members, but there were a few vacancies and all applications should be sent to Mr W J Moss. The annual subscription was ten shillings and sixpence.[18]

There are few records about the sport after this date and it is likely that the club fell into abeyance. In 1975, a group of people met to form a new club, which was to be known as Bearsted Badminton Club. The Secretary and Club Captain was Alan Ferrell and he was assisted by the Treasurer, Bernard Head. The first meeting was held 8 February and it was decided that there would be three sessions a year, each lasting thirteen weeks at the Memorial Hall on a Thursday night. The subscription for the first session was £2.50, but it would be £2.00 for the second and third session.[19] Membership was initially limited to twenty people although this was later raised. After a very successful start, the club continues to thrive, sessions are well attended and tournaments are held on a regular basis.

Badminton has also been played at other local venues in recent times including Eylesden Court and in the Women's Institute hall on a Friday night.

Horse Riding

Horse riding has always been a traditional pursuit in and around Bearsted and Thurnham. In 1934 a riding school had opened at Crismill and E J Masters advertised it in a trade directory. It is probable, that around this date, Bearsted Green Riding School, also opened. It was located at the stables behind the White Horse. This advertisement regularly appeared in Bearsted parish magazine: [6]

> **BEARSTED GREEN RIDING SCHOOL**
> ------------------
> **MILDRED BENNETT**
> Cert. Instructor of the Inst. Of the Horse
> Stables: White Horse Hotel, Bearsted
>
> **Tel. 6165**

Reproduced courtesy of Holy Cross church

After the outbreak of the Second World War Mildred Bennett experienced difficulties obtaining sufficient feedstuffs for her animals. In October 1940 she sought and was granted permission from the parish council to graze her horses on part of the Green.[7] This undated photograph shows the stables she ran behind the White Horse:

Reproduced courtesy of Roger Vidler

As the war continued, Mildred closed the stables and went to work for the Kent War Agricultural Committee. However she continued to be involved with horses and in September 1946, she helped to run a Pony Gymkhana which was held at Nether Milgate. £23 9s was raised for the Nursing Association. After the war, she still continued to organise local gymkhanas and several more were held at Nether Milgate. Charities that benefited included the British Legion Benevolent Fund.[8]

In 1951 a gymkhana was held in Thurnham Court Meadow by kind permission of K W Forknall. The admission charges were Adults 1/- and Children 9d.[9] Gymkhanas continued to be held at Thurnham Court Meadow and Church Meadow in the 1950s but the conditions were not satisfactory, and it was eventually decided to discontinue the event. In the early 1950s, Pauline Moore opened a riding school in Sutton Street. She ran it very successfully, teaching generations of children in the local area the proper methods of riding and the right methods of caring and looking after horses. Pauline decided to give up her licence in 2003, and now has a small livery yard.

Since 1954, there has also been horse riding, a riding school and an equestrian centre run from Cobham Manor in Water Lane, Thurnham. As Cobham Manor occupies around seventy acres of fields, and is close to the North Downs Way, there are many opportunities for exercising horses. There continues to be an extensive yearly schedule of show jumping, and dressage events held at the centre. Riding lessons can be booked and horses can be bought or hired and there is a wide a range of livery options. This photograph shows the main entrance to the equestrian centre:

Reproduced courtesy of Malcolm Kersey

Bearsted Woodland Trust

The origins of the trust lie in the Bearsted and Thurnham Amenity Society which had been set up in 1997 in order to oppose a proposed development of land for housing situated by Mote Hall in Church Landway. In 2003, whilst Bearsted Fayre was taking place, the developer unexpectedly began clearing the land. There was an enormous public outcry to this action. Richard and Dena Ashness, the owners of Mote Hall, then bought the land in order to preserve and protect the area; subsequently generously donating nearly all of it to the community as a 'green space'. After a great deal of exploratory work concerning the options for managing the land, the first meeting of the Bearsted Woodland Trust Management Committee was held in January 2004, and the first public meeting was held in October.

In a very short time, a management team for the trust, led by the imagination and energy of Peter Willson and Richard and Dena, had made phenomenal progress. Within two years, membership of the Trust was over 500 families. Planting schemes in which trees could be individually sponsored and then planted by volunteers were so advanced that Phase Two was well underway.

By 2005, the work of the Trust had caught and engaged Pauline Moore's attention. She bequeathed over ten acres of her land, situated between the A20 and Roundwell. Many local people were touched by this gesture and there was a corresponding surge in applications for membership, which rose to over 700 families in 2006. A further acre of land at the top of Major's Lake and three acres of Barn Meadow in front of Gore Cottage were donated by the original trustees. As the area owned by the Trust had expanded, there could now be a link to a path across the Lilk stream. As detailed in another chapter, after an appeal for funds, a new bridge was built and it was officially opened in September 2007.

In November of that year the Trust entered, and won, the 'People's Millions' competition organised by Meridian Television. £50,000 was also donated by Biffaward and the money was used for 'access for all': paths were constructed around the land. An official opening took place on 12 July 2008 and appropriately, it was Pauline that cut the ribbon at the ceremony. This photograph shows Peter Willson (demonstrating the ease of use for a mobility scooter) leading Hugh Robertson, MP for Mid Kent constituency and other supporters of the trust during the inaugural walk around the paths:

Reproduced courtesy of Malcolm Kersey

Pauline's generous and perceptive bequest means that this land will never be developed as it will be placed in perpetuity with the rest of the Trust land; kept for recreational use by local people, especially children, animals, and those who enjoy an open space. The Trust has leased some land running parallel to Church Landway to the parish council for a nominal fee of £1 per annum for the use of junior 'Under 12' football teams from the 2008 season. It is also hoped to install a play area for children over the age of 4 in 2009. Today, Bearsted Woodland Trust is well established. Its achievements and schemes to develop the woodland area as a facility and amenity for all the community continues to be thoroughly supported.

Traditional pub games and other miscellaneous pastimes

Beetle Drives and Plant Sales

Beetle Drives were first recorded in Bearsted and Thurnham during the Second World War but in the 1950s Bearsted Scouts truly cornered the market. At least fourteen were held in four years at the Women's Institute hall. Perhaps the very simple rules of the game were part of the appeal: [10]

Rules for a Beetle Drive

During this game, parts of a beetle are drawn. The part to be drawn is decided by the roll of a die:

1   for a head
2   for antenna   There are two antenna, so separate numbers are rolled
3   for a body
4   for a leg   There are six legs, so separate numbers are rolled
5   for an eye   There are two eyes, so separate numbers are rolled
6   for a tail

The correct number of the body must be rolled before any other part is drawn. The head legs or tail can be drawn to the body, but the head must precede the antenna and eyes.

The first person to draw all the parts is the winner. Usually, the game is played in groups of four. The first person to complete their beetle shouts Beetle! This stops the play of all the groups and points are recorded on a score sheet. The score for incomplete beetles is also recorded.

The ultimate winner is the person or team who has drawn the most complete beetles during the time allowed and gained maximum points.

The evenings generated much-needed funds for the Scout Group's new headquarters in Roseacre Lane. Tickets were priced at one shilling and sixpence. Organisations such as Bearsted School and the Women's Institute also ran fund-raising Beetle Drives. In later years, advertisements appeared in the parish magazine. Under such headings of 'Yet Another Beetle Drive' there were encouraging sub-titles: [11]

> Plenty of Fun and No Experience Necessary

Reproduced courtesy of Holy Cross and St Mary's churches

This photograph shows a Beetle Drive in progress which was held when Bearsted Scouts invited the Girl Guides to a party in the Women's Institute hall in 1956: [12]

Reproduced courtesy of Kent Messenger newspaper group

Gerry Harris recalled that Beetle Drives were revived in 1977 following the discovery of a substantial beetle-infestation in the roof of St Mary's church. £5,000 was required to remedy the damage, so this seemed to be an appropriate way to raise the money. These, and other events such as pancake evenings (held at Mrs White's house) and a plant sale (held on a corner of Bearsted green), were arranged by Gerry and the late Brian Robbins.

Plant sales continue to take place. The plants are supplied from a nursery in Hythe which has had three different owners over the years but each has remained committed to the event. A small number of items are also donated from church members' gardens. The plants are mainly suitable for hanging baskets and for bedding but there are also tomato and a few vegetable plants, such as cabbage and lettuce. Sales commence at 8.30am, and the event is always tremendously popular; some customers combine this with shopping at Rickwoods and the WI Country Market. In more recent years, the annual sales have raised sums between £600 and £1,000 for the church.

Whist Drives

From the 1930s, and for the greater majority of the twentieth century, whist drives were held in the Women's Institute hall. They provided popular entertainment whilst raising funds for various national and local good causes such as the West Kent General Hospital, Bearsted and District Nursing Association, King George V Memorial Hall and the Women's Institute.[13] In July 1933 an event took place in the garden of Miss Marsham's house at Greystones in Spot Lane in aid of the Archbishop of Canterbury's New Churches Fund.

During the Second World War, the Prisoner of War Fund received the sums raised through regular whist drives. The British Legion also held events just before Christmas in order to raise funds for their annual party for children.

In 1953, regular events were also held at Little Dane in Thurnham Lane, through the generosity of the White Family. Charities to benefit included the British Sailors Society, Cancer Research and Thurnham Church and Sunday School. A bus service was provided for participants picking up passengers in Detling and along Ware Street.[14]

In November 1957 a further series of whist drives overseen by Mr H Humphrey, was well supported. They were held on the first Wednesday of each month at the Women's Institute hall, and aided the Old Folks Association, the Boys Club, the Football Club, the King George V Memorial Hall and the RSPCA.[15]

Artists and Leisure Painting Group

Many of the attractive properties and views in Bearsted and Thurnham have caught the attention of professional and amateur artists. Amongst the most notable of these is Helen Allingham, who specialised in drawings and watercolour images of old buildings. Her picture of The Old Bakery was described as 'a Village Street, Kent' and was first shown in London during an exhibition of the Royal Society of Painters in Water Colours during 1895. Montague Barstow, the husband of Baroness Orczy at Snowfield, was also a professional artist who regularly supplied pen and ink drawings as illustrations for national newspapers. More recently, Michael Chaplin has also produced many attractive studies of the local area.

Richard Odell (who painted the impression of Bearsted and Thurnham Carnival and Fayre in watercolour for the covers of this book) started the Leisure Painting Group in 1996. He recalled that from the outset there seemed to be a good level of interest in the congregation at Holy Cross church. Word quickly spread about the group; it soon became apparent that many others were also interested. Due to the limited space available within the meeting room, a waiting list had to be introduced.

Members appreciate help with their painting techniques, but equally value the social contact brought through meeting with others having a similar interest. In summer, if the weather is fine, the group meets outdoors in the local countryside or in the gardens of some of the fine local houses which are made available through the generosity of their owners. Sometimes they travel farther afield and spend a day in a different environment.

The group holds an annual exhibition at Holy Cross. There is also a selling exhibition on the Green during the Fayre, but this was started quite independently by the Fayre committee. When Richard took over the running of the Fayre exhibition from Sorrel Bagge, members of the group such as Roland Tomalin were then invited to display pieces. The exhibition enables the work of the group to meet a wider audience.

Dancing

During the twentieth century, dancing was always a popular pastime for local residents. After the Tudor House was built in the 1920s, it became a venue for dances. This undated photograph shows the ballroom:

Reproduced courtesy of Martin Elms

In August 1931 a Toc H Flannel Dance was held at the Tudor House Tea Rooms in aid of the Restoration of the Church Tower Fund. Music was provided by Jack Carter's Dance Band.[20] During the Second World War, dances held in the villages were tremendously popular. Doris Britcher was able to recall that at the beginning of the war she was allowed to attend dances which ran from 7 to 10.30pm. Music was supplied via a wind-up gramophone. These were held in the Memorial Hall, a room at the White Horse and at the Women's Institute hall.

Dance nights were very popular with members of the armed forces but there were some held which they were not permitted to attend. Doris, along with many other younger local girls, went to these. She learned the quickstep and waltz, but her favourite was the Palais Glide. In December, two dances were held: the Christmas Dance and one on New Year's Eve. Both of these events finished at 12.15am.

The armed forces which were stationed locally included soldiers camping in Vinters Park and members of the Royal Air Force based at Detling. The dances that they attended at the White Horse were held in a function room which had been added to the building in Victorian times. Sometimes, over a hundred people would cram in to the confined space, dancing the night away to the sounds of an army band.[21] The events were very popular but the soldiers and airmen were not known for their dancing skills; they were quickly dubbed 'football matches'. They were still hugely attractive to the young people of the village, but it is debatable whether the presence of some mothers acting as chaperones was regarded in a similar light! The dances continued throughout the war and were never once stopped by an air raid.[22]

During the 1950s and 1960s, the Women's Institute hall was a popular venue and reflected a national trend. Old Tyme Dance and Square Dancing featured during these decades, and bands such as the Chordites and The Downbeats also performed. As the twentieth century progressed, the nature of popular music changed. The smaller village venues began to be poorly attended as discotheques with recorded music and night clubs offering major bands arrived in Maidstone. Until the fire in 1983, the Tudor House was able to mount some competition and regularly held a discotheque, but by then the era of regular dances held at a local hall with a small band had almost vanished.

Kathryn Kersey, Ian Lambert and Rosemary Pearce

Bearsted and District Local History Society

The 70th Annual General Meeting of the Bearsted and District Local History Society took place on Friday 27 April 2007...

Two important relevancies are to be noted in the above statement. First, it is unusual for a village organisation, unconnected with sport, to be able to claim this longevity and, secondly, each of the seventy Annual General Meetings has a written report extant in the society's archives. There are also (and more importantly) complete minute books stretching back to April 1936 and these make for fascinating reading to local historians. The material in this article is chiefly obtained from research based on these books. Thus, there is a pretty comprehensive record of the events, speakers and outings and work of the society, as well as records of some of the connected personalities; comprising an implicit social commentary of interest to the modern reader. For the sake of brevity without too much loss of important detail, I propose to begin by looking again at the Secretary's report of 2007 so that the reader has an awareness of how things are and how things have been. Perhaps the best introduction to this short 'History of the History Society' is by an appraisal of the seventieth anniversary year meetings.

In September 2006, Sandra Noel gave an insightful account of her father's work as official photographer to Mallory and Irvine's attempt on Everest in 1924. Sandra has a thousand slides made from John Noel's original glass plates. Her father died in 1989, ten years before Mallory's body was found.

Sir Robert Worcester, founder of MORI polls and owner of Allington Castle, came to speak at a ticket-only evening in mid-October. (It was 'ticket-only' because the seating capacity of the Memorial Hall is set at 140). He has lived most of his working life in England and has a passion for castles. He spoke with enthusiasm about his home and the alterations he has made to preserve its history. History needs to be protected and Sir Robert, like so many speakers in our past, protects and shares his heritage.

The October meeting hosted Andrew Wells, who spoke knowledgeably about Leeds Castle, of which he is a Trustee. His slides, many of which were of areas of the castle still not accessible to the public, were much appreciated. After so many years when the castle was closed and unseen by all except those who lived there, it is a great joy that the people of our villages and the rest of the country have visiting rights.

In November, the Tonbridge Mummers led by Geoff Doel and Mick Lynn brought two short plays connected with Bearsted. The Bearsted Play is one of the few recorded south-eastern England Mummers plays still performed. The plays, seasonal and other folk songs made a lively contribution to our twenty first century Christmas preparations.

Jill Cochrane, a television presenter and former resident of Thurnham, shared, in January 2007, her recollections of the making of the Meridian Television programme Country Ways. The audience was delighted to renew acquaintance with this popular broadcaster. The old established members of the society may have been reminded of Bert Gipson, an amateur wildlife photographer and raconteur from Rodmersham who appeared, by popular demand, on the society's programme annually from the 1950s until his death in 1975. Jill, and the late Bert, share a love of nature and an ability to enthuse others. Bert Gipson's slides were legendary and Jill used the more technological advances of the moving image in much the same way; as a vehicle for sharing experiences.

Bob Spain, who had been vice-chair from 1980 to 1983, also returned to share his Reminiscences. Since leaving the society, he has continued his interest and participation in all areas of history as writer, archivist, and broadcaster.

The quality of speakers contributes to the success of the society; this has always been the case. From the beginning, people eminent in their field were happy to speak in Bearsted. Membership is around 140, and there is a steady stream of visitors. The society is affiliated to the Kent History Federation and the Kent Archaeological Society. It is routinely informed of courses and activities at the University of Kent; the Centre for Kentish Studies; Maidstone Museum and Bentlif Art Gallery and local libraries. There is no reason why the society should not continue to flourish for at least another seventy years. So, how did it begin?

Bearsted and District Local History Society

On 25 April 1936, a meeting was held at the Women's Institute hall in The Street to consider the desirability of forming a Local History Group. This was an initiative of the Kent Council for Social Service, following upon some local history lectures given in Bearsted by Dr. Gordon Ward[1]. Mr Whitehead from Bearsted was in the Chair and Mr Monkton also represented the village. Thurnham sent Miss K M Green, Mr Hutchinson, Mr J Hampson, Miss Howden, Rev A O Scutt and Mrs Scutt and Miss Watchman. From Hollingbourne came Miss C Mercer, and from Leeds, Miss B M Weekes. The Kent Council for Social Services was represented by Major Salt. It is not recorded how these representatives were selected or whether they were 'simply' interested parties but they were people of influence in their villages. The Chairman said that the meeting needed to ascertain if there was a desire to start such a group and it is clear that the move was approved. By the end of the evening: [2]

> ...it was resolved that the villages of Bearsted, Detling, Hollingbourne, Leeds and Thurnham be invited to form a united Local History Group...

Mr Hutchinson was proposed by the Chairman to act as Honorary Secretary. Major Salt undertook to ask Mr Fisher to give notice of the meeting in Detling and Mr Arkwright in Hollingbourne. Mr Whitehead undertook to insert a notice in the Bearsted Parish Magazine. The date of the next meeting was fixed for Friday 15 May 1936 at 8pm at the Women's Institute hall. Twenty one people attended that meeting at which Mr Whitehead initially took the Chair. The minutes recorded:

> ...those present then constituted themselves into the Bearsted and District Local History Group and (a) committee was formed.

From our perspective in 2008 there is an attractive historical edge to the secretary's words, for the society thus formed has been in existence without a break except for the war years. Mr Loweth was elected Chairman and Mr Hutchinson stood as Honorary Secretary. The annual subscription was set at one shilling. It was decided that meetings should be held in the four villages in rotation; the first to be Friday 8 October at Thurnham Vicarage. It was also decided to hold a number of informal meetings at each of the parish churches during the summer, the first to be at Bearsted on the evening of Friday 5 June.

The Secretary reported that Dr Ward was unable to lead an excursion but it is unclear when or how an invitation was made to him. The secretary was also asked to write to Dr Ward asking him to lend any materials he had collected for his lectures. He replied very negatively later that month; the letter is shown in its entirety on the next page. It seems entirely probable that this rather stern admonition inadvertently set the society's future course, for during the summer of 1936 arrangements were made for visits to the churches at Bearsted, Thurnham and Leeds under the guidance of their respective priests. In this manner began the custom of what became known as the 'summer excursions'.

The meeting of 23 October 1936 was held at Hollingbourne Village Hall with Mr Loweth in the Chair and Mr Hutchinson as Honorary Secretary. Twenty two people attended. The meeting addressed: [3]

> The history of Hollingbourne parish in the last hundred years and the Secretary was asked to prepare a report of the discussion...

All reproduced courtesy of Bearsted and District Local History Society

Meetings followed in November at Thurnham Vicarage, and on 10 March 1937 at the Women's Institute hall. At both of these assemblies the history of their respective villages in the previous one hundred years was addressed. It was suggested that if there were monies the group should purchase a set of six-inch maps of the area, so it seems that Dr Ward's suggestions may have borne fruit in another direction too!

This is the letter from Dr Ward:

> DR. GORDON WARD,
> 7, PEMBROKE ROAD,
> SEVENOAKS, KENT, ENG.
>
> TEL. 28
>
> 22/10/36
>
> Honoured Sir,
>
> I feel that I cannot very well send you my boxes for purposes of study. You would certainly need to keep them for a long while and I should lose the use of them. I sent one note book to the Rector of Thurnham in July last, it was to be returned 'very shortly' but it hasn't come back yet.
>
> You have a great deal of material in your parishes. Why not get to work on that?
>
> I suggest that you must somehow or other get hold of maps of the area - 6 inch maps.
>
> Number thereon every house or group of houses, or divide up the map into convenient areas bounded by roads and number the houses in each area.
>
> Then find out for each house every single fact you can - when it was built, or altered, who has lived in it, if it has been a shop, or inn, what it has been rated at, etc. Include all the latest cottages. Record any tales about the inmates, especially such as bear on village affairs or have a very human interest.
>
> That's one type of activity. Then there is the scrap book of newspaper cuttings. Get hold of every old newspaper you can; everything printed about the villages or used in the villages. Pictures, photos, etc. But if possible relate everything to the map. For example, endorse all the picture postcards with a note of what map point they are taken from and in what direction the camera pointed. Also date same.
>
> Field names can also be collected and mapped.
>
> Churchyard and church inscriptions are very useful, not forgetting non-conformist bodies, but they need indexing.
>
> For indoor work, making indexed copies of church books, and extracts from diaries, also indexed;
>
> There is so much to do that one hardly knows where to begin. But I'm afraid I can't part with my records.
>
> Yours,

At the April meeting, held at the Men's Institute, the Secretary read a letter from Major Salt inviting the members to appoint a representative to the County Local History Committee. Mrs Lucy was elected. Mr Jessup spoke on the history of place names and then the Summer Excursions were organised: [4]

> ...one at Binbury Manor in connection with the beating of the bounds of Thurnham parish, the other at Stoneacre and the third at Hollingbourne Manor...

There are, unfortunately, no notes on these outings.

The next set of minutes is dated 4 December 1937 and is preceded by an income and expenditure account on a single sheet of notepaper. It records forty subscriptions at one shilling each and the purchase of a minute book at three shillings and ninepence. We see also that Kent Council Social Service received nine shillings and eightpence for stencilling notices and providing envelopes - such are the minutiae which eventually form an historical record! The minutes also show the beginnings of formal organisation. The committee would meet at the beginning and end of the winter season and: [5]

> ...at such other times as was thought necessary...

All reproduced courtesy of Bearsted and District Local History Society

The secretary, Mr Hutchinson, outlined the programme for 1937/8, which included lectures on Gas, Electricity, Water, Rural Planning, and Bearsted records. Group work was divided up into: newspaper cuttings; registers examinations; mediaeval manors. It was also agreed to establish a map fund.[6] The intervening January meeting concerned the Hollingbourne District Council's Rural Planning Scheme, explained by the surveyor Mr Page. With considerable foresight, the reminiscences from older residents in February 1938 also began to be recorded and noted in the minute books, long before the importance of oral history was largely recognised. One interviewee was Mr Card, who recalled his work as an ostler and horse clipper for two major local landowners, Mr Whatman and Mr Tasker:[7]

> He often went to London with Mr Whatman's carriage and horses. The household generally went by rail while the coachman and grooms took the horses up by road. He remembers one winter with a heavy snowfall walking from Ashford to Maidstone to collect the clippers which he had left at Gould Court...

Miss Mercer reported interviewing elderly inhabitants of Bearsted, including Mrs Walkling of South View Villas. Mrs Lucy had also talked with various persons from Hollingbourne and the information gleaned included the recollection:[8]

> ...the great day used to be when the chaff cutting machines came. There used to be a volunteer corps which practised shooting in Musket Lane, and hence its name...

Both reproduced courtesy of Bearsted and District Local History Society

The detailed reporting of this meeting became the standard for the future. The minutes of the history society have almost always been more than straightforward accounts of the formalities of the occasion. In general they are 'mini-history-essays' and posterity is the richer for this style of reporting. Indeed, the three secretaries[9] who have held office since 1948 have been responsible for recording the words and opinions of some of the County's most illustrious and interesting historians.

At the meeting of 24 March 1938, the Secretary reported on the progress of the Group's Scrapbook (regrettably, now believed to be lost) and then welcomed Miss Yeo and Mrs Smashall who outlined the work of the Committee for the Preservation of Rural Kent. The Secretary also introduced an initiative to make a survey of old cottages; to identify old houses and cottages which had been photographed.

Since its inception, the society introduced several initiatives which depended on the enthusiasm and erudition of its members. The Group regularly drew attendance of thirty to forty people, often more. The members participated in active historical research as well as hosting speakers with a range of interests. Some speakers so endeared themselves to the society that their names occur almost annually throughout the ensuing years. These include Brian Philp; Peter Bonnert; Elizabeth Melling; Joyce Roper; Paul Oldham; Ken Gravett; Ivan Green - all experts in various fields of history, archaeology, etc. Added to these speakers are the Chairs and other officers and members who were happy to address their society on subjects in their fields of expertise.

At the second committee meeting in October 1938, it was resolved to hold a local History Exhibition at a local venue the following year. A month later, the Tudor House was agreed upon as a venue and individual members were charged with specific areas of historical research and subsequent exhibits, and other matters such as a bookstall, notices, etc. Other groups were to be involved: Hollingbourne Women's Institute and the Bearsted Cricket Club were mentioned. By March 1939, arrangements were well underway and included a dance at the Tudor House (single tickets 3s 6d, double 6s). All seemed set fair to introduce local history to an audience drawn from the wider community and to put the Bearsted and District Local History Society firmly on the map.[10]

Again, perhaps with some prescience, the secretary reported that Miss Wigan had asked whether the Trustees could be appointed to hold materials in the event of the Group itself disbanding. It was agreed that in such an event, Maidstone Museum would be offered such materials which were felt to be of permanent value. On 17 July, Mr Scott chaired a meeting at which the final arrangements were made regarding the exhibition. These minutes are not signed and they are the last notes taken before the outbreak of war. There is no record of a formal decision to disband the society, nor of the decision not to proceed with the exhibition, but there is a letter from the end of the war expressing views about its cessation.[11]

The page immediately after the report in the minute book of that last pre-war meeting in July 1939 is headed:

> The following were present at the meeting on 26th September '47

Reproduced courtesy of Bearsted and District Local History Society

and is followed by thirty names.[12] This meeting was held in the King George V Memorial Hall, Bearsted, with Rev W H Yeandle in the Chair. This transcript of the meeting is undated and unattributed, but is most likely from the Kent Messenger:

Bearsted and District History Society

About 40 people attended the meeting called to restart the Bearsted and District Local History Society. The Vicar (the Rev W H Yeandle) was elected chairman with Mr F Bevis, The Bluff, Roundwell, Bearsted as treasurer, and Miss McKenzie-Smith, Woodside, Bearsted as secretary.

The committee consists of Messrs B Holworthy, S H Loweth (Bearsted), Mrs Bernard (Detling), Mrs Lucy, the Rev C A R Walmer (Hollingbourne), Miss D Castleman-Brown, Mr J Butcher (Leeds), Messrs Wm Clifford and Sutton Maxted (Thurnham).

The organisation of the history society was formalised in the late 1940s and early 1950s with winter meetings every month from November through to March and with the Annual General Meeting held in September or October. Summer excursions, which were, from the outset, the main thrust of the organisation, were held in May, June and July. In the beginning the excursions were organised by the Secretary and general committee and were often undertaken with a combination of motor bus and private cars and, on occasion, on foot.

Sadly, there are very few photographs of excursions in the society records. This picture below was undated but is of a group of members outside Stoneacre, Otham. This property was acquired by the National Trust in 1928.

Photograph courtesy of Bearsted and District Local History Society

Bearsted and District Local History Society

As an example of excursions, the minutes of 1951 recording three Summer Meetings paraphrased the details: a motor coach and cars transported sixty members to Bishopsbourne on 19 May when the society was entertained by Sir John and Lady Prestige, who had a fine collection of clocks and timepieces. Tea was taken in the village hall in china lent by Lady Prestige. On 16 June, a somewhat smaller party than usual made an expedition to Lullingstone. The cost to forty members was 8s 9d, which included transport, visits to the Roman Villa, the Silk Farm and tea. The third visit of that summer was to Roydon Hall (by invitation of Captain Arthur Cook) and Dukes Place. Tea was served by Mrs White at East Peckham Club. At Dukes Place, Mr Eric Roy, the owner, welcomed the party and they were taken on a tour of the house and grounds. The party arrived back in Maidstone at 8pm. The cost of the outing was 5s 9d including tea.

The society has seen changes, of course, but in general the plans that were implemented in those days at the end of the 1930s have endured and flourished. There are now six winter meetings with an Annual General Meeting in April and four summer excursions. The speakers for the 'lecture season', examples of which are seen in the Secretary's Report of 2007, are varied; the programme containing something for everyone.

The excursions in the summer of 2007 make an interesting comparison with those of 1951: [14]

> On 27 May 2007 a visit was made by coach, and with a professional guide, to the Inns of Court; the Temple and the Royal Courts of Justice and, after a short coach tour, to Lincoln's Inn. The cost to participants was £20.
>
> Kew Gardens and a guided tour of Kew Palace was the itinerary for 16 June at a cost of £24.
>
> On 12 July the Society visited Highclere Castle, at which there was a guided tour of the staterooms, and Whitchurch Silk mills. The fee of £26 included a sandwich buffet.
>
> The September excursion was to the Wimpole Estate in Cambs. The cost of £26 (or £17 for members of the National Trust) included a guided tour of the Home Farm and an introductory talk before visiting the Hall.

Another facet of the society which bears mention is the quality of the Chairpersons over the years. Each of them has brought something of him or herself to the post and has made a contribution to learning and entertainment in the group. From May 1936, until October 1938, Mr Loweth and Mrs Lucy appear to have taken turns to chair meetings. Their combined efforts put the history society onto the path it still follows. Throughout 1939, Mr Scott pushed the organisation forward. He was one of the five original trustees of the King George V Memorial Hall, and the first Chairman of that hall's Council of Management. It was under his chairmanship that plans for the society's 1939 exhibition, (later abandoned), were put into place.

The Reverend Walter Harold Yeandle, Chairman from 1947 was a keen amateur historian. He intended to write a history of the village, and although his early death prevented a publication he left a miscellaneous, and invaluable, collection of transcripts and notes. He died in post in 1952 and Lilian McKenzie-Smith recorded his death in the minutes: [15]

> Aug. 20th 1952.
>
> Our dear Chairman, the Reverend Walter Harold Yeandle, M.A., A.K.C. died, following an operation in the National Hospital, London.
> Members attended his funeral. Flowers were sent. on Monday, 25th August 1952.

Both reproduced courtesy of Bearsted and District Local History Society

Yeandle's notes were catalogued by Dr Felix Hull in 1969 and are available to scholars and researchers in the Centre for Kentish Studies in Maidstone. The society, under his chairmanship, was in a very safe pair of hands although matters of scholarship were not always straightforward, as will be seen in this transcript of a report from the parish magazine in 1950: [16]

> The Pilgrims Way was the subject of an eloquent and amusing lecture by Mr F C Elliston-Erwood, FSA, to a crowded meeting on 24 November. He was in his best form and told with a wealth of detail the reasons why he has retracted some of his opinions about that ancient road under the hills, as published many years ago. He cited a number of authorities to show that the name, 'The Pilgrims Way', was not an old one and at the very earliest did not go back earlier than the reign of Queen Anne. Whilst pilgrims may have used the road, there was nothing to justify the extravagant and romantic tales which have become generally associated with it. Mr Elliston-Erwood's logic and mathematics in debunking the popular ideas about the crowds of pilgrims were most interesting but did not carry conviction to all his hearers, as was shown when Mr F R Scott, of The Friars, Thurnham, proposed the vote of thanks to the Lecturer. Had he not had to leave to catch his train, he would have had to face a considerable barrage of questions and criticism. But whether or not we agreed with his conclusions we were delighted and entertained by his lecture.

Reproduced courtesy of Holy Cross and St Mary's churches

The Rector of Otham, the Rev C T Spurling, a long time member and representative of his village, took over the Chair and stayed until 1960. Lilian McKenzie-Smith's minutes reflect a time of organisation and consolidation under this happy regime.

Dr Felix Hull (then County Archivist) was elected at the Annual General Meeting in September 1960 and he invited Mr Spurling to be his vice-chairman. As might be expected, Dr Hull was instrumental in obtaining several speakers eminent in their field, and also taking the floor himself on several occasions. He was an eloquent speaker on a myriad of topics and also often brought artefacts from the Archives for demonstration purposes. Dr Hull was succeeded in the post by a later vice-chairman, Lieutenant-Commander A Waite, RNR. He, too, was, of course, pressed into service as a speaker during winter seasons; one of his most innovative talks was on the discovery of a clinker built boat, possibly from the tenth century, in the marshes at Graveney, near Seasalter. The members of the society were among the first in the country to see photographs and hear details of the find, in October 1971.

Mr and Mrs Waite retired to Dartmouth in 1975 and Mr L R A (Allen) Grove, from Hollingbourne, and the curator of Maidstone Museum, agreed to become Chairman. Allen Grove, an academic who wore his learning lightly, had been a member of the society for several years and his name is in many of the winter programmes. The first meeting which he chaired, a presentation by Mr Bert Gipson, was attended by 146 people. He was in post as Chairman of the society when in 1977 it was decided to produce a book on the history of the two villages. Some members of the history society and of the Bearsted and Thurnham Residents Association [17]

> ...formed themselves into a committee under the chairmanship of Dr Felix Hull, to piece together fragments of historical information about our two villages....

Reproduced courtesy of Bearsted and District Local History Society

Allen became a major contributor to the book, which was launched on 22 September 1978 and is on most bookshelves in the parishes. A ticket for the launch is shown on the next page. During Allen Grove's tenure, Lilian McKenzie-Smith was made the first Honorary Life Member of the society in 1979. She had been secretary for more than thirty years. (Ian Dalziel became the second recipient of this life-membership in 2008).

In 1985 Allen Grove announced his intention of retiring to give way to a younger man and the Chairmanship was offered to Mr Michael Searle. He oversaw the 1986 'Domesday Project', which was a photographic record of Bearsted and Thurnham in the ninth centenary year of William I's famous survey of England. Several keen amateur photographers from the society offered their services and the result is a file of two hundred and fifty slides and photographs of the villages taken during 1986. They are stored in the Centre for Kentish Studies and are available for viewing with permission of the Chair and secretary.

A ticket for the launch of the book:

> **BEARSTED & THURNHAM HISTORY SOCIETY**
> **BEARSTED & THURNHAM**
> **RESIDENTS ASSOCIATION**
>
> **A**
> **CHEESE & WINE**
> **EVENING**
>
> To mark the publication of
> "The History of Bearsted & Thurnham"
> Friday 22nd September at 8 p.m.
> The Memorial Hall
> Manor Rise, Bearsted
> entrance 50p

Reproduced courtesy of Bearsted and District Local History Society

At the fortieth Annual General Meeting in October 1986, a membership of two hundred and ten people was reported. Robert James was elected as the new Chairman. This was the last time that the Annual General Meeting was held at the beginning of the winter season for, in October 1987, it was agreed that henceforward the election of officers and committee would take place in April and they would commence their duties at the start of the winter season in September. This arrangement still holds today. Robert was a popular Chairman, able always to speak on music as well as a host of other subjects. He was Chair until 1994 when he attained his eightieth birthday.

Robert's successor was Gerry Harris, a keen art historian whose knowledge was, of course, employed on several occasions as part of the programme. He is recorded, in 1997, as being called upon to fill in (with a presentation on Gainsborough and Reynolds) for a programmed speaker at half an hour's notice. He also presided over the sixtieth anniversary celebrations and the society's donation to the restoration of the Queen Victoria Diamond Jubilee memorial; the village pump and cover outside The White Horse.

Marion Pring, from Hollingbourne, was elected as Chair for the start of the Millennium. There was an exhibition of old photographs in the village library and later in the Women's Institute hall, and an update of the 1986 Domesday Project, called The Millennium Project. Hollingbourne had been one of the villages to send a representative to the exploratory meetings in 1936, and the society has always had a good contingent of members from there. Marion's chairmanship was not only welcome but also appropriate.

Roger Vidler was elected to take over the reins in April 2004. Under his auspices there were exhibitions in Maidstone museum and at the Museum of Kent Life. The spring 2005 exhibition in the village library comprised written reminiscences and photographs from members, of life in World War Two. As with most chairmen he has been called upon to speak on his area of expertise and among his interests is the collection of postcards. Roger also inaugurated the extra meeting in October when a 'celebrity' speaker would be invited. The first of these in 2005 was Paul Atterbury, a presenter on The Antiques Roadshow. His reception was a good indicator of how popular these events would become.

In 2006, it was agreed that the society should once more encourage members to research areas of local history and then to publish the results. To facilitate this, a publishing imprint was created and a block of International Standard Book Numbers was purchased. The first book, Robert Fludd of Bearsted, to be published in this manner was written by the author of this article. Robert Fludd, one of the village's most illustrious sons, was born and buried in Bearsted. He was an Hermetic philosopher and probably the last alchemist. This is a portrait of Robert which appeared in the book:

Reproduced courtesy of Angela Legood

And so the Bearsted and District Local History Society continues to flourish. There is much to learn and new generations to learn it. We could end this briefest of brief histories of the history society with a clichéd homily. But perhaps better to echo Dr Gordon Ward:

There is so much to do that one hardly knows where to begin.

Angela Legood

Bearsted and Thurnham Carnival and Fayre

The early years

For many people, Bearsted and Thurnham Carnival and Fayre marks the biggest opportunity in the year to truly be 'at play' and indulge in some pleasurable relaxation. A social and community event held on Bearsted Green can be traced back over many centuries.

In mediaeval times, fairs were often held on Sundays, but not on religious feast days, and were an occasion for a Court of Justice to be held. There is a smattering of references to such courts being held in both the White Horse and the Royal Oak public houses, situated at either end of the Green but there are few formal records.

One of the earliest references to Bearsted Fayre is found in the Quarter Sessions records of June 1654, when William Hudson was accused of stealing sheep from the Isle of Sheppey. In his defence, he said that he bought the sheep at Bearsted Fayre in June from James Grey. There is no indication whether this fayre was held once a year, or more frequently, but clearly it was an animal market, or a hiring fair.[1]

As seen in a previous chapter in this book, between 1817 and 1821, a series of one-day fairs and races for Bearsted and Thurnham took place on the Green. It is interesting that they flourished for five years before being seemingly abandoned. In his Topographical Dictionary of England of 1831, Samuel Lewis makes reference to a fair held on 14 September which was (and still is), Holy Cross day, but Pigot's Directory of 1840 mentions a Pleasure Fair held on the third Tuesday of July.[2]

The precise origins of the modern Fayre are not clear but there were many small fund-raising events being held in Bearsted and Thurnham in the 1920s. It is likely that some of these were held by Bearsted and Thurnham WI to help clear the debt incurred through building their hall in The Street.

In June 1929, Bearsted parish magazine advised that:

> ...a gay garden gathering of parishioners was in contemplation...

which was to be held on Wednesday, 10 July in the gardens of Snowfield, by permission of Major and Mrs Craig. In August, it was reported that the Church Garden Party had gone really well, and expressed gratitude to Major and Mrs Craig for their kindness. Miss Wind's dance pupils provided a delightful hour's entertainment, but the general dancing was not as general as it might have been:[3]

> ...owing to the heat, and the shyness of the swains!

Both reproduced courtesy of Holy Cross church

The following year, Bearsted Parochial Church Council addressed the matter of the Archbishop's Appeal on behalf of the church schools, including Bearsted School. It was recommended there should be a big open air fete and the proceeds to be divided between the Archbishop's Appeal and the school.

A transcript of the advertisement which appeared in the parish magazine: [4]

Wednesday 16 July...
...is the date of Bearsted Fayre at Snowfield

THE COMIC DOG SHOW
is promised to be a 'howling' success
Please get an Entry form and all particulars from Mrs Lance Monckton, Bell House

BOWLS COMPETITION
Mr John White of 'Greenway' will tell you all about this
Entries (1 shilling) close 1st post July 16th

TENNIS COMPETITION
The preliminary rounds will be played at The Mount on Saturday afternoon, July 12th
3d will be charged to non-competitors to view. Entries close July 8th
All particulars from Mr Gregory, Hill View, Tower Lane

MAIDSTONE MILITARY BAND
DANCING
TEAS AND REFRESHMENTS
STALLS
SIDESHOWS &c. &c.

Admission 6d

Please buy your ticket early

Will you help us by getting a poster displayed in a prominent position or by selling tickets?

Mr A S Perrin, Sec

Reproduced courtesy of Centre for Kentish Studies

The parish magazine subsequently reported: [5]

> The 16th July dawned dismally, but none were daunted. The weather gradually improved and intense activity was soon visible in the garden of Snowfield.
>
> At 3pm the Fayre was opened by Mrs Craig and from then, until the dancing closed at 9.30pm, an increasing number of people laboured and spent and enjoyed themselves.
>
> It would be invidious to name any of the multitude of helpers, but exception must be made to express our indebtedness to Major and Mrs Craig for all they have been, are, and will be, we hope to Bearsted, and to those jolly youngsters in khaki – the Bearsted Boy Scouts – who did an immense amount of 'donkey work' in true Scout spirit.
>
> The receipts from all sources amounted to £76 19s 3d and the total expenditure stands at £23 19s 11d, giving a balance of £52 19s 4d. A copy of the balance sheet may be seen at Mr Philip Monckton's house. It has been decided that Bearsted Fayre shall occur on the August Bank Holiday next year.

Reproduced courtesy of Holy Cross church

By April 1931, it had become clear that the tower of Holy Cross church was in need of restoration. Ivy had grown over a large area, and was affecting the stonework. As no other beneficiaries had been put forward, it was decided that the proceeds of the Fayre would pass to the Church Tower Fund. On this occasion, the event was held at William and Dorothy Whitehead's house, The Mount and was opened by the High Sheriff of Kent. £203 17s 6½d was raised, with all expenses paid 'from another quarter' - perhaps this, too, was the generosity of Mr. Whitehead.[6]

In 1932, there were changes: it was held on Holy Cross Day and at a new location. The theme would be Bearsted Dickens Fayre with a firm emphasis on history and a number of participants wore Victorian costumes. Some canvas booths were built and painted to imitate half timbered houses for the stall holders.[7] These photographs give some idea of the Green's appearance during the event:

Reproduced courtesy of Jessie Page

This photograph is undated, but was probably taken during the 1932 Fayre in front of Bell House. It shows that the event was relatively sophisticated as Major Craig is using a public address system that was almost certainly provided by Oswald Jones. Oswald was one of the first electrical engineers in Bearsted and lived at Snowfield Cottage:

Reproduced courtesy of Bearsted and District Local History Society

It is interesting that despite being held on the day which the mediaeval fairs had probably taken place it did not suit the twentieth century, being too late in the year. The net proceeds were only £82, but local organisations to benefit from the Fayre that year included the District Nursing Association, the Sports Club and the Churchyard fund. After 1932, the date changed back to the August Bank Holiday and the event, now called the Fayre, was held on the Green. Mr Whitehead, as chairman, and Mr Perrin, as secretary, continued to preside over plans and the church was credited with making the arrangements.[8]

This photograph of some children from Bearsted School performing a country dance during the Fayre was taken in 1933:

Reproduced courtesy of Barbara Foster

Bearsted and Thurnham Carnival and Fayre

It was not until 1934 that details of the Fayre appeared in the school log book: [9]

> <u>6 August</u>
> Bank Holiday. School closed. A number of the Children gave a display of Country Dancing on the Green in the afternoon (Annual Fair).

Reproduced courtesy of Roseacre School

In 1935, a list of stalls and stall holders was published in the parish magazine: [10]

Fancy Stall, Nursing Association	
Flowers, Produce Stall	Mrs Ambrose, Mrs Thorpe
Cake Stall	Mrs Oswald Jones, Mrs Higgins
Bottled Fruit & Jam Stall	Mrs Mercer
Bathroom and Household Stall	Mrs Philip Monckton, Mrs Shannon
Toy Stall	Mrs Jessel
Sweet Stall	Mrs Cruttenden, Mrs Loweth, Mrs Ashley
1/- stall	Mrs Tompkins, Mrs Wilson, Mrs Wickham
Bran Pies	Mrs Lysons, Miss Hodson, Miss Marsham
Hoop La	Mrs Brook
1d on Square	Mr Rupert Smith
Rodeo Horse	Mr Camfield
Pontoon Darts	Mr Body
Ring and Bottle Neck	Mr Gooch
Pool Wheel	Mr Dibble and Mr Mildren
Spinning Jenny	Mr Bevis
Electric Speedway	Mr T Datson
Penny in Bath	Mrs Joan Blundell
Bagatelle	Miss V Daniels, Mr J Blamire Brown
Nail Driving	Mr White
Cokernut Shies	Mr Presland
Palmistry	Madam Zarah
Pegging the Winner	Mr Litchfield
Swings	Mr Blundell
Roundabouts	
British Legion	
Toc H	
Mat Slide	
Balloon Race	Mr Holtum
Penalty Football Kicking	Mr Fairbrass
Bearsted Draw (Voucher prizes)	
Bowling for pig (2 cash prizes of 10/- each, ladies and gents)	

Reproduced courtesy of Holy Cross church

Bearsted and Thurnham Carnival and Fayre

In 1936 the theme of the Fayre was The Pickwick Papers. A group of people dressed as characters from Dingley Dell entered a float as an entry in the Maidstone Cricket Week carnival to advertise the Fayre. £190 was raised and £95 donated to the fund for the Memorial Hall, Bearsted.[11]

This photograph is one of many taken during Maidstone Cricket Week:

Reproduced courtesy of Evelyn Fridd and Margaret Plowright

In June 1938, plans were unveiled by Mr Whitehead at the Men's Institute to expand and develop the Fayre. There were to be new, more attractive stalls, but this would require many more helpers! The attractions included 'cokernuts', sideshows and stalls. During the event, a cricket match also took place on the Green. Intriguingly, there was also a party of dancers from Finland who gave a display, but quite how they came to be involved in the event remains obscure. Children from Bearsted School also entertained with folk dancing, encouraged by their new headmaster, Robert Skinner. The Fayre was opened by the new owner of Snowfield, Lieutenant-Commander Litchfield-Speer. The opening ceremony also included a speech by the Secretary of the Finnish Legation, who made it clear in what he said that the Finns thought of England as an industrial nation![12]

Once again, a float was entered into the Maidstone Cricket Week Carnival and this photograph was taken outside Sessions House:

Reproduced courtesy of Thomas Gilbert

Bearsted and Thurnham Carnival and Fayre

This poster advertised the 1939 Fayre; the last to be held before the outbreak of the Second World War. Surely there is more than a hint of bravura here, particularly as the growing storm clouds of the conflict approached?

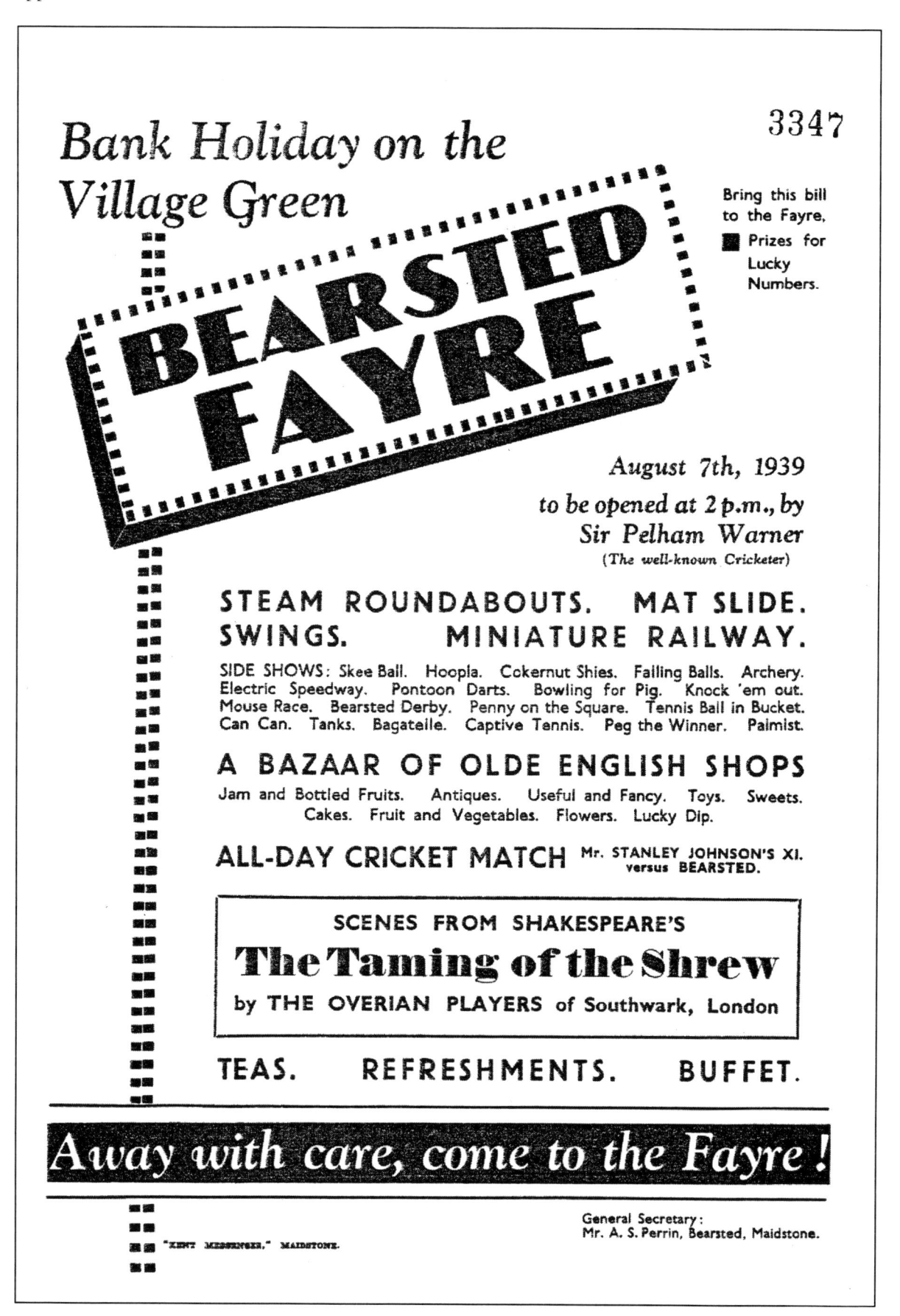

Bank Holiday on the Village Green

BEARSTED FAYRE

3347

Bring this bill to the Fayre. Prizes for Lucky Numbers.

August 7th, 1939
to be opened at 2 p.m., by
Sir Pelham Warner
(The well-known Cricketer)

**STEAM ROUNDABOUTS.   MAT SLIDE.
SWINGS.   MINIATURE RAILWAY.**

SIDE SHOWS: Skee Ball. Hoopla. Cokernut Shies. Falling Balls. Archery. Electric Speedway. Pontoon Darts. Bowling for Pig. Knock 'em out. Mouse Race. Bearsted Derby. Penny on the Square. Tennis Ball in Bucket. Can Can. Tanks. Bagatelle. Captive Tennis. Peg the Winner. Palmist.

A BAZAAR OF OLDE ENGLISH SHOPS

Jam and Bottled Fruits.   Antiques.   Useful and Fancy.   Toys.   Sweets.
Cakes.   Fruit and Vegetables.   Flowers.   Lucky Dip.

ALL-DAY CRICKET MATCH   Mr. STANLEY JOHNSON'S XI. versus BEARSTED.

SCENES FROM SHAKESPEARE'S
The Taming of the Shrew
by THE OVERIAN PLAYERS of Southwark, London

TEAS.   REFRESHMENTS.   BUFFET.

Away with care, come to the Fayre!

"KENT MESSENGER," MAIDSTONE.

General Secretary:
Mr. A. S. Perrin, Bearsted, Maidstone.

Reproduced courtesy of Jessie Page

Bearsted and Thurnham Carnival and Fayre

These two photographs were taken during the event:

The swing boats are visible in this photograph:

Both reproduced courtesy of Jessie Page

Bearsted and Thurnham Carnival and Fayre

The fancy dress competition was always tremendously popular with adults and children. Many photographs of entries for the competition survive, but there are very few named participants. This is a sample of typical entries:

All reproduced courtesy of Roger Vidler

221

Bearsted and Thurnham Carnival and Fayre

The Fayre was successfully revived for the Bank Holiday Week in August 1945. In September, the parish magazine carried the following report: [13]

> Bearsted Fayre was a quite astounding success. It was a grand sight to see the Green swarming with merrymakers really enjoying themselves, and making the most of the first August Bank Holiday since 1939 on which one could feel safe from enemy attack. Visitors came from far and near, (just as now), and spent so lavishly at stalls and sideshows that by the end of the day, takings had amounted to £675 – a notable record. The thanks of the Fayre Committee were expressed to all those who on the day so spontaneously and freely worked with a will to make the revival of the Fayre a great success...

Reproduced courtesy of Holy Cross church

The Fayre continued to be an excellent way of celebrating community life whilst raising funds for good causes. New attractions and stalls were developed - Chris Hunt could remember that his family helped to build and decorate some new booths for the stalls. Cricket matches continued to be held during the event. In the 1950s, a supply of ice cream was readily to hand as the Snow Maid ice-cream factory had opened in Bearsted behind the Men's Institute. Maureen Homewood worked there for a time and recalled that amongst their most popular products which always sold well at the Fayre, were ice-cream cornets and choc ices. The attraction of riding on a miniature steam train, which had first appeared at the Fayre in 1939, continued to be a great success and on one occasion, a beauty contest was held!

This photograph shows the train during the 1950s:

Reproduced courtesy of the Litchfield family

Despite the popularity of the Fayre, problems began to arise. Increasing costs meant that even after considerable sums were taken, once expenses were deducted, there was a disappointing amount of money to be shared between local organisations. In 1955, over £1000 was taken, but after expenses were taken out, only £375 was left, to be shared between twenty five organisations. The parish council became concerned that there seemed to be a lack of interest in the Fayre within the villages. Sam Mendel, chairman of the Fayre Committee, asked the youth of the village to contribute new ideas and give the event some new life.

The committee's concerns were thrown into sharp relief once again in 1957 when it was found that despite again taking over £1,000, costs had risen to such an extent that only £240 profit was achieved! It was decided to abandon a large-scale event. Confusingly for the historical record, the Scouts and Guides continued to run a fund-raising occasion in the summer which, although far smaller and rather low-key, was still known as a fayre or fete.[14]

The later years

In 1977 the Queen celebrated the Silver Jubilee of her accession, and Bearsted and Thurnham decided to mark the event by reviving the Fayre. Since the 1950s, areas of Bearsted south of the Ashford Road, such as the Madginford Estate, had been developed and there were few opportunities for the entire community to meet together. It was hoped that a large event would serve as a means to strengthen links and ties within the parish. Pat Marshall represented the south side: Madginford Residents' Association, whilst Muff and Cecil Banks were leading lights for the north side. A new feature was the introduction of a carnival procession winding its way from the shops on Madginford, through the Landway Estate to arrive at the Green, before the final judging of the floats and fancy dress competitions.

This is the front page of the programme:

> BEARSTED & THURNHAM
>
> *Jubilee*
> *Carnival Fayre*
>
> **BEARSTED GREEN**
>
> **Saturday, 4th June, 1977**
>
> **No.** 00301
>
> PROGRAMME 10p
>
> KEEP THIS PROGRAMME IT COULD WIN £10.00

Reproduced courtesy of Malcolm Kersey

The Jubilee Carnival Fayre was an immense success and there was such enthusiasm, that another one was planned for 1978. The organisation was largely undertaken by Madginford residents, assisted by one or two others. Unfortunately, a visitor to the 1977 event had been struck by a cricket ball, so this part of the entertainment was abandoned. However, this gave more space for stalls all around the cricket square. It was agreed that the profits raised by each stall-holder would be divided with half being passed to the Fayre to be distributed later to local organisations from the village, and to targeted charities.

During December 1993, Cecil Banks retired from the committee, but not before he and Muff were presented with an engraved crystal bowl and bottle of champagne at the Fayre. It was a gesture of thanks for their many years involvement. This photograph was taken at the presentation:

Reproduced courtesy of Kent Messenger newspaper group

<u>Left to right</u>: Jill Cochrane, Cecil Banks, Muff Banks.

In 1994, Geoffrey Sidaway, then vicar of Bearsted, wrote in the Carnival and Fayre programme, that he regarded the event as an outstanding success; viewing it as an essential part of the local yearly round. He also, somewhat ruefully recalled that he was once foolish enough to tell a bride that she could indeed get married in Holy Cross church at 1.30pm on Fayre Day. Her vintage car became locked into the carnival procession and only extricated with great difficulty: a few more minutes, and she would have been judged along with the rest of the floats! One year, towards the end of the 1990s, there was a very violent storm the evening before the Fayre, with thunder, lightning and high winds. This caused a lot of damage to the booths and general set-up. An appeal was put out on local radio and from early in the morning, volunteers and pressed men set to and restored order, so that the Fayre was able to go ahead as usual.

The Queen celebrated her Golden Jubilee in 2003, and as June was the Jubilee month, the Fayre was the culmination of the village celebrations. The front of the 2003 programme was designed by Richard Odell:

Reproduced courtesy of Bearsted and Thurnham Carnival and Fayre Committee

Bearsted and Thurnham Carnival and Fayre

The Fayre carries on each year, thanks to the hard work of the stalwart few and, in particular, Pat Marshall, currently the President and Secretary, who has been involved since its reintroduction in 1977. For many years arena events included maypole dancing by Roseacre School, and a tent-pitching competition between the Scouts and the Guides. This photograph of the maypole dancing was taken in 2002:

Reproduced courtesy of Malcolm Kersey

Profits now are usually counted in thousands of pounds, which are shared by village organisations and one or two main charities, including Maidstone Hospital, the Wisdom Hospice at Rochester, the Stroke Association in memory of Gladys Delves, long serving member of the Executive committee, and the Heart of Kent Hospice at Aylesford. This last, in memory of Rod Freear, treasurer, at the time of his death.

A Presentation Evening is held, usually in October, to distribute donations to applicants, and to enjoy a social evening, bringing together representatives of village organisations. The mayor of Maidstone is usually invited to make the presentations, and Pat Marshall, (mayor in 2002-2003), has had this happy privilege, as have John Horne (2006-2007) and Richard Ash (2007-2008); all residents of Bearsted and Thurnham.

Long may the Carnival and Fayre continue! Perhaps the last words about the event though should be those of Geoffrey Sidaway, once more, who in 1994, so neatly encapsulated what the Fayre is all about for so many residents:

> ...A neatly trimmed village green surrounded by timbered houses. Brass bands, warm sunshine, candy floss, swing boats, wonderful cake stalls. Couple all of this with the sound of the MC's voice over the microphone and it has to be the last Saturday in June. Bearsted and Thurnham Carnival & Fayre is one of the highlights of our year, a real community effort, which, on the day, is literally thousands of people.
>
> This is what community life is, or should be all about: people working together as a team, not only to support local clubs and organisations and raise money for national charities, but above all to have fun together and revel in one another's company...

Reproduced courtesy of Bearsted and Thurnham Carnival and Fayre Committee

Rosemary Pearce

Notes to the Text

A Variety of Amusements

1   pp.20-21, *250 Years of Cricket in Bearsted 1749-1999*
Bearsted Cricket Club 1998

2   i   Entry for Bearsted, *Pigot's Commercial and Trade Directory for Kent, 1826*

         ii   Despite extensive searches of the archives for Kent Fire Brigade, local insurance company records and local newspapers, a record of the date of this fire and of the rebuilding of the public house has not been found.

3   For further information see: http://www.soham.org.uk/history/1814peacefestival

Occasional Holidays and Celebrations (for children of all ages)

1   p.59, *A Calendar of Country Customs*
Ralph Whitlock
Batsford 1978

2-6   i   Bearsted and Thurnham United School log book 1863-1886
CKS reference C/ES 18/1/1

        ii   pp. 406-407, *The History of Maidstone*
J M Russell.
Original printing 1881, re-printed John Hallewell 1978

7   pp.10-11, *The Centenary Magazine 1839 to 1939*
Robert Skinner 1939

8   i   p.86, *Folklore of Kent*
Fran and Geoff Doel
Tempus Publishing Limited 2003

        ii   p.27, 29, The Mummers Play in Sussex, Kent & Surrey
Mumming, Howling and Hoodening: Midwinter Rituals in Sussex, Kent & Surrey
Geoff and Fran Doel
Meresborough Books 1992

9   i   *ibid.* p.44

        ii   *The English Folk Play*
Sir Edmund Chambers
Oxford University Press 1933

10   *op.cit.* p.11, *The Centenary Magazine 1839 to 1939*
An account is given by Mr Walkling, of a Mummers Play, performed during Edward Barnacle's tenure as Master 1879 to 1881. There is no record in the school log book of the play being performed.

11   There is one reference to an entertainment in the school log book:

> 22 December 1927
> After a short programme arranged by the children, the school closed this afternoon for the usual Christmas holidays of two weeks.

Bearsted Church of England School log book 1922-1959
Records held by Roseacre School, The Landway, Bearsted

12   I am indebted to Fran and Geoff Doel for this most authoritative account in:

        i   *op.cit.* pp.90-91, *Folklore of Kent*

        ii   *op.cit.* pp.27-47, *Mumming, Howling and Hoodening: Midwinter Rituals in Sussex, Kent & Surrey*

13   The red and white costume for Father Christmas dates from relatively recent times. Details from an account given by Geoff Doel before a performance by The Tonbridge Mummers at a meeting of the Bearsted and District Local History Society, 23 November 2006

14-15   Bearsted parish magazine, Bearsted 1875-1897
CKS reference P18/28/8-11

16-17   pp.69-73, *A Season at Rosherville Gardens* by George Frampton
Bygone Kent, Volume 7, No 2
Meresborough Books 1996

18   *op.cit.* Bearsted and Thurnham United School log book 1863-1886

19   *op.cit.* Bearsted School log book 1922-1959

Notes to the Text

20   p.10, *British Empire Exhibition Official Guide*

21-22 *Bearsted Parish Council: a miscellany of its history*
R A F Cooks 1977

Coronations and Jubilees

1. Entries for 1887
Bearsted and Thurnham United School Log Book 1886-1893
CKS reference C/ES 18/1/2

2. Bearsted parish magazine 1875-1897
CKS reference P18/28/8-11

3. Bearsted parish magazine, Bearsted 1902
CKS reference P18/28/12

4. Bearsted parish council accounts, Silver Jubilee 1935
CKS reference P18/29/8

5. Bearsted parish magazine 1935-1938
CKS reference P18/28/18

6. p.151, *History of Bearsted and Thurnham*, revised edition 1978
Bearsted and Thurnham History Book Committee

7-8. Bearsted and Thurnham parish magazine, 1977
CKS reference P18/28/33

Introduction to Cricket and Bearsted

1. Information held by Ian Lambert

2. William Alexander, 1767-1816, was the son of a coach-maker in Maidstone. Between 1784 and 1792 he was a student of the Royal Academy. His career included an appointment as a draughtsman to accompany Lord McCartney's embassy to Peking. In 1802 he as was appointed professor of drawing at the Military College at Great Marlow. He was then offered the residential post of assistant keeper of the antiquities in the British Museum in 1808. He died at Maidstone in July 1816 and there is a memorial to him in Boxley church.

   i   pp.397-398, *The History of Maidstone*
   John Russell 1881, reprinted John Hallewell publications 1978

   ii Entry for William Alexander
   A New General Biographical Dictionary
   Hugh J Rose, London 1857

Cricket at Bearsted: The First Two Hundred Years

1. p.iii, *250 years of Cricket in Bearsted*

2-4. *ibid.* pp.20-27

5-6. *Alfred Mynn and the Cricketers of his time*
Patrick Morrah
(First published Eyre and Spottiswoode 1963), Cambridge University Press

7. i   Report of funeral, Maidstone Telegraph, Malling Chronicle and West Kent Messenger, 9 November 1861

   ii *op.cit.* p.27, *250 Years of Cricket in Bearsted*

8-9. *ibid.* p.31

10. Tithe Map and Apportionment Schedule for Bearsted 1840, 1842
CKS reference P18/27/2, 3

11. Application to stop up highway across the Green, Bearsted, September 1875
Bearsted parish council records
CKS reference P18/8/3 1871-1887

12. Bearsted parish magazine, June and August 1896
CKS reference P18/28/11

13-15 i   Entry for Thurnham in 1891 census
NA reference RG12 91

        ii http://www.cricinfo.com/England

        iii *Who's Who of Cricketers*
Edited Philip Barley, Philip Thomas, Peter Wynne Thomas
Queen Anne Press 1981

Notes to the Text

16		p.72, *A School at Bearsted* Kathryn Kersey 2003
17-20	i	*op.cit. Who's Who of Cricketers*
	ii	*op.cit.* http://www.cricmania.com/cricket
	iii	p.147, *A History of Bearsted and Thurnham*
21		Obituary for Godfrey Evans by Derek Carlaw *Kent County Cricket Club Annual 2000*
22-23	i	Report in Kent Messenger newspaper, 1951
	ii	*op.cit.* http://www.cricmania.com/cricket
24		This photograph is a detail from a wider, panoramic image of the Green, Bearsted CKS reference U1401 Z12-13
25		Ian Lambert is the child, fourth from the left, in the group of people seated who are watching the match.

Bearsted Cricket Club: Into More Modern Times

1	*op.cit.* p.75, *250 Years of Cricket in Bearsted*
2	*Wisden Cricketer's Almanac*, 1952 John Wisden & Co Limited

Thurnham Cricket Club

1		p.20, *250 Years of Cricket in Bearsted*
2	i	Regrettably, this reference to cricket in 1819 proved untraceable when this article was under preparation.
	ii	Tithe map for Thurnham CKS reference Dcb/TO/T6B
	iii	Tithe apportionment schedule for Thurnham 1840, 1843 NA reference IR 29 17 39
	iv	Papers concerning court case: Thomas versus Dering, Bart in Queens Bench 1838 CKS reference U41 L1
3		*op.cit.* pp.90-91, *250 Years of Cricket in Bearsted*
4		Match report from Kent Messenger newspaper, 1878
5		Match report in the Kent Messenger newspaper 1905
6		Match reports in the Kent Messenger newspaper, 1914 and 1919
7		Match reports in the Kent Messenger newspaper, 1921 and 1922
8	i	The Lower Brewery, established around 1650 in Lower Stone Street, Maidstone, was bought by Fremlin's in 1929 from Isherwood, Foster and Stacey.
	ii	Match report in the Kent Messenger newspaper, 1923
9		Match report in the Kent Messenger newspaper, 1925
10		The accuracy of this statement and the location has not been verified.
11-12		Match reports in the Kent Messenger newspaper, 1931 and 1932
13		Match report in the Kent Messenger newspaper, 1934
14		Match report in the Kent Messenger newspaper, 1939
15		Match report in the Kent Messenger newspaper, 1949
16-19		Analysis of sporting trends from match reports in Kent Messenger newspaper during 1950s
20-24		Match report in the Kent Messenger newspaper, 1954-1957
25		Summary and analysis by Ian Lambert from reports in Kent Messenger newspaper
26		Match reports in the Kent Messenger newspaper during 1960s
27-29	i	Match report in the Kent Messenger newspaper, 1961
	ii	Summary and analysis by Ian Lambert from reports in Kent Messenger newspaper
30-31		Match reports in the Kent Messenger newspaper, 1962
32-33		Match reports in the Kent Messenger newspaper, 1963

Notes to the Text

34   Match reports in the Kent Messenger newspaper, 1964

35   Match reports in the Kent Messenger newspaper, 1965

36-39   Match reports in the Kent Messenger newspaper, 1967-1968

Milgate Park Cricket Club

1   i   p.41, *A History of Bearsted and Thurnham*

    ii   As an adult, Lewis Cage later owned extensive land holdings in and around Milgate and areas of Sutton Street.

2   i   Prior to 1902, Walter owned Mote Hall (which he later re-named Church Farm) in Bearsted. In November 1902, Walter married Lilian Fitzroy, so Milgate became their married home. (At the time of their marriage, he was aged 58, Lilian was 34). Lilian was the great, great grand-daughter of the Third Duke of Grafton.

       For further information about Walter and Lilian see: http://www.thePeerage.com

    ii   1901 Census return for Bearsted
NA reference RG13 764

3   i   Bearsted parish magazine, August 1896
CKS reference P18/28/11

    ii   Match report in the Kent Messenger newspaper, 1896

4   Undated match reports in the Kent Messenger newspaper during the 1900s

5-6   Match reports in the Kent Messenger newspaper, 1909

7   Match report in the Kent Messenger newspaper, 1912

8   i   Personal reminiscences and research undertaken by Ian Lambert

    ii   The Wigan family team set up by Sir Frederick and James comprised their sons and nephew, plus one nephew by marriage. Correspondence between Kathryn Kersey and Mary Wigan, December 2007.

9   Match report in the Kent Messenger newspaper, 1913

10-16   Match reports in the Kent Messenger newspaper, 1921-1924

Bearsted Football Club

1   Bearsted parish magazine, October 1895
CKS reference P18/28/11

2   Report in Kent Messenger newspaper, 1897

3   Report in Kent Messenger newspaper, March 1906

4   *op.cit.* Bearsted parish magazine, March 1906
CKS reference P18/28/12

5   *op.cit.* Bearsted parish magazine, 1920
CKS reference P18/28/15

6   Report in Kent Messenger newspaper, October 1919

7   Report in Kent Messenger newspaper, September 1919

8   Report in Kent Messenger newspaper, December 1921

9   Report in Kent Messenger newspaper, March 1927

10   The details given here are those listed by Bearsted Football Club. Alternative details suggested for the team change the positions of Gilbert in the middle row with that of Smith in the front row.

11-14   *op.cit.* Bearsted parish magazine, September 1932, May 1934, November 1934 and August 1949
CKS reference P18/28/17

15   Report in Kent Messenger newspaper, 1956

16   *op.cit.* Bearsted and Thurnham parish magazine, August 1957
CKS reference P18/28/23

17   *op.cit.* Kent Messenger newspaper, 1962

18-19   Reports in Kent Messenger newspaper, 1965

20   Report in Kent Messenger newspaper, 1967

21   Information in archive for Bearsted Football Club held by Mike Anthony

22   Report in Kent Messenger newspaper, 1972

Notes to the Text

23	Report in Kent Messenger newspaper, 1974
24	*op.cit.* Bearsted Football Club archive
25	Report in Kent Messenger newspaper, 1978
26	Reports in Kent Messenger newspaper, 1980, 1981
27	*op.cit.* Bearsted Football Club archive
28	Report in Kent Messenger newspaper, 1982
29-30	*op.cit.* Bearsted Football Club archive
31	Report in Kent Messenger newspaper, 1986
32	Information from Bearsted Football Club website: http://www.bearstedfc.co.uk
33	The club was formed in 1916 by workers of the Vickers armament factory at Crayford, Kent.
34-36	Personal reminiscences and research undertaken by Ian Lambert.
37	*The Bears Review*: Bearsted FC Newsletter, 1 December 2004
38-39	Personal reminiscences and research undertaken by Ian Lambert
40	Report in Kent Messenger newspaper, 9 March 2007
41-42	Personal reminiscences and research undertaken by Ian Lambert

Thurnham United Football Club

1   Nearly all the information in this article has been obtained from reports in the Kent Messenger newspaper and from personal memories and recollections of past and present members of Thurnham Football Club.

MPE Football Club

1	Personal reminiscences and research undertaken by Ian Lambert
2	Undated report in the Kent Messenger newspaper
3	Personal reminiscences and research undertaken by Ian Lambert
4	p.126, *Souvenir Centenary Edition Handbook 1992-1993* Maidstone and District Football League
5-8	Personal reminiscences and research undertaken by Ian Lambert
9-10	Table based on statistics found in Kent Messenger newspaper, 1979-1982
11-12	Personal reminiscences and research undertaken by Ian Lambert
13-15	Table based on statistics found in Kent Messenger newspaper 1985-1990
16	Personal reminiscences and research undertaken by Ian Lambert
17-18	Table based on statistics found in Kent Messenger newspaper, 1996-1998
19-21	Personal reminiscences and research undertaken by Ian Lambert
22-23	Table based on statistics found in Kent Messenger newspaper, 2003-2005
24	Personal reminiscences and research undertaken by Ian Lambert
25	Table based on statistics found in Kent Messenger newspaper, 2005-2006

Bearsted Golf Club: People and Personalities

1	*100 years of golf at Bearsted 1895-1995* Clive Horton, 1995
2-8	*ibid.* pp.1-5, 27-30
9	i *ibid.* pp.27-30 ii p.128, *Images of Kent Cricket* John Evans, Derek Carlaw and Howard Milton Kent Messenger newspaper group 2000
10	Luton Town versus Middlesborough, 16 October 1974

Notes to the Text

Bearsted Golf Club and Course: Around and About the Course

1   *op.cit.* pp.27-30, *100 years of golf at Bearsted 1895-1995*

2-3   Several reports of these two incidents were filed. Each differed in detail but the versions reproduced here are now believed to be correct. Some of the details also appear in:

       i   *Aircraft Casualties in Kent, Part 1: 1939 to 1940*
Compiled by G G Baxter, K A Owen and P Baldock
Meresborough Books 1990

       ii   p.211, *Dutifulness and Endurance: Bearsted and Thurnham 1914-1918, 1939-1945*
Kathryn Kersey 2005

       iii   Rudolf was aged 24 and based at either Coquelles or Etaples.
The Revd Arthur Scutt, vicar of St Mary's, Thurnham recorded the same day:

> Much fighting over Thurnham during the Morning Service at 11am.

4   *op.cit.* pp.38-41, *100 years of golf at Bearsted 1895-1995*

The Tudor Park Hotel and Country Club

1   *Four Fires in Thurnham*, Michael Perring
Bearsted and Thurnham Remembered
Kathryn Kersey 2005

Bearsted and Thurnham Bowling Club

1-5   pp.1.0-1.8, *History of the Bearsted & Thurnham Bowling Club: the first 10 years*
Ewan T Rayner, 1994

6-9   *ibid.* pp.2.1-2.6

10-12   *ibid.* pp.3.1-4.7

13-14   *ibid.* pp 6.1-6.4

15-16   *ibid.* pp.7.1-13.9

17   Further notes from Annual General Meetings of Bearsted and Thurnham Bowling Club 1989-2007, compiled by Ian Lambert, 2007

18   *op.cit.* pp.1.11-13.9

19-23   *op.cit.* Further notes compiled by Ian Lambert

24   Details from Bearsted and Thurnham Bowling Club website: http://www.bearstedbowlsclub.co.uk

Bearsted and Thurnham Lawn Tennis Club

1   Notes written by Mr J L Ollett and held in archive of Bearsted and Thurnham Lawn Tennis Club

2   p.147, *A History of Bearsted and Thurnham*

3   Bearsted parish magazine, 1929
CKS reference P18/28/16

4-10   Bearsted parish magazine, May 1930, November 1930, 1931, May 1932, 1935, 1936 and 1938
CKS reference P18/28/17

11   Bearsted parish magazine, 1940
CKS reference P28/18/19

12   i   *ibid.* Bearsted parish magazine, 1941

       ii   Bearsted parish magazine, 1942
CKS reference P18/28/20

       iii   Personal reminiscences and research undertaken by Ian Lambert

13-15   Bearsted parish magazine, June 1946, August 1946 and 1947
CKS reference P18/28/21

16   i   *ibid.* Bearsted and Thurnham parish magazine, May 1948

       ii   Personal reminiscences and research undertaken by Ian Lambert

17   *ibid.* Bearsted and Thurnham parish magazine, 1949

18-20   Bearsted and Thurnham parish magazine, 1951-1953
CKS P18/28/22

Notes to the Text

21   Bearsted and Thurnham parish magazine, March 1954
CKS reference P18/28/23

From Boer to Bulls Eye: Bearsted Rifle Club

1-2   The majority of the information in this article is based on the Minutes and Records of Bearsted Rifle Club and from a conversation with members of the rifle club; Liz Vickers, Vic Matthews, Bill Woolven and the late Dennis Gibbons, 19 October 2006.

3   Bearsted parish magazine, November 1910
CKS reference P18/28/14

4-5   *op.cit*. Minutes and Records of Bearsted Rifle Club, conversation with members 19 October 2006

6   p.142, *A History of Bearsted and Thurnham*

7   *op.cit*. Minutes and Records of Bearsted Rifle Club, conversation with members 19 October 2006

8   Major Leney was connected with the brewery at Wateringbury, and with a mineral water firm in Folkestone, where there is a plaque commemorating his involvement with the Zeebrugge Raid in the First World War.

9   Captain Chapman was appointed as Deputy Chief Constable in 1910. In 1915 he was called up to serve in the First World War, which he did until 1917. It was during this time that he was promoted to Major. In 1920 his title was changed to Assistant Chief Constable, and in 1921 he became Chief Constable. He served until 1940 when he retired through ill-health.

        Information from *Policing in Kent*
Roy Ingleton
Phillimore 2007

10   Bearsted parish magazine, November 1938
CKS reference P18/28/18

11-12   *op.cit*. Minutes and Records of Bearsted Rifle Club, conversation with members 19 October 2006

13   Bearsted parish magazine, June and September, 1939
CKS reference P18/28/19

14   Bearsted parish magazine, 1938
CKS reference P18/28/18

15   Obituary for John Hampson, 30 March 1940, Kent Messenger

16-20   *op.cit*. Minutes and Records of Bearsted Rifle Club, conversation with members 19 October 2006

Roll Up! Roll Up! The Circus comes to Bearsted and Thurnham

1-4   Information on the history of the circus and about Philip Astley from these websites:
         http://en.wikipedia.org/wiki/Philip_Astley
         http://www.circushistory.org/
         http://www.history.uk.com/articles/index.php?archive=56

5   i   The majority of the information in this article has been obtained from John Lawson and other members of the Lawson family.

       ii   Details from website: http://www.johnlawsonscircus.co.uk

Drama in Bearsted and Thurnham

1-2   Bearsted parish magazine, May 1923 and 1924
CKS reference P18/28/16

3-5   Bearsted parish magazine, January 1931, 1933 and 1934
CKS reference P18/28/17

6-7   Bearsted parish magazine, 1939-1941
CKS reference P18/28/19

8-9   Bearsted parish magazine, December 1942 and 1945
CKS reference P18/28/20

10-11   Bearsted and Thurnham parish magazine, 1948-1949
CKS reference P18/28/21

12-15   Bearsted and Thurnham parish magazine, 1950, May 1951 and 1952
CKS reference P18/28/22

16-17   Bearsted and Thurnham parish magazine, July 1956 and 1957
CKS reference P18/28/23